THE BOOK OF MATT

Hidden Truths About the Murder of Matthew Shepard

STEPHEN JIMENEZ

STEERFORTH PRESS

HANOVER, NEW HAMPSHIRE

For information about permission to reproduce
selections from this book, write to:
Steerforth Press L.L.C., 45 Lyme Road, Suite 208,
Hanover, New Hampshire 03755

Cataloging-in-Publication Data is available from the Library of Congress

ISBN 978–1–58642-214-1

3 5 7 9 10 8 6 4 2

This book is dedicated to my mother,
ROSE LEE JIMENEZ,
who paved the way with love and generosity

and to the memory of my grandmother,
JUSTINE GOMEZ,
who taught me to believe.

CONTENTS

AUTHOR'S NOTE

All the material in this book is based on research and investigation that I began more than thirteen years ago in Laramie, Wyoming. My search for sources that could help illuminate the truth behind Matthew Shepard's 1998 murder eventually took me to twenty states and Washington, DC. Portions of this material first appeared in an abbreviated form in a one-hour report I produced for ABC News *20/20* with my colleague Glenn Silber ("The Matthew Shepard Story: Secrets of a Murder," 2004). Following that broadcast, I continued the investigation on my own.

Nearly fifteen years after Matthew's gruesome beating on a lonely, windswept prairie, the story of his murder is not over, despite the fact that two perpetrators — Aaron McKinney and Russell Henderson — were apprehended, convicted, and sent away for life. Tangled secrets of this landmark crime persist. Like hungry ghosts, they gnaw quietly and invisibly at facets of our collective soul that cling to a mythic innocence; to a morally simple world of blacks and whites that is, at best, ephemeral. Together we have enshrined Matthew's tragedy as passion play and folktale, but hardly ever for the truth of what it was, or who he was — much to our own diminishment. As journalist Ellen Goodman observed about the false mythologizing of Private Jessica Lynch's heroic exploits in the Iraq War, "There is something terrible about the alchemy that tries to turn a human into a symbol . . . To turn a human into a symbol, you have to take away the humanity."

While writing this book, I have utilized voluminous public records and media accounts of the Shepard case, including the complete ABC News archive compiled during our investigation. I have also relied extensively on my own interviews with more than a hundred individuals who have firsthand knowledge of the case and/or its principals. These include McKinney and Henderson, the prosecutor, defense attorneys, law enforcement officers from several departments and agencies, judges and other officials, and an array of friends, family members, co-workers, and other associates of both Matthew and his assailants. The prosecutor alone was interviewed for more than 150 hours.

In some instances I have had privileged access to documents and information that were unavailable to journalists who reported on the 1998 crime and the trials that followed, as well as new sources that have emerged in the years since. I have also examined the records of several other state and federal criminal cases whose relevance will become clear in the story that follows.

Pseudonyms are sometimes used when a source would only agree to talk with me on condition of anonymity, either for the protection of privacy or out of legitimate fear of retaliation. In those instances an asterisk follows the pseudonym* the first time it appears in the text. All material not based on my personal observation has been carefully reconstructed from the statements, reminiscences, testimonies, communications, and/or notes of sources. A complete list of those sources is included in the appendix.

Though this is a work of nonfiction journalism, I have occasionally employed methods that are slightly less stringent to re-create the dialogue of characters — words I did not personally hear; nor could the characters themselves recall every word exactly from memory. But my intention throughout has been to remain faithful to the actual characters and events as they really happened.

At the end of the aforementioned ABC News report, *20/20* co-anchor Elizabeth Vargas acknowledged, "There is still a lot about the Matthew Shepard murder that we don't know." Even then, in 2004, there was a good deal more that we, the investigative team, *did know* but were not yet prepared — or permitted — to report. My additional investigation in the ensuing years picked up where that story left off, but the responsibility for all new material and any inadvertent mistakes or omissions is strictly my own.

PART ONE

Darkness on the Edge of Town

ONE

Father and Son

In February 2000 I went to Laramie, Wyoming, to begin work on a story whose essence I thought I knew before boarding the plane in New York. What I expected to find in the infamous college town was an abundance of detail to flesh out a narrative I had already accepted as fact. I went to research a screenplay about the October 1998 murder of gay college student Matthew Shepard — a crime widely perceived as the worst anti-gay attack in US history.

At the time I was teaching screenwriting at New York University and producing documentary films. Like millions of others who followed the news of Matthew's beating and the subsequent trials of his assailants, I was appalled by the grotesque violence inflicted on this young man. According to some media reports, Matthew was burned with cigarettes and tortured while he begged for his life. As journalist Andrew Sullivan later recalled, "A lot of gay people, when they first heard of that horrifying event, felt punched in the stomach. It kind of encapsulated all our fears of being victimized . . . at the hands of people who hate us."

By the time I arrived in Laramie I was a Johnny-come-lately. For more than a year the story of Matthew Shepard's savage beating and "crucifixion" on a remote prairie fence had been told again and again in the national media. The murder trials had ended by early November 1999 and Matthew's killers, Aaron McKinney and Russell Henderson, both twenty-two, had been sentenced to two consecutive life terms with no chance of parole. As far as the media was concerned, the story was finally over.

From the very first reports of the October 6, 1998, attack, major news organizations provided a generally uniform account of the crime and the motives behind it. A sampling of newspaper and magazine stories painted a harrowing picture:

Shepard, 22, a first-year student at the University of Wyoming, paid dearly . . . allegedly for trusting two strangers enough at the Fireside Lounge to tell them he is gay. What followed was an atrocity that . . . forced the stunned community [of Laramie] to painfully confront the festering evil of anti-gay hatred, as the nation and its lawmakers watched.

— *The Boston Globe*

[Police] investigators turned up the following sequence of alleged events . . . Sometime Tuesday night, Shepard met Henderson and McKinney while at the Fireside Bar and Lounge. Shepard told them he was gay. They invited him to leave with them. All three got into McKinney's father's pickup, and the attack began.

— *The Denver Post*

Hungry for cash, perhaps riled by Shepard's trusting admission that he was gay, they drove to the edge of town, police say, pistol-whipped him until his skull collapsed, and then left him tied like a fallen scarecrow — or a savior — to the bottom of a cross-hatched fence.

— *Newsweek*

Albany County Sheriff Gary Puls, who suggested . . . that the beating was being investigated as a hate crime, said . . . the investigation . . . is "aggressively continuing" . . . Laramie Police Commander Dave O'Malley told the Associated Press that while robbery was the main motive, Shepard was targeted because he was gay . . .

— *The Washington Post*

What people mean when they say Matthew Shepard's murder was a lynching is that he was killed to make a point . . . So he was stretched along a Wyoming fence not just as a dying young man but as a signpost. "When push comes to shove," it says, "this is what we have in mind for gays."

— *Time* magazine

While some gay leaders saw crucifixion imagery in Mr. Shepard's death, others saw a different symbolism: the Old West practice of nailing a dead coyote to a ranch fence as a warning to future intruders.

— *The New York Times*

The chilling ordinariness of McKinney's and Henderson's small-town backgrounds reminded me of Perry Smith and Richard Hickock, the murderers in Truman Capote's *In Cold Blood*. In glaring contrast, Matthew Shepard was characterized as "well educated" and "well traveled." He was "a slight, unassuming young homosexual," *Newsweek* said, "shy and gentle in a place where it wasn't common for a young man to be either . . . [he was] sweet-tempered and boyishly idealistic."

I was curious about who Matthew was as a person, just as I was bewildered by the warped motives of his killers. But what compelled me as a writer and a gay man to go to Wyoming was neither the brutality of the murder nor its suddenly iconic place in the national landscape. I first began to feel a visceral pull to Matthew's story when I read the words of his father in a *New York Times* report on Aaron McKinney's sentencing.

In a hushed Laramie courtroom on November 4, 1999, Dennis Shepard delivered a wrenching soliloquy that brought the tragedy home with fresh impact. His words made it clear that his life had been shattered; that nothing could undo the magnitude of his family's loss. With TV satellite trucks and throngs of journalists lining the streets outside the county courthouse, and a SWAT team with high-powered rifles standing guard on nearby rooftops, Matthew's father searched his soul for clues:

How do I talk about the loss I feel every time I think about Matt? How do I describe the empty pit in my heart and mind . . .

Why wasn't I there when he needed me most? Why didn't I spend more time with him? . . . What could I have done to be a better father and friend? How do I get an answer to those questions now?

Minutes later he faced his son's murderer:

Mr. McKinney, your agreement to life without parole has taken yourself [sic] out of the spotlight . . . No years of publicity, no chance of commutation, no nothing. Just a miserable future and a more miserable end. It works [for] me.

My son was taught to look at all sides of an issue before . . . taking a stand . . . Such a stand cost him his life when he quietly let it be known that he was gay . . .

I would like nothing better than to see you die, Mr. McKinney . . . You robbed me of something very precious, and I will never forgive you for that . . .

That Matthew's parents did not seek the death penalty for Aaron McKinney seemed to be a gesture of utmost compassion. Instead they were instrumental in forging an agreement that would allow McKinney to serve two consecutive life terms with no possibility of parole. Months earlier his accomplice, Russell Henderson, had already received the same sentence after agreeing to a last-minute plea bargain.

In exchange for life in prison, McKinney relinquished all his rights to appeal. He also agreed to refrain from talking to the media and was required to transfer any future earnings from his story to a foundation the Shepards had established in Matthew's name. For media and public alike, the horrific story of Matthew's murder came to its conclusion that day. As a screenwriter, I, too, saw a natural ending in McKinney's imprisonment for life. Justice had been served, even triumphed, in a fair trial before a jury of his peers in his own hometown. Like many others, I experienced a somber catharsis when Dennis and Judy Shepard demonstrated mercy after McKinney had shown their son only hate.

On a cold February afternoon in 2000, I picked up a rental car at the Denver airport and made my way north on Interstate 25. I had only been to Wyoming once before, more than a decade earlier, under circumstances that I continued to savor despite my shaky arrival there. The night flight I had taken from Denver to Sheridan ended in an emergency landing after one of the two engines sputtered noisily, then stalled in mid-flight. As the plane jolted and rattled in the inky darkness over the prairie, a lone female flight attendant instructed us to tuck our heads between our legs and grab our ankles tightly because we would be descending fast. No one told us to pray but I could hear frightened murmurs throughout the cabin, including my own.

Somehow the pilots skillfully managed to bring us down on an airstrip in Cheyenne — a breathtaking landing that left no one injured but saw our plane surrounded by rescue crews. *Welcome to Wyoming*, I remember thinking as everyone on board broke into applause.

The next morning I flew on to Sheridan and began a five-week writing residency at a twenty-thousand-acre cattle ranch in the red-clay foothills of the Big Horn Mountains, home of the Ucross Foundation. Ucross, a speck of a town where a bullet-pocked highway sign still reads POPULATION: 25, has been unchanged for decades. Coming from my native Brooklyn, populated by more than 2 million, I immediately felt my senses being blown open by the boundless solitude and a quiet disrupted only by the lowing of cattle and the bleating of sheep or the occasional truck rumbling along Highway 14.

After several weeks there, an unusual inner tranquility merged with my sometimes-distracted yearning for social contact. Some nights, to offset the lonesome silence after hours at my typewriter, I walked over to Porky's, a homey watering hole just across the blacktop from the ranch. Porky's was also a single-pump gas station serving the local ranchers and people passing through. Along with a handful of other cowboy bars at the edge of the Big Horns, the place was bona fide Wyoming. Icy cold longnecks. An old jukebox stacked with Hank Williams, Vince Gill, and Loretta Lynn. Well-worn pool tables. And on Saturday nights a live musician or band cranking out pure honky-tonk. Fresh-faced cowboys and cowgirls barely old enough to drink thought nothing of driving forty or fifty miles for what had to be the sexiest two-stepping in the world.

Even as an outsider it was easy to blend in. People were friendly and unassuming and didn't hesitate to jump into small talk with no introductions. From my spot at the bar I'd watch the couples swaying and gliding across the floor, slowly getting tipsy, flirting coyly like teenagers at a high school dance. A perfectly timed mating ritual, I thought with envy. Most of the cowboys were beefy and well defined. In no time they'd be carrying good-sized guts over their big shiny belt buckles, but right now they were perfect specimens of ruddy virility.

Returning to Wyoming more than ten years later, with still-vivid recollections of its starkly beautiful landscape and bighearted locals, I struggled with the unspeakable brutality of Matthew Shepard's murder. I tried to remember if I had felt safe during my earlier stay in Ucross when I was in my mid-thirties and single. Within the confines of the ranch and surrounding community, yes, I had felt blissfully protected. But I also recalled those nights when I wandered out alone to a few bars and one particular weekend at Porky's when I'd come wildly close to tempting fate. It was my last Saturday night in Ucross, and everyone in the bar seemed to be suffering from a welcome case of spring fever. Brisk wintry smells had disappeared from the air overnight, replaced by something sweeter, more fragrant. I didn't know if it was sagebrush or new grass, but I sucked in the delicious air in long gulps. In a few days I would be back in New York riding the subway.

A good-looking guy named Ron and his winsome girlfriend, Mary Lou, somewhere in their twenties, invited me back to their trailer for more drinking and partying after Porky's closed. Before we left the bar, though, Ron asked me to hop on the back of his motorcycle for a quick spin, while Mary Lou waited. He wanted to show me what a hot bike he had.

Barreling down Highway 14 on that balmy, moonlit night, gripping Ron around the waist as he told me to, I felt exhilarated — all the more so when he pulled off the road onto a dirt trail and cut off the engine. To look at the stars, he said.

Only then, alone with him on the empty prairie, did I realize the danger. It was apparent that Ron was waiting for me to make the first move. Had he ever been with a guy before? Did Mary Lou know this side of him? Maybe he was just shy? Or had he lured me out there to rob me — or worse — under the guise that I'd come on to him?

The two of us stood awkwardly alongside the bike. Even in my light-headed state, something told me to forgo my lust and get back to Porky's as soon as I could. After a long silence I said, "It's amazing out here, Ron—thanks."

He nervously kicked the dirt a few times with the tip of his boot. "Gives you something to remember about Wyoming, huh?"

"We better get back," I answered. "Mary Lou will be sending out a search party."

With a shrug of resignation Ron fired up the bike. "She's back there havin' some fun, I guarantee it."

As we turned onto Highway 14 heading south, the fear lodged in my gut began to dissipate. But there was no way I was going back to their trailer. I'd tell them that I had a lot of packing to do for my trip home.

Back at Porky's the three of us exchanged good-byes with hugs all around. Ron made me promise to look them up the next time I was out that way, but I noticed he never offered a phone number or address.

On my last day in Ucross, I stopped by Porky's to say my fare-wells to Buzzy, the world-weary bartender, who teased me about "the rollickin' good time" I seemed to be having on Saturday night. I asked him about Ron and Mary Lou. From the way they had monopolized the pool table and dance floor I'd assumed they were regulars.

"Never seen them two before," Buzzy shook his head. "Tell you this, they're not from these parts. No way."

Now as I drove on the outskirts of Cheyenne and veered west onto I-80 for Laramie — a wide-open, gently undulating terrain — I tried to hold those decade-old memories at bay. But with thoughts of Matthew Shepard's beating still churning inside, I was sobered by the knowledge that it could have been me. I also could not shake off what I'd read about "the Old West practice of nailing a dead coyote to a ranch fence as a warning to future intruders."

Several miles before Laramie, the highway curved and descended sharply from a peak I would soon come to know as the Summit, where tractor-trailer accidents are common in icy weather and a massive bronze bust of Abraham Lincoln sits on the top of a thirty-five-foot-tall granite base. As the road dropped, it wound through a rocky canyon, giving no hint of the flat, sprawling prairie that lay ahead until it almost reached the valley floor.

I took the first Laramie exit for Grand Avenue and the University of Wyoming, noticing the usual string of fast-food restaurants, an assortment of suburban-style houses in what looked like a new subdivision, and the ubiquitous Walmart. Sitting smack in the heart of the Rocky Mountain West, Laramie has long been dubbed "Wyoming's hometown." One magazine journalist who reported on Matthew's murder wrote that the town "sits in a flat, treeless sweep of high plains bruised by bad weather," yet she also described Laramie as "the friendliest place I have ever been in America."

But as I drove down the Grand Avenue strip that afternoon, past Burger King, Wendy's, Taco Bell, and Taco John's, I could have been in Anywhere, USA.

Aaron McKinney's highly publicized trial had ended three months before and the entire court record in the Shepard case had recently been unsealed, with the exception of McKinney's and Henderson's juvenile files and Matthew Shepard's psychiatric and other personal records. A court-imposed gag order had also been lifted. Although trial witnesses and other principals in the case, other than McKinney, were finally free to talk, the army of journalists that had inundated the town for more than a year had long since departed.

The following morning, while looking through stacks of case documents in a busy reception area at the Albany County Courthouse, a stately limestone building in Laramie's refurbished downtown, I recognized Cal Rerucha, the prosecutor who had won McKinney's and Henderson's convictions. A robust man with thinning hair, then in his late forties, Rerucha had come across in news reports as stern and uncompromising. He also had a reputation for remaining aloof from the media. But as I watched him move about the third floor of the courthouse, making self-deprecating jokes to his staff and others stopping by on county business, he seemed warm and unaffected. Still somewhat intimidated, I asked if he had a few minutes to talk about the Shepard case.

Rerucha invited me into his spacious but plainly appointed corner office, ushering me past his secretary and others working at their desks, then shut the heavy oak door behind us.

It quickly became apparent during the conversation that he was sizing me up and trying to discern my motives for writing about Matthew's murder. He coolly informed me that a slew of other writers and producers had already come to town with an interest in dramatizing the case. I detected an unmistakable note of scorn. Rerucha was clearly not interested in jumping on the Hollywood bandwagon and advised me that "the Shepard family has suffered enough" and he would have "nothing to do with exploiting their pain further."

Despite these remarks, Rerucha spoke with me for nearly an hour. I was further surprised when he offered me his home number and said, "Call anytime."

After a few days of research at the courthouse I left Laramie, laden with notes compiled from thousands of pages of court documents. But I soon turned to Rerucha for additional insight. Over the next several months, in a series of lengthy interviews by phone and in person, a feeling of trust developed. Rerucha described how taxing the Shepard prosecutions had been, including periodic death threats and constant worries for his family's safety. In twelve years of elected office it was also his first death penalty case, with enormous pressure from government officials in Wyoming and Washington, and from the Clinton White House as well.

I knew the Shepard murder had been the focus of national attention, but I slowly realized how much I did not know. Cal Rerucha not only educated me about the legal aspects of the case but also hinted that I should look beneath the surface of what the media had reported.

Our phone interviews almost always began minutes after 5 PM Mountain Time, just after his staff shut down business for the day. Rerucha took his job as a public servant seriously. On principle he would not expend county time chatting with a writer, even about a case that had left a lasting scar on his hometown and, I would come to see, on Rerucha himself.

In one interview he joked that the only reason he was talking to me was that "it's soothing, like talking to a psychiatrist. Otherwise we wouldn't be having this conversation," he added drily.

On another occasion Rerucha chuckled, "You probably wouldn't have made it into my office *period* if you weren't wearing that jacket the day you arrived." He was referring to my favorite jacket — a faded, well-worn tan Carhartt — which he said made me "fit right into Laramie" and didn't mark me as "another media hound from back East."

"Every time those people came to town it was like a swarm of locusts," he scoffed, shaking his head.

Over time I discovered that Cal Rerucha did need to get some things off his chest, but it was not until months after our first encounter that I understood what they were. I made only one promise to him: I would write the story of Matthew's murder truthfully. I also made the disclaimer that once my screenplay was in the hands of Hollywood I couldn't offer any further guarantees.

Rerucha was adamant that he wasn't looking for money or fame. "Lawyers aren't supposed to be celebrities or movie stars, their job is in the courtroom," he lectured me in his affable, yet prosecutorial tone. The one thing that concerned him, though, was accuracy.

"You people in the media say whatever you want, whether it's true or not," he complained. "Betray the public trust and there's not a damn thing we can do about it."

His reservations about the media notwithstanding, Rerucha continued to walk me through countless details of the previous year's courtroom drama I had missed in person, including anecdotes of political maneuvers behind the scenes. A lifelong Democrat in a predominantly conservative, Republican state, he had been elected to his fourth consecutive term as county attorney just weeks after Matthew's murder.

Increasingly, I came to appreciate the immense challenges Rerucha had faced leading Laramie through some of its darkest days. He had

a sizable number of detractors and political adversaries, and a reputation for being difficult and sometimes intransigent — a side of him I
would come to know personally. But overall I admired his ethics and
integrity. As I studied the murder over months and eventually years,
he became both my ally and my guide.

I also searched for other Laramie residents who could provide
insight into how things worked in the town. When I asked about
violent crime, the answers I got were often contradictory. The local
chamber of commerce boasted of a "0%" homicide rate, yet I learned
from Rerucha of other grisly murders in the years immediately prior
to the attack on Matthew. He mentioned — as others had — the
1997 killing of a teenage girl named Daphne Sulk, which had made
only the local news and was quickly forgotten. Rerucha said the Sulk
murder was "the nastiest homicide" he had seen in four terms as
county prosecutor. He strongly encouraged me to take a look at the
case as background to what followed with Matthew Shepard, if only
to compare two ruthless, back-to-back homicides in Albany County,
Wyoming.

Daphne

An hour or so before noon on November 11, 1997, Mark and Michelle Johnson were hunting for pinecones in the snowy woods of Wyoming's Medicine Bow National Forest. The morning was chilly, with a gust of fresh snow blowing through the sun-streaked trees east of Laramie. The Johnsons' mission was to collect enough cones to make Christmas wreaths for family and friends.

Something caught Michelle's eye at the edge of the forest. Jutting from a shallow snowdrift, it looked at first like an outcropping of rock. Moving closer, she recognized the shape of a girl's naked body, partially frozen in the hardpacked earth. The girl's skin was pale blue and appeared to be punctured with bruises. Michelle staggered and turned to her husband. The ruddy glow in her cheeks was gone, and she could hardly get a word out.

In the days before Thanksgiving, news that fifteen-year-old Daphne Sulk had been savagely bludgeoned, stabbed more than seventeen times, and discarded in the wilderness sent a tremor of fear through her nearby junior high school and hometown. The Laramie community also learned that Daphne was pregnant. For a college town of twenty-seven thousand, 93 percent of whom were Caucasian, it came as a still-greater shock when police arrested a thirty-seven-year-old black man, Kevin Robinson, for her murder. Daphne, who was white, had allegedly been his lover. As the story was told in court documents and local newspapers, Robinson wanted her to have an abortion but she refused. Anxious he would lose custody of his two children if word got out that he was the father, he beat and knifed her to death, then dumped her body in a remote wooded area where she was not likely to be found until spring — if ever.

Hideous stab wounds covered Daphne's chest and neck area. Her body was scarred with defensive bruises, indicating she had fought for

her life. A forensic pathologist would later testify in Robinson's trial
that the number of wounds was consistent with an explosion of rage.
Although an autopsy showed that Daphne was barely one month
pregnant, no DNA tests were performed on the embryo to determine
whether the sperm had, in fact, come from Kevin Robinson. It was an
omission over which prosecutor Cal Rerucha and police wouldn't lose
any sleep, since they had abundant evidence incriminating Robinson.

Those who knew Daphne described her infectious enthusiasm, but
recalled that she was also fragile and troubled. The youngest of five
children, she had just started ninth grade at Laramie Junior High.
Roberta Sulk, her mother, surmised that Daphne might have first met
Robinson on the street "on her way to her teen support group."

Before Daphne's body was discovered in the woods, she had been
missing from home as a runaway for eleven days. Police later determined she had spent a few of those nights at an abandoned trailer in
town with another female runaway.

At Kevin Robinson's trial the following year, witnesses would
testify that Daphne boasted of a "secret friend." She had revealed that
she was in a sexual relationship with "Kevin," they stated, and that
he frequently made her perform pregnancy tests in his presence. One
of Daphne's classmates named Miranda, who said she had accompanied Daphne on a visit to Robinson's home, described his eyes as
"glazed over" in a manner that frightened her — as if he were high on
drugs. Daphne told Miranda that if she ever wanted drugs, alcohol,
or tobacco, Kevin was the man to see.

For Cal Rerucha the question of motive was answered when other
friends of Daphne, as well as a few of her teachers, said she had
confided in them that she was pregnant. She allegedly had told several
individuals that Kevin Robinson was the father, and that he was very
upset about the pregnancy and wanted it aborted. But what most
convinced Rerucha of Robinson's guilt were the spots of Daphne's
blood on the door and inside the trunk of Robinson's gold Honda
found by detectives from the Laramie Police Department and the
Albany County Sheriff's Office.

Of all the officers and deputies in both departments, Rerucha
relied first and foremost on Detective Sergeant Rob DeBree of the

sheriff's office, whose instincts he trusted "above all other cops in the county." The two had teamed up on case after case.

A sturdily built man in his forties with a mustache and a curt disposition, DeBree spent most of his off-duty waking hours tending to his ranch on the Wyoming-Colorado border. In local law enforcement circles it was well known that the two men argued incessantly while preparing for a trial, driven in no small part by Rerucha's belabored, if not compulsive, insistence that "not a single witness or piece of evidence get away from us." But as teammates, they shared an aggressive determination to win in the courtroom. Rerucha would be first to admit that he could push DeBree's patience to the limit, not to mention the rest of his staff's.

"You're paranoid, Cal," DeBree groused to him on many an occasion, "and you're driving both of us nuts."

Usually Rerucha got up from his banker's-style oak desk, already damp under the collar of his oxford shirt, and began pacing the floor of his office.

"God-darn-it, Rob, the defense is going to hang us out to dry," he'd snap back peevishly. "I want to go back over every witness statement, a hundred times if we have to."

These routine jousts with DeBree "had nothing to do with second-guessing his judgment," Rerucha recalled in an early interview. "If Rob said something was so, you could pretty much go to the bank with it."

By early summer 1998, seven months of legal wrangling and delays had elapsed since Kevin Robinson had been charged with Daphne's murder, but there was still no trial date. As Rerucha sized up his crowded court schedule and slate of civic duties, he was hopeful he could finish the case by the time his sons went back to school in the fall. Luke, his lanky and athletic older boy, would be in seventh grade, while Max, who stood taller and was more bookish, was a grade behind him.

The atmosphere around the Sulk case had also become progressively more acrimonious. Among Rerucha's political foes there were allegations that he was showing racial bias; there were even those who said Kevin Robinson was innocent.

"Some of the evidence against Robinson was circumstantial, absolutely, but all of it pointed to him as Daphne's killer," Rerucha stated confidently long after the trial was over. Yet other Laramie sources, including several respected attorneys, strongly disputed that view. Even today, they remain convinced that Robinson was "framed" or "set up" while the real killer was protected, presumably by someone with clout. Some found it strange that after Robinson was arrested for Sulk's murder, he was allowed to leave the county jail each day to continue working at his job. He was even permitted to attend his company's Christmas party, returning to his jail cell after the festivities ended.

But behind the town rumors were lesser-known facts regarding Daphne Sulk's history — aspects I only became aware of after I'd been investigating Matthew Shepard's murder for a few years. By the age of fifteen and before Kevin Robinson's name was ever linked to hers, Daphne had made claims to the police that she'd had sexual relations with three different adult males, each of whom served jail time for having sex with her as a minor. Yet her status as a juvenile prevented those records from being made public. Authorities also had credible information that Daphne had been involved with drugs, including methamphetamine. For a time two of the men whom she identified as sex offenders, reputedly meth users themselves, were suspects in her killing; the third offender was in jail when she disappeared.

One story I heard about the Robinson case was said to be too scandalous — or too dangerous — to repeat around town because it involved a prominent family, the Fritzens, who had worked in local law enforcement. Don Fritzen had been a popular county sheriff, while his two sons, Brian and Ben, had served respectively as a sheriff's deputy and a detective in the Laramie Police Department. Don Fritzen's brother-in-law, John Fanning, was also the county undersheriff for several terms and, according to some, a powerful cop who allegedly controlled the town and its surroundings — "just like a sheriff in the Old West, someone you don't want to mess with," one insider cautioned.

Ben Fritzen, Don's younger son, a short, handsome man with a tight, muscular frame, was a lead investigator in the Sulk homicide.

Respected among peers for his keen forensic skills and his network of sources on the street, Ben personally interviewed more than a hundred individuals during the investigation; he was also responsible for discovering drops of Daphne's blood in Kevin Robinson's car.

But seldom mentioned until long after Robinson's conviction was an alleged affair between Brian Fritzen's wife and Kevin Robinson's brother, Royal Robinson, known around town by the nickname "Bug." The affair was apparently a well-kept secret until Brian's wife gave birth to a child fathered by Bug Robinson.

A few Laramie residents who insisted on anonymity contended, "at that point the fix was in." One said the Fritzens, in an old-fashioned vendetta, "promised to get even with the Robinsons if it was the last thing they did."

But rumors notwithstanding, no one dared to question the evident conflict of interest in allowing a Fritzen family member to investigate Bug Robinson's brother for murder. According to Cal Rerucha, he was unaware at the time of any personal connections and therefore had no reason to question Ben Fritzen's role in the investigation. Other locals said, "We've got people in this town a lot more powerful than the Fritzens," and "There are plenty of secrets to go around [in Laramie]," though they also pointed to a decades-old drug scandal that allegedly involved Brian Fritzen. They claimed that Brian, while a police officer, had stolen "a large amount of cocaine" from an evidence locker, "but he got off with a slap on the wrist . . . Instead of charging him, they sent him somewhere for treatment" and allowed him to quietly resign.

THREE

The Little Dude

In mid-summer 1998, as Rerucha prepared the Robinson case for trial, he had another smaller case that had yet to reach the sentencing phase: the burglary of a Kentucky Fried Chicken the previous December. Three young men had broken into the fast-food restaurant on the south side of town and had stolen twenty-five hundred dollars and — somewhat ludicrously — a few desserts.

Among the three known burglars was a twenty-year-old "local troublemaker" with a long juvenile record, Aaron McKinney. In April 1998, Detective Rob DeBree had arrested McKinney in Pensacola, Florida, and brought him back to Laramie to face charges. McKinney had been hiding out on the Gulf Coast for several months with his pregnant seventeen-year-old girlfriend, Kristen Price, living in the home of her mother and working sporadically as a pipe fitter.

Aaron McKinney had been on Rerucha's watch list for years as "someone who showed clear signs of bigger problems to come." DeBree, Ben Fritzen, and other cops had kept an eye on McKinney, too, since they knew that he and his band of friends were using and selling hard drugs. The whole bunch, plus a few of their girlfriends.

Unbeknownst to McKinney, Laramie police had been tipped off to his whereabouts by Kristen Price's mother, Kim Kelly, who reported that he had been physically abusive toward her daughter. Kelly told police she was "afraid of Aaron's violent temper" and was worried for Kristen's safety as well as the soon-to-arrive newborn's.

According to Kelly, while McKinney was living in her Florida home she casually mentioned that she was having a problem with her ex-husband. McKinney advised her on the spot that "he knew people who could straighten it out."

"All I have to do is make a call," he said.

Kelly was dumbfounded by McKinney's barely masked offer to "put out a contract on my ex," but at the time she dismissed his posturing as "a little guy talking like a big shot." He also bragged to Price and her mother of his exploits in California the previous year. He said he had gotten in good with an organized crime family and dropped hints that he had done "jobs" for them, including murder for hire.

"One way to get rid of a body," he told Kelly, "is to burn it, take the teeth out, then bury the body."

Standing five feet, four inches tall, with a skinny build, Aaron McKinney fancied himself a thug and a "gangsta," modeling his words and sometimes his actions after the in-your-face rhymes of his rap-star heroes. Several of his friends would later recall that he was also the brunt of frequent teasing; they called him "shrimp," "pipsqueak," "the little dude," and other terms of endearment.

But despite McKinney's well-honed talent for exaggeration, he had not lied about living in California for a while. He was first invited there by Jay Pinney, a teenage offender whom he befriended while Pinney was in mandatory residence at the Cathedral Home for Children in Laramie. Pinney liked some of the same drugs McKinney did — weed, acid, crack, and methamphetamine — and both liked to party. McKinney also liked to shock people with tales of his friend's childhood in Riverton, Wyoming. But it was Cal Rerucha who first told me about Pinney's history.

At age twelve, Pinney shot and killed a middle-aged neighbor, Delbert Dilts, with a .300 Winchester Magnum. Dilts, a maintenance manager at the town library, had gotten into a minor altercation with Pinney's younger brother, nicknamed "Buggers," while chasing a dog belonging to the Pinney family off his property.

According to Pinney, whom I interviewed two decades later, Buggers came home crying because Dilts "screamed and yelled at him." Without a moment's shilly-shallying, Pinney went and got his father's rifle, trained its scope on his neighbor a hundred yards away, and shot him in the neck, blowing part of his head off. When Dilts's wife, an editor at the Riverton newspaper, returned home after work, she found his bloody remains in a flower patch out front.

Pinney said he would never forgive himself for the man's death, "but I've done everything I can to be a better person."

Since Pinney was not yet thirteen at the time of the murder, he could not be charged as an adult in Wyoming and was sent instead to a juvenile facility for a few years, and eventually to Laramie's Cathedral Home. It was there that he first encountered Aaron McKinney and where the two discovered that "another thing we both liked a lot was guns." Their friendship would later turn sour in California, but before their falling-out Pinney stayed for a while in a crowded trailer in West Laramie where McKinney lived with a couple of his buddies.

"Aaron always had guns," Pinney remembered. "[When] I'd go to [his] place there was usually a pistol on the table."

Pinney, who currently builds supercharger auto engines for an Oklahoma manufacturer, agreed to be interviewed "on the chance it could help other messed-up kids avoid the choices me and Aaron made."

Years before I located Pinney, a confidential source in Wyoming law enforcement had informed me that another person who shared Aaron McKinney's trailer for a period was a convicted felon named Dennis Leroy Menefee Jr. In 1999 Menefee, then twenty-eight, pled guilty to manslaughter for the rape and death of Russell Henderson's forty-year-old mother, Cindy Dixon, while Russell was awaiting trial for Matthew Shepard's murder. The investigation of Dixon's killing, which was led by Detective Rob DeBree, was conducted quickly and quietly, without media coverage, and resulted in a plea bargain that gave Menefee a four-to-nine-year prison sentence. Four years later, he was released.

The lurid tales I was beginning to hear about "Wyoming's home-town" startled me. They made me wonder what kind of netherworld I had stumbled into and how it might have looked to Matthew — a petite, twenty-one-year-old freshman who had attended a Swiss boarding school.

Nonetheless, I followed Cal Rerucha's advice and took a closer look at the 1997 Daphne Sulk homicide, while continuing my research into Matthew's murder. As I examined both cases, I couldn't escape the feeling of being a total outsider in this friendly but frightening college town. Without Rerucha as a guide, I would have been smart to pack up and fly home.

FOUR

Spider's Web

Everyone who worked in the Albany County Courthouse in the late 1990s knew that when Cal Rerucha was nervous he paced. He strode pensively up and down the polished granite corridor outside his third-floor office, his routine interrupted only for stops in the men's room or another refill at the coffee table behind his secretary's desk. It wasn't that he was unfriendly when he was agitated about something; he would still nod hello or mumble a few words of small talk. But you knew to leave it at that.

Rerucha would say he did his best thinking before dawn when much of Laramie, especially its ten thousand university students, had yet to wake up. Hours before his staff set foot in the building, he would arrive and turn on the overhead lights. The office was a sanctuary at that hour.

In summer and early fall it was less gloomy than during the bitter winter months, when coming to the courthouse before sunrise could feel like a form of penance. The long halls, devoid of human activity, felt ghostly, yet he still found comfort in the solitude and focused on the tasks ahead.

This day, September 9, 1998, was different. No amount of pacing could take the edge off waiting for a jury to return a verdict.

Rerucha never liked to "rehearse" his opening and closing statements. No, he'd never call it that, as it implied something theatrical or contrived and therefore less real.

But just before six that morning he had begun walking the hallways of the courthouse, methodically reviewing every point of his case in *State of Wyoming vs. Kevin Robinson*. Cal Rerucha's discipline as a prosecutor was repetition. *Go over your case time after time till none of it feels like a performance. Make it feel like you're breathing the law through the pores of your skin.*

Around ten thirty that morning, in Judge Donnell's courtroom on the second floor, he had delivered one of his vintage closing arguments. His chief investigator, Rob DeBree of the sheriff's office, whose low bullshit quotient, Rerucha believed, was roughly equivalent to his own, assured him he had nailed it.

Still, Rerucha made it a rule to "never underestimate a jury." While he felt certain that Kevin Robinson was guilty of the most heinous kind of murder — killing a fifteen-year-old child who was helpless to defend herself — the physical evidence had only been strong enough to prosecute Robinson for manslaughter and assorted lesser charges. To Rerucha, a devout Catholic, the "lesser" crime of soliciting sexual relations with a minor was not far behind taking another's life. In this case two lives were taken, he argued, since the victim, Daphne Sulk, was pregnant.

By 3 PM the jury still hadn't come back and Rerucha was on the march again. He mentally replayed every point in his closing argument, struggling to satisfy himself that he'd left nothing out that could plant even the tiniest seed of doubt in a single juror's mind.

On this particular afternoon he paced restlessly in the cluster of inner offices off the main corridor. His staffers liked to joke about the hundreds of miles he would log while a trial was going on.

Rerucha had also stopped drinking coffee an hour before. The last thing he needed was to go back in front of District Court Judge Jeffrey Donnell and the jury and be overcome by a need to visit the john again.

He and Donnell had gone to law school together at the University of Wyoming and generally got on well inside the courtroom and out, but, like many of Rerucha's professional colleagues, Donnell often felt his patience wear thin when Rerucha was trying a case. A bearded, old-school conservative known to carry a loaded pistol under his judicial robe while hearing cases, Donnell had no problem ordering his former classmate to sit down and shut up when he got bad-tempered or argumentative.

As Rerucha reviewed the morning's events, he remembered that as he approached the jury box he had nodded courteously to Robinson's attorney, Buddy Carroll, careful not to diminish the gravity of what was before them. Also at the defense table was Carroll's co-counsel, Jason Tangeman, a smart young lawyer with the Laramie firm of Anthony, Nicholas & Sharpe. "Buddy and the Boy Wonder" was the nickname Rerucha and DeBree had coined for Robinson's defenders.

For a few moments Rerucha stopped pacing. He leaned against a file cabinet in the county clerk's office and stared at the passing traffic out on Grand Avenue. Was there anything he'd forgotten in his summation?

"Ladies and gentlemen, we end this case in the same place we began it," he'd told the jury calmly. "With a fifteen-year-old girl whose naked body was found buried in the snow one year ago . . ."

After making eye contact with each juror, he'd pointed to enlarged crime-scene photos on the evidence display he had used during the trial. The most gruesome one showed the pale, frozen corpse of Daphne Sulk.

"The victim was infatuated with an older man whom witnesses have identified as the defendant, Kevin Robinson, thirty-seven years old," Rerucha said, pointing to the defense table. "Daphne was a very fragile girl. She was confused and easily led. You have heard witnesses testify that Mr. Robinson would ask Daphne to take articles of her clothing off and dance for his pleasure and amusement. He treated her like a pet, snapping his fingers to get what he wanted."

Kevin Robinson, solidly built and sporting a neatly trimmed beard, seemed to be listening closely, yet he never flinched or looked away.

"You also heard that Daphne was very upset that she was pregnant," Rerucha continued. "She wanted to keep the baby, Mr. Robinson wanted it aborted. Daphne Sulk had seventeen stab wounds in the chest. What was this child thinking at the time of her first blow? Did she have time to beg for her life? Dr. Allen, who performed the autopsy, told you it might have been thirty seconds, or it might have been minutes. How long is thirty seconds, ladies and gentlemen? If we would take a look at our watches, let's see how long thirty seconds is."

Most of the jurors obliged, glancing down at their watches. As if counting the seconds was not sufficiently dramatic, Rerucha startled them when he hit the flat oak railing of the jury box with his clenched fist. Again and again he brought his fist down, driving the point home with percussive force.

"Blow after blow after blow after blow. In and out the piercing of a knife. Piercing that stops —"

Rerucha paused and looked at his watch, counting the last seconds in silence. Then he faced the jury again.

"— right now. How long is thirty seconds? Is it an eternity? I believe we've proved beyond a reasonable doubt that the defendant purposely, with premeditated malice, killed Daphne Sulk. Some people have said that Daphne was not afraid of Mr. Robinson. Well, a fly is never afraid of the spider's web until it's too late."

In his reverie at the courthouse window, Rerucha wondered if he had overdone it with the spider business. A timid-looking juror in the front row, probably in her sixties, had turned away when he began slamming his fist down. He recognized her from his son Luke's elementary school, where she was a social studies teacher.

Outside on Grand Avenue a few college students rode by on their bikes. Rerucha mused that once the trial was over he'd finally take his mountain bike out again, maybe with the boys. Nothing took his mind off work like hitting the dirt trails on the Warren Livestock property at the east end of town. The sight of wild antelope sprinting across the sage-covered prairie tended to quiet any turbulence still rumbling in him. Even if Robinson appealed, the attorney general's office would handle it. Order would be restored and his family life could go back to normal.

"Cal, you ready?" a gravelly male voice asked.

Rerucha turned to face DeBree. The two had spent long hours building their case and had joined forces on another demanding homicide the year before. DeBree was the best cop in the county, Rerucha thought, but everything about his rugged physical presence said *rancher*. A hankering for the vast emptiness of the high plains seemed to emanate from him head-to-toe. If DeBree were to mosey in one morning and say he was leaving law enforcement to spend the rest of his days herding cattle, Rerucha would not have blinked.

"They're back," DeBree announced with his usual lack of fanfare. "Got a verdict for us."

"They're a good jury, Rob, I just can't read 'em. You think they understood the blood evidence?"

"You spelled it out like the A-B-Cs, Cal, too late to sweat it now," DeBree smiled. "C'mon, let's go face the music."

A restive mood came over the courtroom as the jury foreman prepared to read the verdict. Judge Donnell, who had a mixed reputation for fairness and meting out unforgiving sentences to repeat offenders, scanned the room before signaling him to begin.

As a prosecutor Cal Rerucha lived for charged moments like these, even if they elicited his worst fears. Before giving his full attention to the foreman, he glanced over his shoulder at Daphne's mother, who waited expectantly but seemed bereft of hope. The depth of her loss was still incomprehensible to him, despite his awareness of the most excruciating details of her daughter's suffering. He could barely imagine the rage that would overtake him if someone murdered one of his sons with such hateful abandon.

"We, the jury, find the defendant, Kevin Robinson, guilty of voluntary manslaughter in the death of Daphne Sulk," the foreman stated with a trace of quiver in his voice. "We also find the defendant guilty of soliciting a child to engage in illicit sexual activity, and guilty of taking indecent liberties with a minor . . ."

As Rerucha listened to the verdicts on the remaining charges, he felt a long-awaited rush of vindication and relief. He had always believed more fervently in justice than revenge, but at that instant he couldn't deny his shameless pleasure knowing that Robinson would be locked away for a long, long time. Part of him wished the bastard would rot in hell.

Afterward he quietly exited the courtroom with DeBree, which was as close to a victory parade as the two were likely to see. While Rerucha had won three consecutive terms as county attorney and was poised to win a fourth in several weeks' time, he saw his political career hitting a ceiling. There was always the chance of throwing his hat into the ring for Congress or governor, but he seriously doubted he was up to the fund-raising demands.

Once again Rerucha had driven himself just short of burnout. He desperately needed to catch his breath away from the office; away from thoughts of Daphne and her inconsolable mother, and ten months of dissecting the rage that drove a grown man, a father no less, to inflict seventeen stab wounds on a pregnant teenager.

The Letter

Eight·months after my first conversation with Cal Rerucha in his office and two years almost to the day of Matthew Shepard's death, I returned to Laramie with the first draft of a screenplay. I wanted Rerucha to double-check my facts before I sent the script to a Los Angeles producer with whom I hoped to make a television movie. Since this was my final research trip, I planned to spend a few hours at the courthouse reviewing a file of news clippings on the case that had been faithfully collected by Rerucha's mother. I also wanted to be sure I had copies of all the documents I needed so I wouldn't have to trouble him further.

On a Saturday morning in October 2000, Rerucha took my screenplay and retreated to his office, leaving me in the law library down the hall — a tranquil, wood-paneled study where he had often conferred with Matthew's parents during trial recesses.

As I leafed through articles in a carton of manila folders, I noticed a handwritten letter that appeared to be misplaced. The two-page correspondence was neatly penned on notebook paper and addressed to "Mr. Rerucha." On the bottom of the second page, the letter was signed "Sincerely, A Concerned Citizen." Its anonymous origin immediately seized my interest, but I worried that I had stumbled on something I wasn't supposed to see.

Although the letter had no date, I quickly realized it had been written during Aaron McKinney's trial the previous year. McKinney's lawyers had tried to present a so-called gay panic defense, arguing that an unwanted sexual advance by Matthew Shepard triggered memories of homosexual abuse McKinney had suffered at the age of seven, causing him to react violently. Like others who followed the case I was infuriated by that legal strategy, which sought to place the blame on the victim.

The letter began:

> Dear Mr. Rerucha,
>
> I was shocked to hear that Aaron McKinney's attorneys claim gay panic in their defense . . . Aaron and Russ were quite familiar with gay guys and have frequented gay bars. They became aware of the fact that they had a valuable asset in their pants and that gay guys would give them shelter, food and money in return for a few minutes pleasure . . . Even though [Aaron] was acting the part of "straight trade," he was appalled that he really did like doing it with other guys. Aaron always felt guilty that he let another guy do him. His excuse was: he was only doing it for the money to spend on his girlfriend. Aaron always questioned his own truthfulness as to why he was really doing it. Deep down inside, a small part of him really liked some homosexual action . . .

I was aware by then that one of the alleged "gay guys," whom the author identified as Thomas O'Connor, was a Laramie chauffeur that everyone knew as "Doc," and that Doc O'Connor had also been a friend of Matthew Shepard. Doc was portrayed in several magazine stories as a folksy, somewhat eccentric, cowboylike character who had befriended Matthew a few days before the attack, when Matthew hired a limo to take him to a Colorado dance club.

Yet according to every news account I had read, Matthew had never met Aaron McKinney and Russell Henderson before — they were "strangers."

Could the letter's claims that "Aaron and Russ were quite familiar with gay guys" and that Aaron "really did like doing it with other guys" be some kind of perverse joke? However, if there was any truth to the letter, I had to assume there were other hidden facts around the case. Its author seemed to know Aaron McKinney intimately but felt safer remaining anonymous. Why? What else did he or she know? And where did Doc O'Connor fit? Was he the link between Matthew and his killers, despite his repeated public statements to the contrary?

I was also concerned that I had betrayed Cal Rerucha's trust by reading a confidential communication. Although we had become friends, I wasn't ready to discuss the letter with him yet. I needed time to consider its contents and decide what they meant for the screenplay I had just completed. An anonymous letter is hardly reliable as evidence, but the allegations it contained — and its mention of Doc — deserved further investigation.

Pushing aside my anxious thoughts, I quietly photocopied the letter and returned the original to its folder.

That afternoon I had lunch with Rerucha at the Overland restaurant in Laramie's downtown historic district, alongside the once-bustling Union Pacific rail yard. I was puzzled when he commended my screenplay.

"Most of it rings very true," he said, "especially the trial scenes."

He assured me that I was "on the right track," which only confused me more. But I also appreciated that just as I had chosen to remain silent about the letter, his duty as a prosecutor obliged him to be prudent in the extreme.

Two days later as I was preparing to leave town, I asked Rerucha for directions to the secluded fence where Matthew's fatal beating had taken place. For reasons I could not explain I had never wanted to visit the site before. Perhaps I was superstitious about returning to the scene of such a hopelessly brutal crime. But I felt drawn there on the day of my departure and was surprised when Rerucha offered to drive me himself.

I had spent a good deal of time in Laramie by then, yet could not remember a day when the town's pristine high-desert surroundings looked more inviting. The cloudless sky was a luminous azure, and the air crisp and dry with a light autumn gust. Even the dull, brush-covered hills had an almost otherworldly radiance in the noonday sun.

As Rerucha steered his Oldsmobile sedan onto a rutted trail at the edge of the prairie, he waved to a state trooper who was parking his patrol car in the driveway of an adjacent ranch home. Rerucha's attention drifted for several seconds. Gazing into the distance, he shook his head and muttered something, then explained that on the night

Matthew was attacked the same trooper, Dan Dyer, had just arrived home in his vehicle, parking in exactly the same spot, when he noticed a pickup with its taillights out heading into town. It would turn out to be Aaron McKinney and Russell Henderson fleeing the crime scene, while Matthew was left behind, bleeding profusely in the bitter cold, slumped against a fence post.

The road in front of us suddenly gave way to rockier terrain. Rerucha parked there, and we got out to walk the rest of the way. Cresting a low embankment a few steps ahead of me, Rerucha looked into the gully below and discovered that the fence was no longer in its place — it had been moved.

He wasn't surprised, he said, as the owner of the property had grown weary of a steady stream of visitors trudging across his land. The pine fence where Matthew had been found pistol-whipped and unconscious was now something of a shrine for travelers passing through town on the interstate and more committed pilgrims who trekked from farther away.

Within minutes Rerucha and I found the fence in a nearby ravine: a simple, crosshatched log barrier with a spray of dried roses dangling from one of its beams, their color bleached pink by the sun.

As we stood there silently for several long minutes, I thought of the college freshman who had fallen off his mountain bike on an October evening two years earlier, believing at first that he'd come upon a Halloween scarecrow. But then he saw blood shining on Matthew's face and ran to get help.

I also remembered fragments of Dennis Shepard's bittersweet words as he faced Aaron McKinney in court.

"You left [Matt] out there by himself but he wasn't alone," Dennis had said. "There were his lifelong friends. The beautiful night sky with the stars and the moon . . . and the sun to shine on him one more time. One more cool, wonderful, autumn day. And through it all, the smell of sagebrush and the scent of pine trees from the Snowy Range. And the wind, the ever-present Wyoming wind."

Standing in that place, I felt as if I were being challenged to take a second look at the whole case; to somehow pick up where Cal Rerucha had left off. Rerucha's mission as prosecutor had been the pursuit of justice, but if there were more complex truths behind Matthew's murder — as I now suspected — was it a justice that was lacking or incomplete?

What I thought would be the end of a journey, the completion of my screenplay, was only a prologue. With the letter unearthed at the courthouse, a multitude of new questions surfaced. If Aaron McKinney, who reportedly targeted Matthew because he was gay, was not "straight" himself, what else was going on that October night when he unleashed his rage?

Robbery was well established as a motive during McKinney's trial, yet according to the accepted version of events he and Russell Henderson had not known Matthew previously. But given the casual ease with which the three young men were seen leaving the Fireside Lounge together, there had to be something missing from this picture.

After returning home, I delved once more into the hefty archive of research material I had assembled. I was intrigued by portions of McKinney's transcribed confession to police on October 9, 1998, which had been under seal for more than a year along with hundreds of other case documents.

Asked by Detective Rob DeBree about his conversation with Matthew at the Fireside bar shortly before the attack, McKinney stated, "He said he could turn us on to some cocaine or something, some methamphetamines, one of those two, for sex."

Media coverage at the time made little mention of drugs as a possible factor and did not report that an exchange of drugs for sex had allegedly been discussed that night. McKinney also told DeBree and Detective Ben Fritzen, to whom he confessed, that he hadn't used methamphetamine in more than two months. Yet both officers were aware from previous investigations that he was a longtime meth user and dealer. Why was the subject of meth raised only briefly with McKinney and then dropped for the remainder of his confession?

I was further baffled by Cal Rerucha's admission to me shortly before I left Laramie that he had declined an invitation from the Clinton administration to go to Washington, including a visit to the White House. In his usual terse fashion all Rerucha would say was that a couple of his law enforcement colleagues, who had teamed up with Judy Shepard to lobby for a federal hate crime bill, were "upset" with him for not joining them in the capital. For an elected Democratic official to rebuff the Clinton administration seemed like political suicide to me, but evidently Rerucha had his reasons. What were they?

With questions like these mounting, I decided to reexamine Matthew Shepard's murder with the eye of a journalist, a decision that unwittingly grew into a decadelong investigation.

SIX

"Life Training"

During my first year attempting to research Matthew's murder as a journalist, I worked independently and only part-time while continuing to teach. But each time I returned to Laramie, I became more troubled by the things I was hearing — and more confused.

One Wyoming law enforcement official with intimate knowledge of the murder case agreed to talk with me, but only on condition of anonymity because he said he feared for his family's safety. In a strained voice he told me of two individuals who might harm his wife or kids while he was away from Laramie working. One of the named individuals, who had suspected criminal ties, "might put a hit on them," he said. The second individual, whose name I recognized, held a high-ranking position at the county courthouse.

But despite his fear, the official stated unflinchingly, "Shepard's murder had nothing to do with his sexual preferences" — an assertion I would come to hear often during interviews.

I was stunned by his claims. Threats of mob-style violence for talking openly about the murder? If Matthew's killing had "nothing to do with his sexual preferences," what was behind it then?

Until I interviewed this official, it had never occurred to me that organized crime or local corruption might have helped conceal vital truths around the murder. But very quickly I realized that I'd better proceed with extreme caution.

As I asked around Laramie for information on Aaron McKinney and Russell Henderson, I found a number of their peers also unwilling to talk on the record. A few became hostile when I inquired about their drug activities. Many of my early phone calls and letters to potential sources went unanswered; doors were sometimes shut in my face; and a few who agreed to meet with me never showed up. But on the irregular occasions when I got lucky, a single interview could lead to several new sources. Some were willing to go on the record, or at least allow me to use their name to enlist the cooperation of others.

The aforementioned law enforcement official who requested anonymity tipped me off that I should contact a Laramie attorney named Glenn Duncan. Duncan had been disbarred from practicing law due to an alleged misuse of client funds, but before his fall from grace he had worked for a time in the firm of Wyoming legal powerhouse Gerry Spence. Skeptical of Duncan's credibility yet also intrigued, I arranged to meet him in his relaxed office near the University of Wyoming campus.

A husky, middle-aged man with a forceful handshake, Duncan began the conversation by telling me that he was only consenting to an interview "on the slim hope that someone in the media finally tells the truth about Shepard's murder." Although he would prove to be a reliable source of information on Aaron McKinney, he warned that I had my work cut out for me "because of all the misinformation out there."

Two and a half years before the murder, Duncan had tried to help McKinney break his addiction to drugs — mainly methamphetamine — and had nearly succeeded, he said.

In their private conversations, McKinney had confided to Duncan that "he felt [like] a worthless piece of shit" and was "full of resentment" for the local surgeon who had botched his mother's hysterectomy, causing her death when McKinney was sixteen.

I had already heard from Cal Rerucha and others about the wrongful death settlement of nearly one hundred thousand dollars that McKinney had received in 1995, and how fast he had blown through the money.

But regarding McKinney's low self-esteem, Duncan added, "Aaron would pick fights that he couldn't win."

Before meeting Duncan, I'd been told by another McKinney friend about a night when a group of their cohorts were hanging out at "The Buck," a popular downtown saloon near the railroad tracks.

McKinney had spotted the surgeon's son, Richie Shine, in the bar and attacked him in a rage. McKinney's friends quickly jumped in and pulled him off Shine, who fled. Seething with profanity, McKinney promised to catch up with the whole Shine family.

According to Duncan, in April 1996 he invited McKinney to a "Life Training" workshop in Fort Collins, Colorado. During a weekend of intensive group sessions, "Aaron started seeing the lies your mind [can tell] you," Duncan said. But by Sunday, McKinney failed to show up for the morning meeting. Duncan went looking for him and "encouraged him to face his shame," then drove him back to Fort Collins for more "Life Training." For a brief period afterward, "Aaron seemed determined to change," but the weekend intervention didn't last and he was soon back on drugs.

Duncan said he knew nothing specific about McKinney's dealing activities, yet he was convinced that aspects of the Shepard murder had been "covered up." When I asked why he felt so strongly, he cited his unrelated experiences as a lawyer in the railroad industry, where he had "witnessed" corporate cover-ups of accidents and deaths involving railway workers.

The more time I spent in Laramie, however, the more frequently I heard rumors of a cover-up around the murder. Many, like Duncan, questioned the real motives behind the crime and whether Aaron McKinney and Russell Henderson were the only participants in the plan to rob Matthew.

The mother of one of McKinney's male friends, who said she had known Aaron "since he was a teenager," stated that she'd watched both young men and several others in their circle succumb to methamphetamine addiction and eventually to dealing to support their habit.

"Aaron ended up getting into meth and his whole personality started changing," she recalled. "He was more narcissistic . . . in that he had to have those drugs . . . He had to have money and he had to have drugs . . . [They] just basically took control of his life. And if you tried to talk to Aaron about it he would just get angry and tell you to mind your own fucking business."

These frequent allegations that McKinney was involved with drugs
— and that Laramie itself was rife with corruption — seemed to be
more than local gossip. But at the same time, none of the sources I
had spoken with claimed to have direct knowledge of a drug component to Matthew's murder nor did they offer hard evidence to support
the theory of a cover-up.

SEVEN

Doc's Frontier Village

A few months before I met Glenn Duncan and heard about Aaron McKinney's abortive "Life Training," I'd located a former employee of the Fireside Lounge who had worked on the night Matthew left the bar with Aaron and Russell. The employee, Dillon*, whose name I found in a court file, had been questioned at length by police but had avoided contact with the media. At first he was taken aback when I called his mother's listed number in Laramie and left a message for him. Luckily she hadn't asked who I was or why I was calling.

Had he known it was a journalist writing about the Shepard murder he "never would've returned the call," Dillon told me later. But after repeated assurances that I would not use his name in print, he agreed to meet for an early breakfast at Reenie's Beanery, a friendly, home-style restaurant in West Laramie. He said the place was a little out of the way, and we weren't likely to draw attention there.

Reenie's was crowded on the snowy morning I arrived, mostly men in thick flannels and work clothes packing in a big breakfast to start the day. It was easy to pick out Dillon because he was the only person sitting at a table alone. Tall and clean-cut, then in his late twenties, he could have been another local about to brave the frigid weather working on a highway crew or plowing the town streets.

Dillon got friendlier once I explained that I was looking into aspects of the Shepard murder that had perhaps been neglected or overlooked. But I was also aware that he was speaking in a very low voice, as if he was worried that someone might be listening to our conversation. Slowly he recounted his memories of seeing Aaron, Russell, and Matthew at the Fireside that October night — from the time Matthew arrived "between 10 and 10:30 PM," to Aaron and Russell's arrival about an hour later, and the uneventful departure of the three sometime after midnight.

According to Dillon, Matthew was "sitting next to the wait-station, next to an older woman, but for the most part [he] sat by himself." He said the woman, who had blond shoulder-length hair and looked like she was in her mid-thirties, never moved until the bar closed, long after the three men had left together. It was the first time I had heard of a blond woman at the bar. As far as I knew, she hadn't been mentioned in police reports; nor had I come across anyone fitting her description on the official witness list.

Dillon also recalled seeing Aaron and Russell at the Fireside "the week prior," which appeared to be the same evening on which a female friend of Russell claimed she had waited in the truck while Aaron and Russell went inside so Aaron could conduct "some business." Dillon thought he had seen both men in the bar "10 to 15 times," with more frequent visits in the weeks preceding the attack. Later, Aaron himself confirmed to me that he had dealt drugs at the Fireside and other bars but denied any involvement by Russell in his dealing activities.

Before we finished breakfast, I told Dillon I was investigating the role sex and drugs may have played in the murder. He urged me to "look into Doc O'Connor in Bosler," but he cautioned me to "be very careful cause Doc can get nasty."

"He's into all kinds of things up there," Dillon said. "Trust me, he can be violent when he wants to."

Dillon himself had been brutally assaulted outside the Fireside one evening after Matthew's murder, though he declined to say who his attacker was.

In a more subdued tone he confided that the reason the whole truth of the murder never came out was, "there are some cops in town who want it that way." I was baffled, but before I could probe further he revealed that several members of his family had been respected police officers in Laramie, "so I know what I'm talking about." I could see Dillon wanted to leave it at that, so I didn't press him.

I also didn't tell him that I already had an interview scheduled with Doc O'Connor for that afternoon. Doc and I had spoken several times on the phone but he'd let me know right off that he would only talk openly in person. After hearing Dillon's warning, I thought about canceling the interview. I was conflicted. It was obvious that

Doc knew more than he told the media, though his reasons for with-holding information were a mystery. In any case, it seemed impossible to write a more accurate account of the murder without hearing his story. But there was no one I could ask to go along with me; nor would Doc be pleased if I showed up with a companion. He had already insisted I come alone.

After breakfast, as I shook Dillon's hand outside Reenie's, he told me to let him know if there was anything else he could do. I got into my compact rental car, dwarfed in the parking lot by several heavy-duty trucks, and turned onto Snowy Range Road, heading back to the Holiday Inn where I was staying to collect my thoughts about Doc O'Connor. I had asked Doc the day before if we could meet in town but he was firm; if I wanted to see him I had to drive out to his place in Bosler.

Moments after leaving Dillon, I noticed a police car in my rearview mirror, close enough to see the young male cop who was driving. Our eyes met briefly but I was sure I hadn't been speeding. I assumed he would turn in another direction once we got to the intersection of I-25 and 3rd Street, which led downtown. Instead he continued to tailgate me until we pulled into the parking lot of the Holiday Inn. I felt my heart begin to race. The cop made no attempt to hide that he was following me.

As a precaution when I checked into the motel, I had asked that my name and room number not be given out. But I was suddenly nervous about going to my room alone, even in broad daylight. Instead I parked quickly, hurried into the lobby and past the front desk to a restroom in an adjacent corridor, and tried to calm myself.

Was the cop someone Dillon knew? Maybe checking me out to be sure I was the journalist I claimed to be?

I hadn't bothered to look more closely at the car to see if it bore the insignia of the Laramie Police Department or the Albany County Sheriff's Office. Or maybe the cop was a state trooper? Did Cal Rerucha ask him to keep an eye out, knowing I was looking into things that had caused the community a lot of distress? Or was something else going on? Was I being warned to stop what I was doing, pack up, and leave town?

I stood anxiously in front of the restroom mirror and soaked a paper towel in cold water to wipe the sweat from my forehead. I saw how scruffy I looked, with a week or more of beard growth, an appearance I had deliberately cultivated for return trips to Laramie. It wasn't much of a disguise — hooded gray sweatshirt, jeans, old Timberlands, a University of Wyoming Cowboys ball cap, and the faded Carhartt — but the last thing I wanted to do was announce the arrival of a reporter from New York.

When minutes passed and the cop didn't walk in behind me, my body temperature began to cool. The worst of my panic was over, but I still reached into the zippered pocket of my jacket for a little white pill, a five-milligram Ativan, and swallowed it with a palmful of water from the faucet. For a few seconds I thought of the debilitating panic attacks Matthew had experienced and his sardonic shorthand for pills just like this one. "Mother's Little Helpers" he called them, borrowing from the Rolling Stones song of the same name.

I still couldn't make up my mind about Doc but I composed myself and returned to the lobby, hoping to find the police car gone. Instead the young cop was hunched over the front desk talking to a female clerk and looking over a sheet of paper. As I walked past, they seemed a little flummoxed but gave me a friendly nod. Was that my registration form he was reviewing, or was my paranoia spinning out of control?

I left the Holiday Inn and drove north on 3rd Street into the heart of Laramie's downtown. When I finally convinced myself that I was no longer being watched or followed, I felt enormous relief. The last thing I wanted to do was trouble Cal Rerucha in the middle of a busy workday, least of all to expose my fear. But the sense of being an unwelcome stranger didn't go away.

Driving past rows of charming little storefronts and historic brick facades — the very picture of a western, all-American college town — felt surreal, as if I had drifted into the dreamlike landscape of David Lynch's *Twin Peaks* or *Blue Velvet*.

I thought of Matthew again and how Laramie might have looked to him as a smart and worldly yet confused twenty-one-year-old. I also speculated about some of the dangers he might have succumbed to before his encounter with Aaron McKinney and Russell Henderson at the Fireside bar.

Any suggestions that their meeting that night could have been planned around drugs, or some combination of drugs and sex, had been dismissed by the media, based largely on the opinions of a couple of Matthew's friends.

"There was some speculation that [Matthew] was buying drugs from Aaron and Russell, but his friends find that implausible," an article in *Vanity Fair* stated. "Matthew's friends also find it hard to picture him being sexually drawn to Aaron or Russell. Nor do they think that Matthew was interested in a threesome."

And I continued to wonder where Doc O'Connor fit.

Before driving to the tiny town of Bosler to meet Doc, I decided to call Cal Rerucha for a word of advice. I was sitting in my car outside the county courthouse on Grand Avenue, still struggling with the anxiety that had taken hold of me that morning. I was about to leave town on a lonely two-lane road, headed eighteen miles north to a place I'd been told resembled a ghost town from the Old West, replete with ramshackle cabins, a former saloon, and a whorehouse. Doc, who owned most of Bosler, had renamed the property "Doc's Western Village," hoping, as he later told me, to attract visitors there as a tourist destination. Central to the site's appeal would be showcasing the twenty-five-foot white stretch limousine "that Matt Shepard used to ride in."

For his part, Doc contributed significantly to the mythologized view of Matthew that the media quickly adopted as its own.

"Matthew knew he was going to . . . get beaten or strangled — he wasn't sure which," Doc told one reporter. "He said, 'When I get done in because I'm gay, if one gay person and one straight person come together and stop to think that we're both people, that would be something' . . . And then, four days later [after the attack], the whole country comes together. He's bigger than kings and queens. One person told me he wanted to look it up in the Book of Revelation."

But in other interviews Doc seemed to contradict himself. He told a different reporter that he didn't think the murder had anything to do with Matthew being gay, and said he was still fond of Aaron and Russell.

In the years before and after the murder, while he waited for prospective investors in his "Western Village," Doc ran assorted other businesses on the main street — dealing in antiques, used cars, furniture, and, according to some sources, illicit items as well.

But talking with Cal Rerucha for a few minutes allayed my fears. He assured me that "a visit to Tom O'Connor's won't be life-threatening," yet he also indicated in a roundabout way that Doc had been involved in marginal activities for decades and that his rambling pronouncements shouldn't be taken at face value.

I told Rerucha I would call him as soon as I got back to town. "If you don't hear from me, I hope you'll send some deputies out," I said half joking.

I couldn't find the courage to mention the cop who had tailed me to the Holiday Inn.

"Tom's an interesting fellow," Rerucha added with some hesitation. "Who knows, maybe he'll have something to say."

Later I learned that Cal Rerucha had been Doc's attorney back in the 1980s when he'd been in private practice. Doc had sold him the antique oak desk in his courthouse office — where we often sat for interviews — "at a bargain price." According to Doc, it was an heirloom that had belonged to his great-grandfather. Rerucha seemed certain that his former client had no part in Matthew's murder, yet he also intimated that if anyone knew what was really behind it, Doc did.

Following the directions to Bosler that Doc had given, I pulled off Highway 30 into a scrubby driveway that led to several outbuildings and trailers. Uncertain about where to go next, I dialed him on my cell phone.

"Just pull in where I told you," a raspy male voice answered at the other end. "Park there on the left and come to the door right in front of you." Before I could respond, the connection went dead.

The windows of the single-story building nearest me were covered with wrinkled shades; some were torn and yellowed with age. No sign of life inside or anywhere else.

I got out of the car slowly. Just then a thick metal door on the side of the house opened and Doc O'Connor's surly voice bellowed from within, "What's the matter, can't you boys from back east follow instructions?"

Seconds later I stood with Doc, a craggy-looking man with a graying mustache and short ponytail, in a corner of his ranch-style bedroom where we faced a bank of video monitors and computer screens. Staring back at us were black-and-white surveillance pictures of my parked car outside, from every possible angle. I tried to maintain a friendly composure, pretending not to be intimidated or even surprised.

"Don't worry, you're safe here," Doc teased. "If anyone tries to get past these cameras, I've got my rifles."

Studying his face and eyes I could see that he must have been a knockout as a young man. During another visit with Doc months later, as he nursed a rum and Coke at his kitchen table, he confirmed as much when he pulled out a dusty leather-bound album with photos taken in his twenties.

Slowly, over several long, meandering conversations, he loosened up and spoke of things in his past he had long kept hidden: from his adventures performing in porn films and the glories of being paid "big bucks" for sex with Hollywood movie stars and a married bank president to encounters with the infamous gangster "Chauncey" Smaldone and the Denver mob.

"I was a hustler," Doc confessed unabashedly.

According to Doc, he first met Aaron McKinney when Aaron was sixteen or seventeen — one of several local young men with problems whom Doc took under his wing, though some in Laramie allege that his motives have not always been altruistic.

In mid-summer 1998, several weeks before Matthew's attack, Aaron, his girlfriend Kristen, and their infant son lived in an apartment on Doc's property in Bosler "rent-free." The arrangement they had was that Aaron would do "odd jobs" for him, Doc explained as he gave me a tour of the dim, windowless apartment, situated in a huge warehouse across the road from his home.

Many of my early interviews with Doc occurred in out-of-the-way places. Sometimes he would offer to take me out in one of his stretch limos "for a drive out to the mountains," but I politely declined. He said he wanted to show me Centennial, Wyoming, a rustic town about thirty miles from Laramie, and Woods Landing, another remote spot where he had driven Aaron and a few of his friends for parties in the limo.

For a long time Doc continued to say that he had just met Matthew a few days before the attack and that he "never saw Aaron and Matthew together." But as new sources began to tell me a different story, Doc's story began to change, too. He acknowledged that Matthew had, indeed, visited him in Bosler with his friend Alex Trout months before the murder, although Doc was quick to add, "Matt didn't say very much, so I didn't really remember him."

Doc also described a rowdy incident in the limo with Aaron and two unidentified male friends — long before Matthew was killed.

"They dropped a couple of girls off at home first and told me to take them to Woods Landing," he recalled. "I got paid to be the driver and mind my own business, which I always did, until I heard someone break a champagne glass in the back. I slid the window open and told Aaron he'd have to pay me for the glass."

Doc stared at me, pausing for effect. "The three guys were buck naked back there, playing around together. Aaron said, 'No problem, Doc, I'll take care of it.' I just shut my window and didn't say another word."

Only after I questioned Doc intermittently over months did he concede, "Matt may have been one of the guys in back [of the limo] with Aaron . . . I can't say for sure."

I also asked Doc numerous times about one of the many businesses he owned, called Lincoln Escort Service. He answered with a straight face that it was "a service to escort big trucks with heavy loads on the interstate." I told him that an "escort service" means something altogether different where I come from.

But Doc stuck to that story, even after boasting that he had arranged to bring Denver-based female strippers to Wyoming to perform in a bar there.

"They call 'em 'exotic dancers' now, but they do the same thing they've always done," he said with a cool shrug.

I was reminded again of the anonymous letter I found at the court-house long before, stating that Aaron "was acting the part of 'straight trade'" and "his excuse was: he was only doing it for the money to spend on his girlfriend." Did Doc run an escort service that employed young males like Aaron and perhaps Russell, too? And where did Matthew fit in Doc's schemes, if at all?

What I thought was just an innocuous suggestion by Doc in an early interview would later lead me to a seedy hustler bar in Denver called Mr. Bill's, as well as a few other gay bars along the city's Broadway strip. Those late-night excursions prompted me, in turn, to go back to Doc with more questions — and more confusion.

For reasons I did not understand, Doc had also divulged that shortly after Matthew's attack he had hired a prominent defense attor-ney to represent him. If Doc had nothing to do with the murder and Cal Rerucha had never brought charges against him, why did he need a lawyer? Each time I broached the subject, Doc deflected my ques-tions by shifting to something else.

"There are some things you'll never get me to talk about," he swore.

Doc made no attempt to hide his fear that "someone might put a bullet in my back some night when I'm driving home from the Eagles," a Laramie fraternal club in which he'd been an active member and trustee for decades. He always drove into town and back home again on Highway 30, the same deserted, two-lane county road that first took me to Bosler to meet him in 2002.

EIGHT

Palomino Drive

During the summer of 2002 I also began a series of extensive phone interviews with Aaron McKinney, who was then incarcerated at the Wyoming State Penitentiary. It would not be until 2004, however, after he was transferred to a prison in Nevada, that correctional authorities allowed us to meet face-to-face. Aaron's father, Bill McKinney, a long-haul truck driver whom I first met in June 2002 in the snack bar of an Arizona golf course, facilitated my introduction to him.

Initially the elder McKinney was gruff. He told me he was still bitter over the media's treatment of his son, which he felt had compromised the fairness of his 1999 trial. He also complained that reporters had taken his own remarks out of context, in order to cast him "as an anti-gay redneck, just like Aaron."

According to an article in *The Denver Post* a few days after the attack on Matthew Shepard, Bill McKinney stated, "The news has already taken this up and blew it totally out of proportion because it involved a homosexual. Had this been a heterosexual these two boys decided to take out and rob, this never would have made the national news."

Bill McKinney's words — along with a televised interview that week in which Aaron's girlfriend, Kristen Price, claimed that "[Aaron and Russ] just wanted to beat [Matthew] up bad enough to teach him a lesson not to come on to straight people" — amounted to pouring gasoline on a blazing fire. Within days more than fifty vigils, marches, and demonstrations protesting the attack on Matthew took place around the nation. After such blatant statements by Aaron McKinney's father and girlfriend, was there any reason to doubt anti-gay hate as the motive?

Whatever other traits Bill McKinney and his son may share, their sharp facial features and eyes bear an uncanny resemblance, right down to their tight, slightly upturned lips when they're pissed off about something. After meeting Aaron in person, I could never be in his father's presence without having the discomfiting sense that Aaron was there, too.

Bill McKinney only agreed to talk with me, he said, "because you seem to have an open mind on the case, with more questions than answers." I couldn't help but wonder just the same: Would he have given me the time of day had I disclosed up front that I'm gay? One personal paradox of revisiting Matthew's murder was my decision to remain closeted with several sources, at least early on. I was concerned that my investigation might be perceived as having a gay agenda and that sources in Wyoming might hesitate to open up. But it later became apparent that Bill McKinney knew I was gay from the start and was unfazed.

Over many cups of coffee at Shari's twenty-four-hour restaurant on Laramie's North 3rd Street — and despite my initial skepticism — I slowly warmed to Bill's no-nonsense disposition. Never once did he suggest his son was anything less than fully culpable for his explosive violence against Matthew Shepard. On the contrary, he volunteered, "Aaron has always had a terrible temper, going way, way back."

But like others, Bill McKinney was unconvinced that hatred of gays was behind the attack. He reminded me of something I had heard from others in Laramie: that at the time of the murder both Kristen Price's mother and the mother of Russell Henderson's twenty-year-old girlfriend, Chasity Pasley, were in lesbian relationships and "there was no evidence whatsoever of Aaron or Russell expressing anti-gay feelings."

"Aaron lived in the same house with Kristen's mother for months and they never had a problem," Bill recalled.

When I asked him if it was possible that Aaron had been sexually involved with other males, he said he had "no knowledge of it" but appeared to shrug my question off as dumb or irrelevant.

"Come on, Steve, we've all experimented one way or another," he added without the slightest diffidence. "Most people that tell you they haven't are full of it."

Had Bill McKinney not screened me and given his okay, Aaron would not have agreed to an interview. He made that clear in our first phone conversation on August 1, 2002. Both of us began talking with some trepidation, as we knew the call was being recorded by the Wyoming Department of Corrections. This was also the first time Aaron violated the oath of silence that was part of his 1999 sentencing agreement. Immediately following his conviction, he spared himself the possibility of a death sentence by agreeing, among other conditions, to refrain from discussing the case with the media.

By the time of our first interview, I had been commissioned by *The New York Times Magazine* to write an article reexamining the murder. Any moral reservations I had about persuading Aaron McKinney to talk with me were overshadowed by the host of troubling questions that his trial had left unanswered and the media never bothered to probe. A few renowned legal scholars even argued that the suppression of his right to free speech was unconstitutional.

As I began communicating with both Aaron McKinney and Russell Henderson that summer, my foremost challenge was convincing each of them to talk openly when they had nothing to gain, beyond helping to set the record straight. And could I depend on anything they told me when each had lied often in the past?

During many hours of phone interviews with Aaron in August and September 2002, he was mostly cooperative, yet blunt and unintimidated — as if he had no time to waste on formalities. He acknowledged in short order that he'd been a drug dealer for three years prior to the murder and that he'd done "some fucked-up things." But what he regretted most, he said, "is that I'll never be able to be there for my son," who was then four.

When I eventually brought up Matthew Shepard and asked how they first met, Aaron's tone changed. He grew more sullen and cautious. He said that on the night of the crime "Matt came over first" at the Fireside bar.

"Matt was just tryin' to buddy up," he stated offhandedly, without elaborating further.

I was surprised to hear Aaron use the more personal *Matt*. Among his family and friends Matthew Shepard went by Matt, but in court documents and media accounts he was consistently referred to as Matthew.

"I'd been up for about a week," Aaron mentioned out of the blue. "I didn't know I was doin' it. I thought I was beating the dude up." Then, with barely a pause, he asked me for a second or third time, "So what else can I help you with? Is that all your questions for me?"

Aaron liked to abruptly change subjects on me like that, stopping his remarks midstream to ask if I had "any other questions" or "what else do you need to know?" Sometimes a long silence would follow, or I'd hear him talking cheerfully to other inmates in the background.

Aaron had already informed me there were "certain things" he wouldn't talk about, including the names of people with whom he had dealt drugs. "No talking out of school" was how he put it.

But when I finally grew comfortable enough to confront him about his conflicting stories — and some outright lies — he brushed me off by switching subjects again, or telling me another inmate needed to use the phone. In nearly every conversation, there was the unstated threat that he'd hang up on me and that would be it.

Yet the longer we spoke, the better I got at knowing when to press Aaron and when to back off.

I asked him several times if he had known Matthew Shepard before the crime and his answer was always "No." But it was obvious that the question more than irritated him; it put him on edge. He had a similar reaction when I asked about Doc O'Connor. Although he admitted knowing Doc, he was vague at first about whether we were referring to the same person.

"You mean the old dude who lives up there in that weird little town, what's it called again?" he asked unconvincingly.

"Bosler," I answered.

"That's it," Aaron said with feigned surprise. "Yeah, I know who you mean. What about him?"

Why was he being evasive about Doc O'Connor? Several weeks before the murder, Aaron, Kristen, and their newborn son had moved into a makeshift apartment on Doc's property. They only lasted a short time at Doc's before they moved back into town to the Ranger Motel, where the manager was a friend of Bill McKinney. But soon they relocated once more, this time to an apartment owned by Aaron's boss — roofing contractor Arsenio Lemus. Oddly, though, when they were arrested a few weeks later, both Aaron and Kristen gave the police Doc's phone number as their own.

I had been told by friends of Aaron that he often hired Doc's limos for parties, going back years before the murder. It was no secret that Matthew also liked to hire Doc's limos, but I couldn't find any solid information linking the three men — just scattered rumors.

There was, however, a small item in a police report that connected Matthew to the Ranger Motel. His close friend Alex Trout told police that the last time he had seen Matthew alive was at the Ranger bar the night before the attack. Yet a few days later in a TV interview, Trout changed his story and said that the two had only talked of getting together.

My attempts to question Aaron about sex put me in even more volatile terrain than asking about his drug activities. During a phone interview I read him the anonymous letter I had found, which identified Doc and stated that Aaron acted the part of "straight trade" but "[he] really did like doing it with other guys."

Aaron was furious about the letter. "Total fucking bullshit, all of it," he said. "None of it's true."

But the first thing he wanted to know was whether I had shared the letter with his father. When I assured him I hadn't, his relief was palpable. He insisted that I not get into "any of this sex stuff" with his father.

According to Aaron, the only "messing around" he'd ever done with other males was when he was a boy growing up on Palomino Drive in Laramie — "the usual kids' stuff," he said more than once.

On one of my early visits to the town, I drove through the quiet, nondescript subdivision where Aaron had grown up, only to realize its proximity to the fence area where Matthew was beaten. As a boy, Aaron had frequently played with his friends on the same stretch of prairie bordering the subdivision. A strange coincidence, I thought, that this was where he told Russell Henderson to drive the truck during Matthew's abduction. The truck belonged to Aaron's father, but Aaron couldn't drive it because his license had been revoked.

I recalled from conversations with Bill McKinney that he and Aaron's mother had divorced when Aaron was five. I had also read in articles that Aaron's mother locked him in the basement when he misbehaved. Bill McKinney nonetheless placed the blame for Aaron's juvenile troubles jointly with himself and his ex-wife.

"I was always on the road when he was a boy, hardly ever there," he said. "His mother was physically at home, but she wasn't really there either. She didn't know how to raise him."

As I continued to think about the location of Matthew's beating, I reexamined a letter Aaron had smuggled to Russell in jail after their arrest, advising him of a scenario they should use to explain the attack:

> Hey Homeboy . . . When we go to court, if they try us together or seperate [sic] . . . they should hear you say what I said so this is what I told them, me and you was gettin fucked up at the bar and when we was fixin to leave Matt Sheppard [sic] asked us for a ride home, so we gave him a ride . . . and when we got out there he tried to get on me and I started kicking his ass . . . At no time did we know he was gay until he tried to get on me . . . The reason Matt told us he lived in imperial heights is because He wanted to get me in a dark place so we could get funky. That's all I got for now I'm sure I'll think of more later . . .

Ironically, Imperial Heights was the subdivision where Aaron grew up. Matthew lived in a different part of town, close to the university.

Aaron's letter also revealed other inconsistencies in both his version of events and the one put forward by his girlfriend, Kristen Price — unsubstantiated alibis that became the basis of official accounts of the murder.

According to Price's statements after the crime, Aaron told her that Matthew had made a sexual advance *in the Fireside bar*, embarrassing him and Russell in front of their friends. Yet in his jailhouse letter Aaron instructed Russell, "At no time did we know he was gay until he tried to get on me *[when we got out there in the truck]*. . ." (italics mine).

In light of Aaron's claim that he had not known Matthew previously, his use of the more familiar *Matt* in the letter also caught my attention again.

Trying to untangle Aaron's contradictory statements was exasperating at times, especially as I began to gather information from other sources suggesting that he and Matthew were, indeed, well acquainted. In both his recorded confession to police and my many interviews with him, Aaron offered up multiple versions of his motives, the events that led up to the crime, and the murder itself. He seemed to enjoy playing a game of cat and mouse with me, pretending not to see the many discrepancies in his story.

I asked him if he could explain the portion of his recorded confession when he told police that Matthew had offered drugs in exchange for sex. Aaron said he "never made that statement." When I asked if I should send him the official transcript of his confession so he could have a look, he responded blankly, "No, you don't need to send it."

In my frustration I turned to Bill McKinney a few times, hoping he could convince Aaron to be more truthful. Bill was sympathetic but had no solution to offer.

"Aaron's been lying since he was a kid," he said. "Believe me, you're not the only one. He lies to me, too . . . One thing I always tried to teach him, and I think I failed miserably, is the difference between honor and loyalty. Aaron still confuses the two. He would rather be loyal to something or someone, to anything really, even if it's a lie. Then he convinces himself it's honor."

After a thoughtful pause, Bill McKinney added, "When I ask him about that night [of the murder], he tells me he doesn't remember."

NINE

Wildfire

In my search for the truth of Matthew's murder, I tracked down a number of his friends, especially those who had spent significant time with him in the summer and early fall of 1998. Some had moved from Laramie and were reluctant to talk. A few said they had spoken to the media previously but were angry at being misrepresented. And nearly everyone I contacted seemed skeptical — if not fearful — of my attempts to uncover hidden aspects of the killing.

One of Matthew's close friends whom I was eager to meet was Alex Trout. According to Cal Rerucha, the earliest reports of an anti-gay hate crime had originated with Trout, then twenty-one, and another longtime friend of Matthew named Walt Boulden, a college instructor in social work who had turned forty-six on the day of the attack. According to *The Denver Post*, Boulden described himself as a sort of big-brother figure to Matthew.

Trout and Boulden apparently had no firsthand knowledge of the crime, but in their shock at Matthew's near-fatal beating they began to spread the word immediately, before police had fully launched an investigation.

I interviewed Trout the first time on June 12, 2002, at a family-style restaurant in Rochester, New York, where he was working as an assistant manager. Beyond what Rerucha had told me, my interest in speaking with Trout came from reading police reports in which he'd claimed that Matthew had been involved with methamphetamine.

A report by Detective Sergeant Jeff Bury, which was sealed by the court until after Aaron McKinney and Russell Henderson were convicted, noted: "[Trout and Boulden] stated that . . . when [Matthew] was in Denver, that he had gotten into some cocaine use and had also participated in some methamphetamine use." Trout and Boulden's mention of cocaine and methamphetamine couldn't help but remind me of Aaron's later statement to police that Matthew had offered "some cocaine or . . . some methamphetamines . . . for sex." Yet from everything I had examined in the case record, it appeared that some police investigators — for unknown reasons — had chosen to ignore evidence of a possible drug component.

Short and boyish, with wide eyes and a moist handshake, Trout picked me up at the Rochester airport in his car and drove us into town. Almost as soon as we began talking, he said he would have "nothing to do with" my investigative efforts if I intended to write that "Matt's murder was [about] anything but anti-gay hate." I told Trout I was interested above all in who Matthew was as a person, which had been missing from most of the media coverage. He agreed, but I could see I was going to have to tread very lightly.

Another friend of Matthew had already informed me that the Shepard family had excluded Trout and Boulden from Matthew's highly publicized memorial service at the family's hometown church in Casper, Wyoming. That, too, stirred my curiosity since both men had been close to Matthew for several years and had first learned of the attack when Matthew's father phoned Boulden from Saudi Arabia. Trout had also helped Matthew move from Denver to Laramie the previous summer, driving a U-Haul along with a third friend, Ronnie Gustafson.

According to Trout, one of the first things he and Boulden did after hearing that Matthew had been severely beaten was call Jason Marsden, a gay reporter friend at the *Casper Star-Tribune*. They also contacted gay organizations in Wyoming and Colorado. Very quickly the Associated Press and other national media picked up the news of a presumed anti-gay attack.

"Once it started, it took off like a wildfire," Cal Rerucha recalled, "nothing was going to stop it." Rerucha said the story of a hate crime was also fueled, in part, by a couple of Laramie law enforcement officers "who couldn't resist being in front of the [TV] cameras."

When I later interviewed Jason Marsden, the reporter friend, he gave a slightly different account than Trout had given.

"I was sitting in the newsroom at my desk and there was a little bit of commotion around the fax machine," Marsden told me in July 2004. "I saw a couple of the senior editors conferring over something . . . [They] . . . laid this press release from the Albany County Sheriff's Office on the desk and said, 'We've received this press release recently about a young man having been attacked in Laramie and the tipster who alerted us . . . tells me that he is a friend of yours. His name is Matt Shepard. Do you know Matt Shepard?'"

Marsden, who had just seen Matthew "about four or five weeks before that in Laramie," said he was stunned.

I asked Marsden, "When . . . there was mention . . . that the attack could have been motivated at least in part by Matt being gay, was that something that was part of that initial press release?"

"It was not in the initial press release, just the bare details that he had been found and [was injured] . . . and left overnight," he responded. "But some of those friends in Laramie . . . had begun calling reporters, trying to talk to the detectives . . . and pretty quickly came to the conclusion that there was a likelihood that he had been targeted for being gay . . . I did talk to [Trout and Boulden] that day. I can't — I wish I could remember better the exact chain of events . . . But it happened very quickly in there; the press release, phone calls . . . They were very worried that the police might not take it seriously . . . that [Matt's] credibility as a victim . . . would be in some way diminished because he was gay and they were very concerned to make sure that that didn't happen."

Despite a few small discrepancies, Marsden's account of how the story of a hate crime got started confirmed Boulden and Trout's versions — and also Cal Rerucha's. According to Rerucha, "[Trout and Boulden] were calling the County Attorney's office, they were calling the media and indicating . . . we don't want the fact that [Matthew Shepard] is gay to go unnoticed."

In an ABC News interview a few days after the attack, Boulden, whom Matthew had allegedly befriended as a fifteen-year-old teenager looking for a mentor, stated simply, "I know in the core of my heart it happened because [Matt] revealed he was gay. They targeted him because he was gay." Similarly, Boulden told the University of Wyoming student newspaper, the *Branding Iron*, that he was convinced the crime was clearly motivated by hate. "There is no maybe," he said.

Yet Cal Rerucha, who had met with Boulden and Trout shortly after the crime, later stated unequivocally, "I don't think the proof [of a hate crime] was there . . . That was something they had decided."

As Alex Trout drove me back to the Rochester airport on the afternoon of June 12, 2002, he admitted — after several hours of conversation — that he had personally struggled with addiction to crystal meth, but at the same time he refused to talk on the record about Matthew's drug use. Trout also acknowledged that he had dabbled in prostitution and the pornography business. His revelations that day only provoked more questions, which I raised with him in several follow-up phone interviews in 2002 and 2003.

Perhaps most surprising was Trout's disclosure that he and Matthew had visited Doc O'Connor, the limousine driver, at Doc's home in Bosler months before the murder. This contradicted Doc's repeated statements to the media that he had met Matthew for the first time on Friday, October 2, 1998, just a few days before the attack. Trout also claimed that Doc had "stalked" him sexually, which he said he had reported to police, and that Doc had called him "a million times" asking him to have sex with "a long-haired male friend" while Doc videotaped it.

If Trout was telling the truth, however seamy, why had Doc lied about when he first met Matthew?

Soon after interviewing Trout in Rochester, I met two other gay male friends of Matthew who had grown up in Laramie and had briefly dated him. One of them admitted that he, too, had been addicted to methamphetamine and was in recovery. The other agreed to an interview but would not allow his name to be used because he said he feared retaliation from Laramie cops. When I looked puzzled, he told me he had personally sold drugs to some cops in the town. I was all the more startled because I'd been hearing similar accusations while interviewing friends of Aaron and Russell.

Why had the scores of journalists who had originally covered the crime never bothered to pursue the drug angle? The lone exception was a 1999 *Harper's Magazine* article by reporter JoAnn Wypijewski, who questioned the possible role of Laramie's drug underground and other factors, including a rumored sex triangle. But Wypijewski's questions had to go unanswered because her article was published two months before Aaron McKinney's trial, at a time when all witnesses and principals in the case were still under a court-imposed gag order and records were sealed. Later, when I met Wypijewski — a generous, fiercely dedicated journalist — she encouraged me to follow her tracks and gave me several tips on where to dig.

Admittedly, my nascent investigation was beginning to feel more dangerous. As I continued piecing together Matthew's activities in the days and weeks before the attack, I located several other sources. Among them were Tina Labrie, a fellow student of Matthew at the University of Wyoming who had met him at a Laramie picnic on the Fourth of July weekend, 1998, and eventually became his close friend and confidante; and Phil Labrie, her ex-husband.

Two weeks after meeting Alex Trout, I spent a day and a half talking with Tina, then thirty, in the Colorado mountain town of Estes Park, where she was living with her two children. Earthy and personable, with a soft, round face and wavy brown hair, Tina said she had worked hard to put some distance between her family life and an often-insatiable media in the four years since Matthew's murder. Although she had initially given "a couple of interviews," including one to *Vanity Fair*, she subsequently decided to withdraw from the intense public attention.

"I didn't like how it felt," Tina later elaborated. "[In order to] heal and deal with things personally, I just kind of shut everybody out . . . Most of the people doing the interviews didn't understand [the shock and grief] and they didn't want to give anybody any space . . . They [were] all converging on this . . . almost like a battlefield. Like this tug of war. And that was really uncomfortable . . . They wanted to just superficially kind of put it all into one thing. And miss everything else about [Matt], you know."

Until I met Tina, who had been introduced to Matthew by a mutual friend named Kathleen, the little I knew about her had come from media accounts and a formerly sealed police report document-ing events on Wednesday, October 7, 1998. That evening Tina phoned the Laramie Police Department to say she hadn't heard from Matthew since Monday the fifth and was worried about him. In her report, Detective Gwen Smith wrote:

> On 100798, I received a call at my residence from dispatch requesting I contact Sergeant Jeff BURY in relation to an ATL ["Attempt to Locate"] that had been called in on a subject, Matthew SHEPARD. Dispatch advised that SHEPARD had been located tied to a fence in the Sherman Hill[s] area. I contacted Sergeant BURY, who requested I talk to a Tina LABRIE . . .
>
> At approximately 2030 hours, I went to 1007 Lyon and met with Tina LABRIE. Also present was her husband, Phillip. Tina told me that she was concerned about Matthew SHEPARD, an acquaintance she had known since July of 1998. She said that in the past week and a half, Shepard had been acting "not himself," had become somewhat paranoid and began drinking heavily. He also changed the places he used to hang out and was now frequenting Elmer Lovejoy's, the Third Street Bar and Grill and the Fireside Bar . . .
>
> Tina said that she was concerned, as she had been unable to reach SHEPARD on his cell phone for the past two days. She said this was very unusual, as he always had his cell phone with him and had always been easy to contact before. The last time Tina spoke with SHEPARD was Monday evening, 100598, between the hours of 6:00 and 8:00 PM. She took him to a grocery store, as he had been feeling ill and not wanting to drive there himself . . .
>
> Tina continued by telling me that . . . Matthew . . . had also been spending large amounts of money, which was very unlike him. She said he would call Doc's Limo Service to drive him home from the bars if he was too intoxicated. He also rented the limo for a trip to Fort Collins, which Tina

accompanied him, where he went shopping, had dinner, and then the limo returned them to Laramie.

After receiving that information, I did tell Tina and Phillip that Matthew had been located and that he had apparently been assaulted and was injured and was on his way to Poudre Valley Hospital in Fort Collins . . .

In my initial interviews with Tina in September 2002, she was outgoing and thoughtful as she shared memories of her friendship with Matthew. She also talked at length about the weekend before the attack, including the trip they took in Doc's limo on Friday, October 2 to the Tornado, a gay dance club in Fort Collins, Colorado. Tina's recounting of that night, of their return to Laramie in the early-morning hours, and of Matt's anxiety and deepening depression over that weekend was more or less identical to what I had read in *Vanity Fair*.

After many hours of conversation, I sensed that Tina had more to say but was not willing to stray from her comfort zone. I also had many more questions I wanted to ask but knew that most would have to wait. Just as I'd become aware of contradictions and discrepancies between what Alex Trout had told the media and what I discovered interviewing him myself, I detected niggling inconsistencies between Tina's version of events and the "official" narrative reported by police and the media.

In the aforementioned police report, the limo excursion Matthew and Tina had taken was summed up in the simplest of terms: "[Matthew] also rented [Doc's] limo for a trip to Fort Collins, which Tina accompanied him, where he went shopping, had dinner, and then the limo returned them to Laramie."

In fact, the purpose of the limo trip was to go to the Tornado, a nightclub that Matthew, Alex Trout, and others in their circle often patronized, yet the police report had made no mention of the Tornado or of Doc being the driver, and had described the trip instead as involving "shopping" and "dinner." Had it been a simple omission or maybe just a routine summary of facts? From what Alex Trout had revealed about meth and his alleged "stalking" encounters with Doc, however, I realized again that references to drugs and sex were mostly absent from official accounts.

But it would not be until almost a year later, after Tina Labrie grew more comfortable with me, that she began to fill in more details of what had been troubling Matthew in the days before the attack — confirming some of what I had suspected but could not yet prove.

"Matt said he always ended up with the wrong people, involved with drugs, then would go someplace else and start over," Tina told me in August 2003.

She would also have more to say about the ride she and Matthew took in Doc's limo. After they spent the evening at the Tornado, Matthew invited a group of friends for a late-night snack at Denny's — Doc included. But afterward Matthew's mood darkened again.

"During the limo ride home [Matt said] . . . that sometimes Alex really annoyed him because he could be quite a speed freak," she recalled.

It was the first time Tina had mentioned meth ("speed," "crystal," "crank," etcetera) in connection with that weekend.

She said Matthew had also expressed suicidal thoughts in the limo, prompting her to spend the night at his apartment. Moreover, by the following morning, he had taken a near-overdose of prescription drugs, which she felt was precipitated by his worries about money.

But what, if anything, did Matthew's depression and money concerns have to do with Aaron McKinney and Russell Henderson, and their ill-fated encounter three days later? And where did Doc fit in this murky picture — if he had a place at all?

Despite my accumulation of tantalizing new details, I felt like I was still stumbling around in the dark or, worse, chasing my own tail.

Since Aaron was still denying that he had ever met Matthew previously, I redoubled my efforts with sources who were well acquainted with Aaron, hoping they would be more forthcoming. I also conducted numerous phone interviews with Russell in late 2002 and early 2003, but he, too, insisted that he had never met Matthew before and steered clear of discussing anything involving Aaron.

"There are two things I don't want to talk about," Russell told me emphatically. "I don't want to talk about Aaron and I don't want to talk about that night."

In my frustration I wanted to blurt out, *Why the hell are we talking then? Do you think I spent all this time negotiating with the prison bureaucracy so we can have a friendly social chat?*

Even when I avoided mention of Aaron and tried more tactfully to discuss specifics of the crime, Russell would often say, "You'll have to ask Aaron about that."

One of many questions gnawing at me was whether Matthew's meeting with Aaron and Russell at the Fireside had been planned in advance. During Aaron's 1999 trial, Cal Rerucha had argued that Aaron and Russell lured Matthew from the bar by pretending to be gay.

"McKinney and Henderson watch Matthew Shepard, becoming like two wolves watching a lamb," Cal had stated in his closing argument, "and they go into the bathroom together for this purpose . . . [According to Kristen Price's trial testimony] . . . when Mr. McKinney came home [later that night] . . . he said . . . when we came out of the [bathroom], we had hatched a plan that we would pretend that we were gay . . . so we could get Mr. Shepard out of the bar so we could rob him . . . [They] pretended they were homosexuals. Once the hook was set, they reel Mr. Shepard in just like a fish to the bank."

But in Aaron's taped confession to police, I found what appeared to be another small but revealing slip-up in his story:

> **Detective DeBree:** Let's go back again one more time to the [Fireside] bar.
> **Aaron McKinney:** All right.
> **Detective DeBree:** You meet [Matthew Shepard] and . . . how did you meet him?
> **Aaron McKinney:** It was the fag? The queer, yeah? We were meeting in the bar?
> **Detective DeBree:** He was a homosexual, yeah.

Aaron's use of the words *we were meeting* instead of the past-tense *we met* seemed to indicate a previous plan or intent to meet Matthew in the bar.

Aaron McKinney: Okay. He approached us.

Detective DeBree: Okay.

Aaron McKinney: I was drinking a beer.

Detective DeBree: What did he say to you?

Aaron McKinney: Asked us what we were drinkin', what we were doin'.

Detective DeBree: Bought you some drinks?

Aaron McKinney: No, he didn't buy us nothin'.

(More Q & A follows here.)

Detective DeBree: You guys more or less led him to believe that you were homosexuals yourselves and you'd take him for a ride?

Aaron McKinney: Well, I never told him I was gay at all.

Detective DeBree: Did Russ?

Aaron McKinney: Not that I know of.

Beyond Aaron's own words, however — including his mention of a possible drugs-for-sex deal with Matthew — other sources had informed me that the Fireside was one of the Laramie bars where Aaron regularly sold meth. He also sold at the Library and Ranger bars, which Matthew frequented as well.

According to a longtime female friend of Russell who requested anonymity, during the week before the attack she had accompanied Aaron and Russell when they drove to the Fireside one evening. She said she had waited outside in Bill McKinney's truck while the two went into the bar, but "it was clear Aaron was doing some business" and "Russell was just trailing along with him." She was certain the drug stop-off had taken place before Friday, October 2, but after Russell's twenty-first birthday on September 24 "because he wasn't allowed into the bar before then."

Other sources had also informed me that Aaron, Russell, and a couple of their friends had started bingeing on meth on Russell's birthday and that the binge continued for more than a week — until the weekend before Matthew was attacked. But since no one was willing to go on the record, even anonymously, I still had no way to confirm it.

TEN

The Bad Karma Kid

The more I explored the circumstances surrounding Matthew's murder, the more aware I became of a conspicuous absence at the center of the story, an absence other journalists before me had noted: the character of Matthew himself.

From the torrent of media reports following his attack and death in October 1998, to the widespread coverage of Aaron McKinney's trial a year later, the same basic set of facts was repeated over and over. Perhaps the most prevalent image of Matthew was that of "an all American son." As Dennis Shepard had stated eloquently at the time, "Matt was not my gay son, he was my son who happened to be gay." Overnight, however, the compelling identity of "everyone's son" was exploited by an array of interests that mythologized or desecrated Matthew — or both.

Among gay activists, Matthew was anointed the heroic martyr to a pressing human rights cause. Religious Right fundamentalists, meanwhile, deplored him as the embodiment of sin in a morally corrupt world that had grown increasingly tolerant of homosexuality. But who was the real Matthew Shepard? And why was so little known about this young man whose fatal beating captured the attention of millions of people worldwide? Was it the graphic violence of his reported crucifixion and the evocative surname *Shepard* that created an almost religious taboo on depicting him as a complex, flesh-and-blood human being?

Early in my research I had pored over every media story I could find, hoping to learn more about Matthew. But it quickly became apparent that the few journalists who had attempted to examine his life in more than a summary fashion had been hindered in their efforts by sealed court records and witnesses who had been ordered to remain silent.

The most incisive accounts were the *Harper's Magazine* report by JoAnn Wypijewski and a *Vanity Fair* article by Melanie Thernstrom, both published in 1999 before McKinney's trial. According to Thernstrom,

> The mythologizing of Matthew . . . has left him oddly faceless. No one has seemed interested in publishing the details of his life — as if they would detract from his martyrdom. But pity is not understanding, and Matthew's sorrow did not begin at the fence.

Judy Shepard, Matthew's mother — a blond-haired introvert from small-town Wyoming who transformed her grief into a career as a dedicated gay rights activist to honor her son's memory — appeared to agree. In a speech to a national conference of journalists one year after the murder, she stated that the biggest flaw in the media's coverage was its portrayal of Matthew.

"I try very hard to take away that saintlike persona that you have given him, and I hope that everybody sees that he was just a young man in search of his life," she said. "He was depicted as being tied to the fence in the manner of Christ, which really didn't happen. But nobody seems to want to write about how it really did happen . . ."

Wypijewski's illuminating *Harper's* account, while inconclusive, seemed to invite further digging into the murder's complexities; it also served as an inspiration for my own subsequent reporting. Describing her attempts to find out more about Matthew, she wrote,

> Ask around [in Laramie] for impressions of Matthew Shepard and you find as many characters as there are speakers: a charming boy, always smiling and happy; a suicidal depressive who mixed street drugs and alcohol with Effexor and Klonopin; a good listener who treated everyone with respect; "a pompous, arrogant little dick" who condescended to those who served him; a bright kid who wanted to change the world; a kid you'd swear was mentally defective; a generous person; a flasher of money

. . . a sexual seeker; a naïf; a man freaked by his [posi-
tive] HIV status or at peace with it; a "counterphobic" who
courted risk rather than live in fear; a boy who, his father
said, "liked to compete against himself," entering races he
couldn't win and swimming contests he'd finish "dead last
by the length of the pool" just to prove he could do it; a
boy never quite sure of his father's approval . . .

My curiosity and my questions about Matthew only multiplied
with time. Along with media accounts, I examined police reports,
court documents, trial transcripts, and the poignant "victim impact
statements" written by Matthew's parents — all with the aim of piecing together a more truthful and complete biographical portrait. But
it was not until I became well acquainted with several of Matthew's
close friends that I began to appreciate the intricacies and subtleties
of his personality.

Matthew Wayne Shepard was born in Casper, Wyoming, the capital
of Wyoming's oil belt, on December 1, 1976.

More than two decades later, in a statement he wrote in preparation for the murder trials of Aaron McKinney and Russell Henderson,
Dennis Shepard summoned up his earliest memories of Matthew,
who was born prematurely after a long labor. Reminiscing about the
first time he was able to lift his son's head and the thrill he felt in the
maternity ward as he gazed through a window at his firstborn son
sleeping in a bassinet, he wrote, "I was so proud that I could have
exploded!!"

He remembered "Matt's first steps" and the "first bug" that had
captured his curiosity. Matt had responded, his father said, by spending "two hours watching a caterpillar crawl through the grass and up
a tree."

"His nickname was 'Dandelion Head,'" Dennis added, "because
his hair looked just like a dandelion after it has gone to seed and is
waiting for the wind or a child to pick and wave around to watch the
seeds float through the air."

Dennis and Judy Shepard also acknowledged that their son's life had been burdened with difficulties from the beginning. In addition to being a "preemie," Matthew had often been sick as a child. He was given hormone treatments for delayed puberty; he suffered from attention deficit disorder; and for several years prior to his death he'd experienced severe depression, anxiety, and panic attacks. (The Shepards have a second son, Logan, who was born four years after Matthew.)

After attending Crest Hill Grade School and Dean Morgan Junior High in Casper, Matthew went on to Natrona County High School, where he was a sophomore when his life — and his family's — underwent big changes. In 1993 Dennis, who worked for Aramco, the world's largest oil company, was transferred to Saudi Arabia. The Shepard family promptly moved their home to Dhahran on the Persian Gulf.

Lean with rugged good looks, Dennis Shepard was later described by *People* magazine as "a roughneck oil rigger turned construction-safety engineer."

"I come from trailer trash, traveling construction workers," Dennis stated unassumingly.

Strangely, some of the other media coverage on Matthew's attack characterized Aaron McKinney and Russell Henderson similarly as "rednecks" and "trailer trash," yet it was also reported that Matthew and his assailants came from utterly disparate worlds, "from two different sides of the tracks."

Since there was no American school in Dhahran, a largely Western enclave of about sixteen thousand, Matthew's parents sent him to TASIS — a boarding academy in Lugano, Switzerland, near the Italian border — for his last two years of high school.

In retrospect Dennis and Judy Shepard may have had other reasons as well. With each passing year, Saudi Arabia was becoming a less and less secure place for Americans to live. In June 1996, while the Shepards continued to make their home there, a US Air Force base near Dhahran was the site of a terrorist attack. Nineteen people were killed and more than five hundred Americans were wounded.

At the time of the attack, Matthew was in Raleigh, North Carolina, undergoing psychiatric treatment for depression and other unspecified symptoms. He had already completed the first semester of his freshman year at Catawba College, also in North Carolina, but had been forced to withdraw from classes during his second semester.

The media would later offer a variety of explanations regarding Matthew's depression. According to the version repeated most frequently, his emotional troubles stemmed from a violent episode he had suffered in 1995 while he was in Marrakech, Morocco, on a senior class trip with schoolmates from Switzerland. In the early-morning hours he reportedly ventured out from a hotel on his own and was attacked by a gang of young men in the city's Old Quarter. Helpless to defend himself, Matthew was brutally raped six times and robbed.

Both family and friends said the attack had left him traumatized and that he'd never really recovered. Some speculated that the incident might have created a "counterphobia," or a subsequent tendency for Matthew to counteract his fears by courting danger.

But in a television interview with Katie Couric on the *Today* show a few months after his son's murder, Dennis Shepard described Matthew's history of difficulties more opaquely.

"I called him 'The Bad Karma Kid,'" he told Couric. "Because if you were sitting right here, and I was sitting right here and a piano was coming down on top of my head, for some reason the wind would blow and it would land on him."

"He would take the blow so you didn't have to," Couric responded.

"Yes," Matthew's mother agreed.

"Yeah," his father said. "It seemed like he took the blow on a lot of things like that."

Matthew Shepard left behind a few insights of his own into how he saw the world as a boy and young man, notably in autobiographical assignments he wrote for school when he was a teenager, but also in letters he wrote as a nineteen-year-old college freshman at Catawba.

"Dad travels a lot," Matthew remarked tersely at age fourteen, more than a year before the family's move to Saudi Arabia. Next he recorded highlights of a road trip the family had taken around the West in the summer of 1991: They visited Mount Rushmore and

Devils Tower; stopped at the Custer Battlefield ("Little Bighorn") and Medicine Wheel; and drove to North Dakota to see the Badlands.

Matthew also touched blithely on the medical condition that was said to account for his diminutive size. "Last year, I received 4 hormone shots as a part of a growth study group," he wrote. "They hope to learn more about delayed puberty as well as diabetes." ("Delayed puberty" describes the condition when an organism has passed the usual age of onset of puberty with no physical or hormonal signs that it is beginning.)

But in a classroom essay earlier that year, shortly after he turned fourteen, Matthew revealed a side of himself that was both reflective and restless. He wrote about his fascination with theater, which had first taken hold of him in the fifth grade:

> The theater provides me with an escape from everyday living and, at the same time a different perspective [on] that life . . .
>
> Acting allows me the opportunity to escape the daily peeves and enter a world where I know who I am and what the future holds. As I struggle daily to define the seemingly never ending question of "Who am I," theater helps to answer that question not only by being a defining characteristic of my personality and interest but by allowing me to live someone else's life on stage.

Whether acting in local theater productions or just working on a stage crew, Matthew was often surrounded by adults and college students, with whom he apparently felt right at home. For the next six years, until the family moved to Saudi Arabia, he was actively involved with both the Casper College theater group and an adult community theater in town.

"Theater was an escape for Matt," Dennis Shepard agreed.

"I felt the regrets of a father when he realizes his son is not a star athlete. But it was replaced with a greater pride when I saw him on the stage. The hours that he spent learning his parts, working behind the scenes and helping others, made me realize that he was actually a better athlete than a person playing sports . . . I have never figured out how he was able to spend all those hours at the theater during the school year and still have good grades.

"Because my job involved lots of travel, I never had the same give and take with Matt that Judy had," his father acknowledged. "Our relationship, at times, was strained. But, whenever he had problems, we talked . . ."

Dennis also spoke admiringly of the "special bond" Matt and his mother seemed to have. "Judy was mother, father, nurse, teacher, cook, counselor and anything else that was needed . . ." he said. "[She] was Matt's anchor through all his problems."

Mother and son enjoyed movies, theater, their home church of St. Mark's in Casper, and "a good joke." The two spent hours together talking about politics, Hollywood gossip, or the latest fads; Judy also helped Matthew with homework, worked with him on his physical therapy, nursed him when he was sick, and drove him to and from the theater when he was working on a play.

"He was always worried he might do something to disappoint her [but] he seldom did," Dennis recalled.

"At the same time, he would aggravate her to death. [Matt] was a typical son. There were good days and bad days with him. Arguments, mistakes and punishments were made. He was constantly being told to pick up his clothes and clean up his room, even at college. It seemed that he would start an argument just to see how much he could get away with before getting in trouble. In the end and through it all, was his love for her. Judy wasn't just his mother; she was a friend. Judy was his confidant. When he had problems or just needed a shoulder to cry on, she was there. When he had good news, she was the first to hear."

In victim impact statements like those excerpted above or in his words spoken aloud in court, Dennis Shepard also shared tender reminiscences about their family camping and fishing vacations; the love of Wyoming's outdoors that he shared with his two sons and their paternal grandparents; and the final hours he'd spent with Matthew washing his red-and-black Ford Bronco in Laramie.

Looking back on the summer of 1998 when he was home from Saudi Arabia and they spent their last vacation together, Dennis described himself as his son's "hero worshipper."

"I once told Matt that I was jealous of him," he remembered.

But regarding those final hours together, Dennis said, "I told Matt that he was my hero and . . . the toughest man I had ever known," and he praised his son's ability "to continue to smile and keep a positive attitude during all the trials and tribulations he had gone through. I also told him how proud I was because of what he had accomplished . . .

"The last thing I said to Matt was that I loved him and he said he loved me. That was the last private conversation that [we] ever had . . ."

One of Matthew's lesser-known "trials and tribulations" occurred near the end of that summer vacation, during the family's last camping trip together — in northwestern Wyoming. On the evening of August 18, 1998, Matthew went by himself to the Silver Dollar Bar in the town of Cody. A violent incident took place that night that was not only fraught with complications but also misrepresented in later media stories about the Laramie attack.

While drinking at the Silver Dollar, Matthew asked several times if he could join a few bar employees — including a bartender named Chris Hoogerhyde — for an after-hours trip to nearby Newton Lake where they planned to drink beer and look at the stars. Although Matthew had just met Hoogerhyde and the others, they agreed to let him tag along. After they got to the lake, however, Matthew and Hoogerhyde had an angry confrontation. Matthew had apparently expressed some interest in Hoogerhyde, who rebuffed his overture and punched him in the face.

When I first read about the Cody incident, I was disgusted by its brutality and the apparent homophobia behind it, not to mention the obvious parallels with what befell Matthew in Laramie less than two months later.

According to a report in *Time* magazine, "Shepard said his jaw had been broken by a man in a bar who decked him when he realized he was gay." A few months later, an article in *Vanity Fair* stated similarly, "Later the bartender told the police that Matthew had made a pass at him and that he had therefore been compelled to hit him." These and other stories — together with accounts of Matthew's traumatic rape in Morocco — accentuated the impression that he was a perpetual victim of gay bashing.

Several first-person reports, including police and hospital documents, courtroom testimony, and my own subsequent interviews, verified that Matthew had, indeed, been punched by Hoogerhyde at the lake — so severely that he had to be treated in a hospital emergency room. But Matthew also filed a complaint with local police stating he had been "raped" by three men. He said he wanted to press charges.

In reality, the hospital physician who examined Matthew found no physical evidence that he had been sexually assaulted. And by the next morning Matthew withdrew his complaint and stated he had been too drunk to remember what happened.

Some would try to explain the episode in psychological shorthand, speculating that Matthew had experienced "flashbacks of Morocco," which caused him to make false accusations that he had been raped again. Yet the available evidence from that evening suggests a very different story from the one Matthew originally told — and the media repeated.

According to Chris Hoogerhyde's testimony in Aaron's 1999 trial and my own interview with Hoogerhyde by phone — both of which confirmed what police had been told by Leslie Surber, a witness who worked at the Silver Dollar — Matthew made persistent sexual overtures to Hoogerhyde, who is straight, as they sat with friends by the lake. Hoogerhyde said he had repeatedly declined Matthew's offers to take a walk around the lake and to join him behind a parked vehicle for oral sex. But it was not until Matthew grabbed his arm that he lost his temper and punched him in the face, Hoogerhyde said.

A previously sealed police report also appears to substantiate Hoogerhyde's account. At 4:38 AM on August 19 police received a phone call from the Holiday Inn in Cody regarding "a male guest in the lobby who is bloodied [and] says he was assaulted." The report by Officer Scott Steward states:

I responded to the West Park Hospital to take a report of an assault. I was met at the hospital by Officer Barry Ivanoff. Ivanoff informed me that there was a male subject in the E.R. that is claiming to have been raped by three male subjects. I talked to Dr. Polley, the physician examining the victim, Matthew Shepard.

Polley indicated that he did not see any evidence of a sexual assault.

I spoke with Shepard and he stated that he had met this lady and three guys at the Silver Dollar and had left with them and went to a lake. Shepard stated that one of them told him to pull his pants down and when he did the man stuck his penis in him. Shepard had a swollen jaw and split lip. I asked Shepard what happened to his face. He stated, "I think I got hit when I tried to resist."

Shepard continued on to say, "Things are real sketchy because I had been drinking." I asked Shepard to describe the people. Shepard stated that he couldn't describe them. I asked Shepard what happened after he was sexually assaulted. He responded saying, I think they took me back to my motel at the Holiday Inn.

I asked Shepard to fill out a statement and I would talk to him later.

. . . On 082198 Shepard came into the office and stated that he had talked to a lady named Leslie and found out that she was the one that drove him out to the lake . . . Shepard informed me that he did not wish to press charges as he did not remember the night very well.

. . . At approximately 14:40 hrs I met with [Leslie] Surber and a male subject identified as Chris Hoogerhyde . . . Surber stated they went out to Newton Lake after closing the Silver Dollar. She stated that Matthew was whining and said he didn't have any friends and wanted to go with them.

. . . I asked about the assault and Hoogerhyde stated, "Yes I hit him and I'm sorry." I asked Hoogerhyde to tell me what happened.

He stated as follows: We were out at the lake and Matthew started talking about being gay and how he liked men. He just kept talking about it and wouldn't leave it alone. I don't mind gays, I live with two lesbians. Matthew asked me to take a walk around the lake with him and I told him no. He then said, what are you afraid of do you think I might try something. I told him that I thought I could probably take care of myself, besides that, it's a big lake and I don't want to walk around it. We sat there for awhile and he kept asking me to walk around the lake. He then asked me to walk behind the van with him. I told him that I was not going anywhere with him and he grabbed my arm so I hit him. I felt bad for hitting him, but he wouldn't leave me alone. We then took him back to his motel.

. . . Hoogerhyde and Surber both said that Matthew had stated several times that he had been raped 6 times in Morocco.

No further action taken.

Evidently, after Aaron's defense attorneys learned of the Cody incident and other instances in which Matthew had apparently acted in a sexually aggressive or antagonistic manner, they thought they'd found credible support for their theory of "gay panic."

In addition to Hoogerhyde, a different trial witness who had been present at the Fireside bar on the night Matthew was attacked, Mike St. Clair — also straight — would testify for the defense that Matthew, a total stranger, had solicited him sexually. Matthew "said something about 'head' . . . and licked his lips" suggestively, which St. Clair found "really offensive," though he reacted less vehemently than Hoogerhyde had.

A thorny subject like this one is difficult to bring up in any forum, let alone attempt to analyze. But quite apart from the reprehensible strategy of the McKinney defense team, it does seem useful to explore whether Matthew did, in fact, exhibit a pattern of deliberately — or perhaps unconsciously — provoking confrontations that had a potential to turn violent. This is not a matter of "blaming the victim" but rather a conscientious attempt to understand the complex relationship that sometimes exists between victims and perpetrators.

Were the incidents with Hoogerhyde and St. Clair examples of Matthew's inclination to combat his fears by inviting danger — that is, a "counterphobic" reaction — that came from being sexually assaulted in Morocco?

Or did Dennis Shepard's notion of his son as "The Bad Karma Kid" hint at a different — or perhaps parallel — dynamic at work?

Along with Hoogerhyde and St. Clair, I also interviewed a former Laramie bar owner, Jason Palumbo, who had known Matthew as a patron at his bar, Club Retro. I was surprised to hear from Palumbo that he had "permanently banned Matt from coming into my place" after an altercation he had with "a very large bouncer who worked at the door." According to Palumbo, "Matt grabbed the bouncer's crotch and made some wise-ass remark . . . We were just lucky the guy didn't explode."

After Matthew's camping vacation ended on a depressing note — his shattered jaw was now being held in place with a wire — he joined his parents and younger brother, Logan, for a family reunion in Minnesota. They also dropped Logan off at the boarding school he was attending and then tackled the next thing on his parents' agenda before they returned to their home in Saudi Arabia: "settling Matt in Laramie" for his first semester at the University of Wyoming.

ELEVEN

The Blue Masque

The somewhat idealized image I had of Matthew's relationship with his father would later take on a more complex cast when I read letters Matthew had written to his college friend and lover Lewis Macenze while at home in Saudi Arabia over Christmas 1995. The media had barely mentioned Lewis in the aftermath of Matthew's attack.

A slim, handsome, and articulate African American man — the son of a minister — he first met Matthew in September 1995 at the start of Matthew's freshman year at Catawba College in Salisbury, North Carolina. Macenze was a senior at Catawba and his father served as pastor of a local church.

Reading Matthew's letters, I realized the fracturing impact of his continual separations from his father:

> My dad had to leave early this morning . . . I told you he was always gone. I don't know when he'll be back.
>
> . . . I promised myself there would be no screaming this holiday between my father and I . . .
>
> He hasn't lost his temper at me yet – no yelling, which in itself is a miracle . . . One thing I can't stand is being yelled at . . . Anything that needs to be yelled can just as easily be said and I'll understand it just as well.

I first got acquainted with Lewis in emails and phone conversations, and later interviewed him in Tulsa, Oklahoma, where he was working as a motel clerk. We also met up a second time in North Carolina so he could help me retrace Matthew's steps there.

Initially reticent, Lewis gradually helped me see facets of Matthew I hadn't glimpsed before — aspects that were largely missing from the deluge of media coverage and much of what has been written since. He shared letters, photos, and other memorabilia, which he has kept devotedly stored in an antique wooden box since Matthew's death. But it was Lewis's painstaking journal writings and poems that provided the most telling chronicle of his relationship with Matthew, and the extent to which his grief is still an open wound.

One journal entry was written shortly after their first encounter in September 1995:

> [Matt and I] met at the initiation of new members to the Blue Masque, Catawba's theater arts group . . . My job was to blindfold the recruits and get them lined up before we stuffed them in cars and drove them out to the camp-site. As I walked around, I came across this scrawny fresh-man who was complaining that he had to pee. Because he was cute, I volunteered to escort [him] to the nearest tree. In our brief time away from the group, we talked and I learned his name and that he spoke German, which I do, too; I quickly felt das sting auf cupid!

According to Lewis, he and Matthew bonded quickly as friends and confidants. They "talked nonstop" about their vastly different backgrounds, yet thrilled at their mutual love of theater and the performing arts, and their common interest in politics. Over the next several months Lewis wrote of their courtship, as they slowly became lovers:

> On this campus of 800 students, there are only a few openly gay ones. My friends Kristine and Amy are desper-ately trying to fix me up. Amy convinced Matt to meet her at the computer center at the exact time I was to meet Kristine, who just happened to be at the next station. We all talked until the girls disappeared. I asked Matt to join me outside for a cigarette.
>
> He's so classy in his designer jeans, smoking Dunhill's. We sat at the old bell tower, chatting, smoking, laughing as if we've known each other for years. He told me of his

family, his travels and studies, and I of mine. We sat under
the bell tower for hours watching the night go by. (October
3, 1995)

It's my 21st birthday. I didn't get to go out drinking or
even make it to my party because I was in rehearsal until
almost 1 AM. I was surprised to see Matt sitting in front
of the dorm with a single birthday balloon and a Mickey
Mouse doll waiting for me. I was going to drop off my
bags, then walk to get some cigarettes and was delighted
that he wanted to come.

When we returned to the dorm, there were those few
seconds of uncomfortable silence: not wanting to end the
night, not wanting to make the first move. I finally invited
him up to my room for some boxed wine where the conversation continued. We sat on the floor: me Indian style,
he wrapped around me. Our pact was to keep the night
innocent and we did. Just talked and kissed, then slept . . .
(October 26, 1995)

Until I met Lewis, I had come across surprisingly few references to
Matthew's dating experiences, boyfriends, or a love life of any kind.
As JoAnn Wypijewski shrewdly noted in her 1999 *Harper's* article,
there was an all-too-easy tendency "to caricature [Matthew] as a
child-saint, because to think of him as a man evokes a sexual experience no one wants to know."

In April 1996, shortly before Matthew withdrew from Catawba to
undergo psychiatric treatment in the city of Raleigh, he and Lewis
attended a campus political event together. Matthew had already
confided in Lewis about his sexual assault in Morocco as well as other
issues that had been troubling him. But the bright tone of Lewis's
journal entry gave no indication that Matthew was depressed:

What a fantastic Tuesday! Matt and I went to see [Republican
senators] Jesse Helms and Bob Dole speak today at the
gymnasium. The highlight . . . was watching Libby Dole

and how she worked the crowd, and even though we were supposed to be outside protesting with the others we both enjoyed her to the point of wanting to become Young Republicans. Then Jesse reminded us why we weren't.

We held hands throughout the event, trying to bring attention to ourselves and left the building like that when some reporter came up to us and asked if we'd give an interview. It was weird talking to the guy, Matt and I like a real couple finishing each other's thoughts. (April 9, 1996)

TWELVE

Indian Springs

Other than Matthew Shepard himself, no one involved in the Laramie tragedy perplexed me more than Russell Henderson. At the start of my investigation, I accepted as fact that he and Aaron McKinney had participated more or less equally in beating Matthew, an impression first solidified in the onslaught of media coverage following the attack.

Time magazine, citing unnamed police sources, reported: "McKinney . . . apparently taking turns with Henderson, began pounding Shepard on the head with a .357 Magnum revolver." Other leading news organizations stated conclusively that both men beat Matthew. According to *The Denver Post*, "the assailants kept hitting him . . . until they believed he was dead." Yet two weeks after Matthew died, *U.S. News and World Report* said it was Henderson who "allegedly" pistol-whipped him.

Aaron McKinney and Russell Henderson were repeatedly compressed by the media into a single personality with an identical set of motives. *The New York Times* was one of the few news organizations to hint at serious character differences. "If Russell Henderson was a quiet follower," the *Times* stated ten days after the attack, "Aaron McKinney was a man with a short fuse." But long after both men were convicted, confusion persisted over the real nature of Russell Henderson's involvement.

Even Cal Rerucha was uncertain about how involved Henderson had been in beating Matthew, or whether he had taken part at all. Rerucha was quick to point out that under Wyoming law Henderson was still legally responsible for the murder even if he never assaulted Matthew. Yet long after he had won the convictions of both men, I could see Rerucha was still troubled — morally if not legally — by what part Henderson had played in the chain of events that brought about Matthew's death.

Nothing I could find in Russell Henderson's personal history seemed to fit with the sadistic violence of the murder. In contrast, Aaron McKinney had a reputation around Laramie for his volatile temper as well as a long juvenile record. As a boy, McKinney had allegedly abused animals for the fun of it.

After Henderson's arrest for the 1998 attack, his landlord, Sherry Aanenson, described him to a reporter as "quiet, polite, just your average male" and "the most American kid you can get." "I have a hard time imagining him coming up with anything like this on his own," she stated. "It seems extremely out of character . . ."

Carson Aanenson, Sherry's husband, couldn't make sense of Henderson's involvement either. "The gay issue had never been an inkling of a concern," he said.

In several conversations with Cal Rerucha, I revisited the question of Henderson's role in beating Matthew. Sitting behind his hefty oak desk in the county courthouse, Rerucha explained that his chief investigator in the case, Detective Rob DeBree, had all but convinced him that "Russell must have held Matthew down while McKinney beat him or he took part in the beating himself." DeBree based his opinion, Rerucha said, on the substantial amount of Matthew's blood found on a silver Boss jacket belonging to Russell.

"If Russell wasn't in close proximity to Matthew during the beating, blood couldn't have spattered on his jacket that way," Rerucha recalled thinking at the time. "We just assumed McKinney and Henderson were covering up the real amount of Henderson's involvement."

I was intrigued by the doubt I saw in Rerucha's pinched expression and the subtle change of tenor in his voice. As he glanced at me across his desk, he pointed with his index finger to an area just over his mouth. "The gash above Russell Henderson's lip had a half-moon shape," he said plainly, "just like bruises found on Matthew Shepard."

I had seen Henderson's scar in courtroom photos and had simply accepted, like others, that it came from an unrelated street fight he and McKinney had gotten into with two young Hispanic men shortly after they left Matthew at the fence. I was also aware from court transcripts that at Henderson's sentencing in April 1999, six months after the attack, he stated openly for the first time that he had tried to stop McKinney from beating Matthew. According to Henderson, McKinney turned on him in a fit of rage, striking him across the face with the same .357 Magnum he was using to beat Matthew. But until Rerucha mentioned Henderson's scar I had never given it much thought.

Although police reports showed that Russell Henderson received nine stitches in a Laramie emergency room that night, I was still leery of his motives. Was his new story just a ploy to win sympathy and a more lenient sentence? Henderson had been facing a possible death sentence for months. Why would his attorney wait until the hour of sentencing to reveal that he had been pistol-whipped by Aaron McKinney? Henderson himself initially told police he had been hit during the later street fight. Why should he be believed now?

Yet Cal Rerucha, who had won his conviction, was now implying that he believed "Russell finally told the truth" when he admitted being assaulted by McKinney with the murder weapon. By the time of his admission, though, Henderson had already accepted a plea bargain for two life terms — a decision he made in the final stages of jury selection while under a threat of the death penalty.

Upon hearing Rerucha's doubts, my catalog of questions multiplied. What about Henderson's bloodstained jacket? Was Detective DeBree right when he said Henderson "must have" been more involved in beating Matthew? Did he take turns with McKinney as widely believed?

My first attempt to communicate with Russell Henderson was through his grandmother Lucy Thompson, a soft-spoken daycare provider who had raised him along with her late husband, Bill. Lucy was polite but discouraging when I phoned her in 2002, more than three years after the murder. She said she had been hounded incessantly by the media and had "no faith whatsoever in journalists." Although I promised to respect her privacy and not quote her without permission, I could tell she had heard it all before.

After calling Lucy intermittently over weeks, she finally allowed me into her tidy, single-story ranch home on Laramie's South 26th Street to talk for what she assured me would be no more than ten minutes. "If I feel uncomfortable I'm going to ask you to leave," she warned me at the front door. It was early evening and her circle of young children had already gone home for the day.

Around Laramie I had heard several people declare, "Lucy's raised half the kids in this town." Cal Rerucha praised her as "a beloved fixture of the community for decades" and said she could provide genuine insight into Russell's life. It was a life Rerucha himself knew intimately since he had advocated on Russell's behalf in family court when he was a boy. Rerucha described how Lucy and Bill Thompson had rescued their grandson from the neglect of an alcoholic mother and a string of violent men who had passed through her life — men who had also abused Russell.

We sat in Lucy's cozily furnished living room talking for almost two hours, surrounded by framed photos of her four daughters, several grandchildren, and others in her family. Before the conversation was over I had no trouble comprehending her distrust of the media. The intrusions of reporters and camera crews during thirteen months of court proceedings in late 1998 and 1999 had been so unremitting, she said, that she nearly suffered a breakdown.

Lucy eventually confided that she had been prepared to call the sheriff's office and have me removed from her home if I behaved as others had. With a slightly mischievous glint in her eyes, she held up the portable phone resting on the arm of her chair. But as Lucy grew to trust my intentions, other conversations followed. Early on she arranged for me to meet Gene Pratt, the president of her Latter Day Saints congregation, and Deanna Johnson, a close family friend. Both had been close to Russell since he was a boy and agreed to advise Lucy regarding their impressions of me.

Pratt and Johnson asked pointed questions about what I hoped to accomplish and whether it would cause the family more pain. Lucy informed me afterward that they had reported back to her favorably, but still she was not optimistic that her grandson would talk with me.

"It's Russell's decision and I know he'll make the right one, but he needs time to think about it," she told me. "It's up to him."

Several other individuals who were close to Russell during his adolescence — relatives, friends, employers, co-workers, and a former girlfriend — had stated in court documents that his world fell apart at age fifteen when his grandfather died. An employee at the Laramie post office, Bill Thompson was said to be the only male Russell bonded closely with or trusted. The two hunted and fished together, and during his early teen years Russell helped administer daily dialysis treatments to him. According to Lucy, "Russell adored his grandfather and Bill had the same feelings for him. When Bill passed away, so did a big part of Russell. It was painful to see how much he hurt.

"I'm not making excuses for Russell, he must pay for what he did," Lucy added in a sad but resolute voice. "Matthew Shepard's life was taken so terribly and his family will always suffer missing him. I pray for the Shepards every day because I know the hurt they feel. But there's a lot more to Russell than what many people think. He's not the cruel person he's been made out to be."

Even Cal Rerucha told me more than once, "We almost had a success with Russell, he almost made it."

Rerucha's use of we implied personal regret, if not responsibility, for the system having failed Russell in his passage to manhood. His observation registered with more poignancy when Lucy showed me a picture of Russell at age fifteen on the front page of Laramie's *Boomerang* newspaper, taken shortly before his grandfather died. Standing at attention in a pressed khaki uniform covered with merit badges, he is beaming with pride as Wyoming's governor presents him with an Eagle Scout citation.

Yet the belief of many that Russell Henderson's world only came apart with the death of his grandfather was not entirely convincing to me. Was that, too, another myth of the Laramie tragedy?

After waiting months for a reply to several letters I had written him, I received a short typed note:

> Mr Jimenez
> I have taken a long time to send this because I have been debating on whether or not I want to see you or not [sic]. I have changed my mind a hundred times. I finally decided that it should not hurt to talk to you. Please understand

that for right now I want everything that I say to be "off the record". . .
Respectfully,
[signed] Russell A. Henderson
#19624
Rawlins, Wyoming

Had it not been for Lucy, my letters to Russell most certainly would have gone ignored. But it took three of his devoted guardians to persuade him to communicate with me, even off the record.

By the time of our first face-to-face interview in the spring of 2003, Russell had been transferred from the Wyoming State Penitentiary to an austere prison in the Nevada desert. He was then in the fifth year of his double life sentence.

One purpose of the interview was to find out how involved Russell really was in the violence inflicted on Matthew Shepard. Matthew had been beaten so severely with the barrel of McKinney's gun that his skull had been crushed. It was a topic Russell had been wary of discussing in letters or phone conversations when he knew they were being monitored by prison authorities. But because of my persistent doubts, I had questioned him relentlessly anyway. His story was always the same:

> I have told you everything I know. I would even take a polygraph test to prove it to you. Maybe since I've been plastered all over the T.V. as one of the killers . . . people . . . want me to be more involved than I really was . . . Believe me, this life that I now have to live would be a lot easier if that were true . . . I hope that someday you will believe me but I understand why you don't . . .

High Desert State Prison, tucked on the outskirts of Indian Springs, Nevada, was a one-hour drive through barren, clay-colored hills from the extravagantly outsized Bellagio hotel in Las Vegas where I was staying for two nights. *The New York Times Magazine* had given me a modest travel budget but at the last minute I'd gotten a low-priced package deal online. Leaving behind the flashy commerce of the Strip, I soon found myself surrounded in every direction by clear cobalt skies, which made the horizon itself seem like a mirage.

I arrived at the prison wearing jeans and a pale denim shirt, my head buzzed close to the scalp, and was promptly advised that I was being turned away because my attire was virtually identical to the inmates' uniform. An affable female guard with some rank smiled at my dilemma. "Your haircut doesn't help," she ribbed me. But she was also quick to give directions to a Super Walmart back down the highway, close to the edge of Las Vegas. "If you hightail it, you can buy yourself a new suit of clothes and be back here in just over an hour," she promised.

Sure enough, when Russell Henderson was escorted into the visiting area later that morning he looked exactly as I had earlier, right down to his shaved scalp. Russell is shorter than average, about five foot seven, with a compact, slightly stocky build. As he joined me at a drab metal table in the middle of the room, I felt the steady gaze of his glassy blue-green eyes. Russell seemed intent on quickly assessing everything about me before I had a chance to do the same to him. Maybe it was a survival skill picked up in prison, but from what I had already learned secondhand he had spent much of his life in a state of high alert.

As we faced each other across the table and slowly got acquainted, Russell's answers to my questions were clipped and flat. In earlier phone conversations, he had also come across as exceedingly introverted and guarded.

Near the end of that first visit, I asked how he was coping with two life sentences. Without a grain of self-pity, Russell answered, "I belong here for what I did." I'm not sure what I expected him to say but I heard none of the usual convict's complaint — that he was "innocent" or "got fucked over by the system" or was "framed" by someone else.

There was much I hoped Russell Henderson would clarify that day and the next morning when I returned. Instead I left the Nevada prison somewhat disappointed by his reticence. At his April 1999 sentencing, Russell had admitted that he drove the truck the night

Matthew Shepard was robbed and beaten, and that it was he who tied Matthew to the fence, albeit on the instructions of Aaron McKinney. Yet Russell also told me explicitly on several occasions that he "never raised a hand" against Matthew. "[I] never struck him, never hit him," he repeated at a later date. "I never even pushed him. Never even shook his hand."

Since Russell had agreed to a plea bargain and never presented concrete evidence to support his version of events, why should he be believed now?

After visiting him, I arrived back in my Las Vegas hotel room more puzzled than ever by his matter-of-fact, yet seemingly candid account of the crime that landed him in prison for the rest of his life. I also felt a lingering sense of confinement as I stared out the window at an opulent necklace of mosaic-tiled swimming pools in the perfectly manicured gardens many stories below. That evening, while drifting through the packed hotel casino in search of a restaurant — hundreds of slot machines chirping loudly and flashing their colored lights — the sensation of being trapped on a surreal journey of my own was exacerbated.

In Russell's next round of letters, mixed with answers to my ongoing questions about the murder, he charted his daily prison routine for me: finishing classes for his high school diploma; basketball workouts; fantasy sports competitions; planting a vegetable garden in parched desert soil; and drawing portraits late at night in his cell with pencils and a sketch pad sent by his grandmother. His activities sounded more campuslike than the infernal atmosphere usually conjured up by *maximum security*. But by then I was coming to understand that Russell is expert at masking his pain.

Long before he and I met, I had heard a rumor in Laramie that his first year at the Wyoming State Penitentiary was a nightmare; that he had been placed in segregation for a time for his own protection. There had been talk of a "Mom" and "Dad" taking ownership of him as their "boy," which he steadfastly denied to me. If true, it was a humiliation he clearly did not want me writing about.

After my initial visits with Russell, I would not admit to anyone but myself the discomfort sparked in me as I got to know him personally, or the empathy I had begun to feel. Most of the time I simply retreated to a more detached professional stance, in part to protect my work on the story but mostly to protect myself from becoming attached to him. At age twenty-five, with two life sentences and a reputation as a contemptible anti-gay killer, Russell's predicament was nothing if not bleak.

THIRTEEN

Alibi

One person I was still very eager to talk to was Kristen Price, Aaron McKinney's former girlfriend and the mother of his son. Because she was prosecutor Cal Rerucha's "star witness," she had been sequestered outside Wyoming for nearly a year while awaiting McKinney's 1999 trial. "We wanted to be sure nothing happened to her," Rerucha explained drily. "Without her testimony, our capital case against McKinney would have been weak."

Not long after McKinney's conviction, Price and members of her immediate family vacated their Florida home and vanished as if they had been swept into a witness protection program. After I finally managed to locate Price's mother, Kim Kelly, who reluctantly agreed to act as an intermediary, I grew impatient with the many preconditions she insisted upon for meeting her daughter. But I also realized from her nervous communications that she was genuinely worried about the safety of her daughter and grandson. She said there had been "boxes of letters with threats against Kristen" while the case was going on in Laramie.

Five years after the murder, Price and her family were living in seclusion in a quiet midwestern suburb. They had gone to extreme lengths to put those events behind them, so the prospect of a journalist looking into them again was disconcerting. Late-night emails that Kelly sent me before our first meeting conveyed high-strung emotions bordering on paranoia, which I didn't dismiss. She said she was afraid "other people might find us, just like you did."

As a safety measure I hired a recently retired FBI agent to accompany me as a driver, on the outside chance someone hostile or unknown had gotten word of the interview. It was the first time I felt the need for a bodyguard while investigating Matthew's murder.

Facing Kristen Price and her mother in a window booth at a brightly lit chain restaurant, I appreciated why Cal Rerucha had placed so much stock in Price as a witness. Despite my suspicion that she had told bald-faced lies to the police and the media and that she may have perjured herself on the witness stand, I found something ingenuous about her; her openness and maturity surprised me.

A pert, wholesome-looking brunette, Kristen said she decided to talk to me because she had not resolved her emotional distress over Matthew's murder. She was "still deeply upset" that she had helped conceal evidence after learning of the crime from Aaron, and especially that she had not notified authorities that Matthew was left tied to a fence, which might have saved his life.

But Kristen also echoed her mother's fears and expressed the same concerns Aaron had. She was worried that telling the truth might put their four-year-old son in danger.

By the time I met Kristen, Aaron had already revealed to me his extensive drug-dealing activities during the three-year period preceding the murder. He was also adamant about not naming his dealing cohorts or "talking out of school." When I mentioned this to Kristen, her mother interrupted.

"Aaron would definitely keep his mouth shut, to protect Kristen and their son," Kelly said.

In our initial interviews in 2003, Kristen admitted that she had fabricated significant portions of her original story to the police and the media in October 1998, including the claim that Matthew made an unwanted sexual advance at the Fireside bar — an incident that never happened. Her hope then was to win sympathy for Aaron.

"I would have said or done anything at that point to get him out [of jail]," she stated.

As a young mother at the time, Kristen was also desperate to avoid prison herself as an accessory to murder. Later, as the prosecution's main witness, she helped diminish the role of methamphetamine in the case. But now, as she changed her story about Aaron and Russell's anti-gay motives, she revealed that her life with Aaron had revolved around buying, selling, and using meth.

"It was an everyday thing," she confessed, shaking her head plaintively.

Another reason she wanted to "come clean," Kristen said, was that she had been battling her own addiction "on and off" since leaving

Laramie and was still struggling to put that chapter behind her. Like
Aaron, however, she would not name names or provide details about
his chain of suppliers or those he was selling meth to at the time of
the murder.

From the very start of the Shepard investigation, a couple of key
police officers had consistently downplayed Aaron's involvement with
meth and denied it was a factor. Yet several other knowledgeable
sources informed me that, among other activities, Aaron had traveled
to a California meth lab as a courier — a federal meth-trafficking
offense — and that he and other young dealers in his circle had even
sold drugs to local cops.

In reality the drug trade in Wyoming, and Laramie in particular,
was not something new. Since the 1980s a handful of local dealers
had prospered, abetted by corruption on the part of some respected
businesspeople, attorneys, physicians — and police.

According to a close friend of Matthew Shepard who grew up in
Laramie, "The cops are as involved with drugs in this town as the
citizens are."

Several years before Matthew's murder one cop who would later
work on the case was investigated by state law enforcement agents for
concealing a cache of $160,000 in drug proceeds in the basement of
his Laramie home. To the chagrin of state officials familiar with the
investigation, the cop was never charged with a crime and remains a
sheriff's deputy today. Apparently, local police offered no complaints
since the confiscated drug money was used to buy new equipment
and uniforms.

Until the mid-1990s cocaine was the top drug of choice in the
Rocky Mountain West, including Wyoming. Within a couple of years,
however, an epidemic of methamphetamine addiction and meth-related
crime took hold in Wyoming (and many other parts of the country),
and for more than a decade held the state in its devastating grip.

Before I met Kristen Price and her mother, Aaron McKinney had
already admitted to me that his "gay panic" story was a lie and that
Matthew coming on to him sexually was not the source of his murderous rage. But I suspected as much long before his disclosure. It was

not simply the rumors I had heard that he was gay or bisexual and a hustler. It was also the lengths Aaron had gone to enlisting others in his half-baked alibi, including his jailhouse letter instructing Russell Henderson on exactly what to say.

According to Aaron, he had already come up with his gay panic alibi before his arrest and persuaded Kristen and Russell (and indirectly, Russell's girlfriend, Chasity, an art student at the University of Wyoming) to go along with it. In his confession to police, Aaron held to that basic story they had agreed upon, but he made a few critical changes. The most glaring discrepancy was that instead of saying that Matthew made a sexual advance on both him and Russell at the Fireside bar, as Kristen alleged, Aaron said the reason he exploded was because Matthew grabbed his leg in the truck as the three men were driving through town.

All four accomplices would eventually admit to me that they had lied about the crime's motives in a concerted attempt to cover up. They also revealed how they had gotten rid of all their drug paraphernalia, successfully concealing that evidence from police investigators.

"I figured the police would come look in [my] apartment . . ." Aaron said. "I needed to get everything out of the house that [could] get me in any kind of trouble."

In phone interviews with Aaron, I sensed that he was growing more comfortable with me. Or at least he was more willing to discuss specifics of his drug-dealing activities, as long as I was also talking to other clued-up sources on the outside, whose information he could simply confirm or deny. Aaron's refusal to be a snitch — or to be perceived as one — was something he was vigilant about.

I was therefore surprised when he confided that his "real plan" on the night of the crime had been something altogether different. He claimed that a roofing co-worker had tipped him off about "another dealer" in town who had six ounces of methamphetamine, worth more than ten thousand dollars on the street. Aaron said he had planned to steal all the meth, believing it would not only solve his money problems but also provide him with an ample personal supply of the drug. It was only when he couldn't pull that robbery off that he decided to rob Matthew "instead."

It was a story — or another lie — I hadn't encountered before, including in Aaron's confession. It served to throw me off course a bit and left me guessing as to why he might have mentioned this other robbery plan. Was there any truth to it or was it just another attempt to deceive?

Despite my many phone interviews with Aaron, I was also still apprehensive when I got word from Nevada correctional authorities that I could finally meet him in person. Cal Rerucha had told me more than once that his worst fear was that "Aaron will kill again if he's given the chance. Prison won't stop him. Next time it'll be a guard or another inmate."

Forty-five miles from Las Vegas, in the same desolate prison where I'd met Russell, a guard escorted me into a dank holding cell not far from the main visiting area. Aaron, then twenty-six, was waiting for me there.

He quickly stood up to shake my hand, pursing his lips and smiling sheepishly. Although the guard positioned himself several yards away, I'd felt anxious about being left alone with Aaron.

Almost immediately, though, I felt disarmed by his small size and timid demeanor. I saw in his glazed eyes the look of a lost adolescent, someone who would need protection to survive within those unforgiving walls, despite pumping weights religiously to beef up his chest and arms.

As we sat talking on a narrow metal bench welded to the floor, I was eerily aware that this young man alongside me had slammed a seven-inch gun barrel into Matthew Shepard's skull over and over until his brain stem was crushed. That Aaron McKinney was not coming across as unrepentantly evil made my emotions all the more confused.

For a moment I speculated about his capacity for remorse and atonement. But later I would be embarrassed to admit to anyone but myself that I sensed fragility in Aaron, however distorted or damaged.

Was he playing me like a con artist, eliciting pity and compassion when none were deserved?

During his incarceration in Laramie's county jail while awaiting trial, Aaron had shamelessly autographed his name as "Killer," and, according to a jailhouse snitch, he threatened to take a pregnant female guard hostage.

Long after our first prison meeting in Nevada, I was haunted by a photograph of Aaron taken during his 1999 trial, which I had seen in *Vanity Fair*. Clad in a bright orange jumpsuit, Aaron leered menacingly past the camera lens. His gaze — piercing yet remote — seemed to invite intimacy while simultaneously repelling it.

"It looks like his eyes are dead — dead inside," Matthew's mother was quoted in the article. "I believe there are people who have no souls."

I could not theorize about Aaron's psychological makeup or judge whether there was anything redeemable in him. It was a pointless exercise, as he seemed destined to spend the rest of his life in prison. But many who followed his trial felt cheated by an outcome that spared him the death penalty. Lethal injection was too good for McKinney, they said.

Several times during my investigation, however, I was forced to thoroughly reconsider my understanding of Aaron McKinney's character and his motives. One catalyst was my research into the relationship between methamphetamine addiction and violence, under the tutelage of an internationally renowned substance abuse expert at UCLA Medical Center.

But on another occasion it was Aaron himself who gave me pause. In a filmed interview he spoke with unexpected candor about his accomplice, Russell Henderson.

"It's really hard for me to talk to Russ, to see him in this situation, knowing that I'm the one that put him here," he said. "I ruined that guy's life. He was a good kid. Squeaky clean . . . He didn't do nothing [sic]. The only thing that man's guilty of is keeping his mouth shut."

FOURTEEN

The Mile High City

Before Doc O'Connor moved to Bosler, Wyoming, in 1979 and began to remake the crumbling old railroad town into his "Western Village," he had run several businesses in Denver, where, by his own account, he'd already gained a reputation as something of an outlaw, "at least in my personal life anyway."

The two enterprises Doc had owned that he was proudest of were a used-furniture and antiques shop, and an adult bookstore. With little modesty, he hinted that a lot more had gone on in the bookstore than selling porn and adult novelties. Doc had liquidated the Denver businesses years before, but one of his more recent ventures, "Doc's Class Act Limousine Service," still kept him connected to the Mile High City, where his mother and other family members made their home.

According to Doc, he had several customers in Laramie "that liked to hire a limo to take 'em down to Denver for a night out on the town," a drive of just over two hours. He owned two stretch limousines; one was silver, the other white. With their plush interiors, well-stocked bars, tinted windows, and "a super discreet chauffeur" — usually Doc himself — "people could relax and not have to worry about how much alcohol they knocked back." They could also get frisky if they wanted, Doc said, since a thick, opaque window stood between the driver up front and passengers in back. "I invented 'Don't ask, don't tell,'" he boasted more than once.

It was well known from Doc's extensive media interviews following the Laramie attack that both Matthew Shepard and Aaron McKinney frequently hired his limos. But after I was told by Dillon, the former Fireside employee, that Doc was involved in "a lot more than meets the eye" — some of it allegedly illicit — other Laramie sources informed me that Doc was also the proprietor of another business, which he advertised on his website (comeandgetit.com) as "Lincoln

Escort Service." Although I was skeptical of much that Doc had to say, the scraps of verifiable information he regularly tossed my way took me off-guard. His admission that he had been a hustler himself, coupled with the anonymous, still-unsubstantiated claims that Aaron McKinney and perhaps Russell Henderson had secretly plied the same trade, prompted me to do some trawling around in Denver. A logical place to start was the city's gay bars and nightclubs, especially those with a reputedly hustler clientele.

But four years had elapsed since Matthew's murder. How likely was it that current bar patrons would remember if they had ever seen Doc or one of his limos around? Or Aaron and Russell for that matter? Doc volunteered that several other chauffeurs had worked for him the year Matthew was killed, so he had "no way of knowing what went on in the limos when I wasn't driving."

Doc's knack for anticipating my questions and even reading my thoughts irritated me. He made me feel like the inexperienced, amateur investigator I actually was. He, on the other hand, was a crafty salesman and an expert at sticking to his version of things, whether true or not. Yet I had the persistent sense that Doc wanted me to get to the deeper truths behind Matthew's murder, for reasons that eluded me. He openly acknowledged his affection for Matthew as well as Aaron and Russell, but what else was he hiding, and why?

I spent my first night in Denver barhopping on Broadway, just south of the state capitol and the popular gay neighborhood of Montrose. By the time I ordered a beer at the third establishment on my list, which featured scantily clad go-go boys dancing on the bar, I was convinced that I had succumbed to a very stupid idea. How could I possibly get information this way? Surely this wasn't real reporting. Who the hell was I trying to fool? Only myself, I assumed.

As part of their sweaty routine, the dancers jumped off the bar and mingled with customers, grinding their hips before us with dollar bills poking out of their jockstraps and briefs. I tried talking with two of the young men, shouting in their ears over the pounding house music. I said I was a journalist and mentioned the name *Matthew Shepard*. Both of them stared at me seductively, but their eyes also chastised me for being a middle-aged party pooper. It was apparent that as far as they were concerned I was talking about ancient history. Embarrassed, I slipped each of them the obligatory dollar bills they were waiting for, to which one responded with a peck on my cheek and the other a pinch on my rear end.

I was desperate by then to call it a night and go back to my hotel room. Rummaging through the downtown bar scene felt like a dead end or, at best, a waste of time. But since I probably wouldn't return there, I decided to stop briefly at the last place on my list — the accurately but blandly named Broadway. A source had advised me that the bar had changed owners in recent years, though its regular crowd of mostly hustlers and johns had remained the same. At the time of Matthew's murder, it was known as Mr. Bill's.

Once inside the packed, smoky bar, I began to feel just as I had trying to solicit information from go-go boys down the street. What the f--k was I doing there? What was I trying to prove? Clearly it was time to go home. Instead I bought a beer to silence the clamor of critical voices. But I was also single then and had taken notice of the bearded, well-built bouncer straddling a stool near the entrance. Maybe that's what really drew me to Broadway, to feed my own lust. I wasn't attracted to most of the guys wandering around the bar, but the bouncer was another story. Wearing a plaid flannel shirt, snug jeans with a gash of ripped denim across one thigh, and a studded western belt, he also had a warm, inviting smile.

As it turned out, there was no quandary to confront. Minutes after I began talking to the bouncer, he confided that he was happily committed to a lover who would be waiting for him at home when the bar closed. He wanted to know where I was from and what brought me to Denver. I said I was a journalist doing undercover reporting for a possible story on gay hustlers — which was partly true. I also asked if he had worked there back in 1998 when the bar was called Mr. Bill's.

No, he'd only been employed there for a year, the bouncer said. He suggested that I try to find a former manager named Duane who had worked at Mr. Bill's for more than fifteen years. "He and his partner run a kitchen at a veterans post somewhere in town," he added. "A VFW, I think. Duane's the guy you want to talk to."

The next morning in my hotel room, I was still full of doubt. Searching the Denver bar scene at random seemed to be a gratuitous detour, especially when Matthew's murder had occurred in Wyoming. But something else had crept into my mind the night before. As I lay in bed, I couldn't stop thinking about the murder of another gay man from Laramie that I had come across in my research — a 1993 killing that had never been solved. The victim, a forty-seven-year-old psychology professor at the University of Wyoming named Steve Heyman, had apparently come to Denver on a recreational trip and was murdered with extreme brutality. His body was thrown into speeding traffic from a bridge that crossed Interstate 70. What little was known about the crime was that Heyman had visited a few gay bars in the same Broadway vicinity where I had just been. There was brief speculation that he was the victim of anti-gay hate, but when police turned up no leads the case was essentially forgotten.

Along with many gay males of my generation whose coming out was made possible by the urban bar environment that began to flourish in the 1970s, I feared the kind of violence that killed Heyman. The nightmare of meeting a new acquaintance in a bar or disco and ending up robbed or beaten, or worse, occurred with numbing regularity among gays. But I also had a vague hunch that Steve Heyman's murder in November 1993 and Matthew Shepard's five years later had more in common than their shared gay identity and being from the same Wyoming college town. At the moment, I felt ill equipped to contemplate those parallels further, or the more daunting prospect of investigating another grotesquely violent crime. Like the murders of Matthew Shepard and fifteen-year-old Daphne Sulk, however, Heyman's killing was plagued by mysteries and unanswered questions.

I phoned three veterans posts in Denver that morning — all Veterans of Foreign Wars (VFW) — and found out that none had kitchen facilities. On my final call, I had a surprise when I asked if Duane or Rob was working in the kitchen. Seconds later, a raspy, smoker's voice picked up the phone. "This is Duane," he announced politely.

Almost as soon as I introduced myself and asked if he remembered seeing photos of Matthew Shepard's attackers in the news four years earlier, he interrupted me. "Yes, absolutely," he said. Duane quickly confided that he had "recognized them" from Mr. Bill's bar. His first reaction, he recalled, was "shock" at the realization that "these guys who killed that kid came from inside our own community."

I was momentarily speechless.

"Mr. Bill's was all about hustling," Duane went on. "They'd hang around the pool table between turning tricks. They were doing the twenty dollar jobs" — which he called "the low end" of the trade.

Already my mind was flooded with questions. I had gotten the strong impression from Doc O'Connor that Aaron McKinney had dabbled in hustling, yet Doc said nothing about Russell Henderson, only that Russell had been in the limo a few times partying with Aaron and a couple of their friends.

Duane wanted to check with his partner Rob first but said he didn't see any problem with both of them sitting down for an interview. He told me to phone him back in a few hours. Instead of asking Duane more questions I decided to end the call, as I was worried he might change his mind.

Late that afternoon, I met Duane Powers and Rob Surratt at VFW Post #1 on Bannock Street in Denver, just blocks from the bar formerly known as Mr. Bill's. When I arrived, they were tidying up the kitchen at the end of their workday. Both men were lean and of medium height and had the worn look of old-time cowboys — or old bartenders who had worked too many all-nighters. As soon as the pair started talking, one could have mistaken them for brothers. They had a rough, easy banter, bossing each other around with good humor and finishing each other's sentences.

Over a round of beers at a table in the bar area, where there were just a handful of patrons, Rob, a former bartender at Mr. Bill's, confirmed in broad terms what Duane had told me on the phone. He pointed out that the only reason they had taken notice of Aaron and Russell was "they stood out from other hustlers cruising tricks" in the bar. "We knew they weren't locals," Rob said.

As I probed further, Rob and Duane admitted they had no personal knowledge of the activities Aaron or Russell engaged in once they left Mr. Bill's. But Duane, who claimed to have tended bar and managed there for eighteen years, said he had little doubt about what the two men had come there for. He repeated what he had stated previously about "the twenty dollar jobs" and added, "[They were] getting a blowjob in some guy's car, then coming back again to have a few beers and shoot more pool, then do it all over again. They just had a different routine than the pros who'd been around a long time."

Duane surprised me once more when he offered to call "the real Mr. Bill," the bar's former owner, to see if he'd be willing to talk to me. Since I was leaving the next morning for Laramie, I thanked him but suggested we wait until my return. There were other questions I wanted to ask Duane and Rob but thought it best to postpone them. Did they know Doc? Had they seen his limos around Mr. Bill's? I also wanted to ask about drugs, a subject that could make them, and "Mr. Bill," uneasy. I had no reason to doubt their allegations of hustling — which gave credence to other discoveries I had made— yet it seemed equally plausible that Aaron had gone to Mr. Bill's to sell drugs, as he was known to do at bars in Laramie. Away from his hometown, where he was already on the radar of local cops, he was less likely to be apprehended.

In phone interviews, Aaron seemed insulted when I asked if he had ever hustled guys. But as I listened to Duane and Rob, I recalled again what Aaron had stated in his confession about a possible exchange with Matthew of "some cocaine or . . . some methamphetamines, one of those two, for sex."

I wanted to ask Duane and Rob specifically about crystal meth and how prevalent it was at Mr. Bill's and other bars in the area. I decided that could wait, too, but before we parted I turned to Duane, who had worked at Mr. Bill's longer, and asked if he had ever heard of Steve Heyman, the murdered professor from Laramie. Duane shrugged; the name didn't seem to register.

Then I mentioned how Heyman died, his body bludgeoned and dumped on the highway. Immediately Duane nodded and said, "I know exactly who you're talking about." Heyman had been a regular at Mr. Bill's when he was in Denver and apparently liked hustlers.

Homicide detectives had long believed that Heyman met his killer in a local gay bar and that there may have been more than one assailant, but nine years had passed and no suspect had been charged.

Murders like this were not uncommon: A gay man meets a hustler; the hustler promises sex in exchange for money but his real plan is robbery; and the robbery turns deadly.

I was reminded once more of something that had been said about Aaron in the anonymous letter: "he was acting the part of 'straight trade.'"

Had Steve Heyman gotten tangled up with straight trade? Had he perhaps known his assailant(s) previously?

Some suggested Heyman's murder was a hate crime, but in light of things I'd been learning in Laramie it also seemed reasonable to ask: Was there a possibility drugs had been involved?

FIFTEEN

Tristen

My reexamination of the circumstances surrounding Matthew's murder was a frustrating series of fits and starts. There were many dead ends and many occasions when I thought I should simply abandon the effort. Perhaps the most discouraging moment came in spring 2004 when *The New York Times Magazine* killed the article that I'd been working on for two years. Wasn't that telling me something? If the world's newspaper of record no longer wanted to publish the story, why should a novice journalist like me keep on?

Several friends had also urged me to "get on" with my life and career, subtly inferring that a self-respecting gay man and liberal shouldn't be tampering with the accepted version of Matthew's murder *anyway*.

But if I try to discern a rationale for my persistence with Matthew's story, I can see in retrospect that a new lead would invariably appear or a break would occur just as I was on the verge of giving up. I was also constantly surprised by the source of these new leads, as they often came from the most unexpected places.

Tristen was a case in point.

In early April 2004 Aaron McKinney and Russell Henderson sent me copies of an unexpected letter each of them had received from a "T. Henson" of Gulfport, Mississippi. Both men, still incarcerated at High Desert State Prison in Nevada, claimed they did not know anyone by that name, though Aaron hinted in his roundabout way that maybe the correspondence "could help" my investigation. The letters, dated March 24, 2004, were similar but not identical; they were typed, single-spaced, and less than a page long.

"Dear Mr. McKinney," the letter to Aaron began. "It has taken me many years to finally decide to write to you. I have so many questions and I really don't know where to start . . . I was dating Matthew Shepard when you did what you did to him. If you just needed money you could have asked him and he would have called me and I would have gave [sic] you the money so you wouldn't have hurt him. I wish you could have seen him in the hospital and what it has done to many of us . . . I even tried taking my own life. For the loss of missing him so much."

The letter to Russell Henderson began similarly, yet the writer immediately asked the question, "Why Matt?"

"He would not have done anything to hurt anyone," Henson continued. "And if it was for money all you had to do was ask and he would have gave [sic] it without any problems. My doctor says it is time I at least write to you and Aaron. So I can try to overcome this. You both took my life when you took Matt away from me."

When the letters were forwarded to me, I had already been researching Matthew's murder on and off for four years. But I had never come across the name T. Henson before or any reference to their dating relationship. If Henson was the person he professed to be, it seemed strange that none of Matthew's friends I had interviewed ever mentioned him. There had also been no mention of him in the year-long media coverage or in any of the court documents.

As I compared the two letters more carefully, I noticed a few subtle differences. In his letter to Aaron, Henson stated, "you could have asked [Matt] and *he would have called me and I would have gave you the money* so you wouldn't have hurt him" (italics mine). Yet to Russell he wrote, "If it was for money all you had to do was ask and [Matt] would have gave it without any problems."

Henson's statement to Aaron implied that Matthew didn't have "the money," but that he, Henson, would have provided it had Aaron only asked. Why, on the other hand, did Henson tell Russell that Matthew "*would have gave [the money] without any problems*"? (Italics mine.)

My curiosity stemmed from knowing that Matthew had been very anxious about money on the weekend before the October 1998 attack. Yet incongruously, he had also spent about eleven hundred dollars in cash on the night of Friday, October 2, hiring Doc O'Connor to drive him in a stretch limo with his friend, Tina Labrie, to a Colorado dance club. According to Tina, Matthew became increasingly preoccupied and depressed as the evening went on.

"He mentioned on the way down . . . 'Do you think this is selfish of me?'" she recalled. "'I'm spending all this money [on a limo service] and . . . I could be giving this to . . . poor starving children somewhere.'"

But during a later interview, Tina spoke more candidly about Matthew's state of mind that evening. "He was really worried . . ." she explained. "It just seemed like there was something bugging him, something on his mind . . . kind of those fears of who do I trust and who don't I trust."

Concerned about Matthew, Tina slept over at his Laramie apartment that night. The following morning, she overheard an upsetting phone conversation he was having with his mother, who was in Saudi Arabia. The subject was money.

The fact that Henson raised the issue of money in his letters to Aaron and Russell more than five years later made me reconsider what it was that Matthew was so worried about. What was behind his "fears of who do I trust and who don't I trust"?

After the call with his mother ended abruptly, "Matt began to cry uncontrollably and panic," Tina said, then went into the bathroom and "took a lot of his anti-anxiety medication."

> I asked him, how much did you take. And at first, he didn't want to tell me. And then finally he told me how much he took . . . I said this would kill most people, you know. I don't remember the milligram dosage but he took up around fifteen [pills] . . . I was like, do I need to take you to the emergency room. He said, no, no, no, just monitor me. And I was like okay. I took his cell phone and nothing happened . . . He was fine. It amazed me.
>
> . . . He said he was having a harder and harder time being able to relax, being able to sleep, being troubled by nightmares . . . One of those pills would have probably put me out for two days. And here he is, eating them like candy. Like [he] can't survive without them.

Tina also reminded me again of Matthew's size; that he weighed only 105 pounds.

The first time Tina described his near-suicide-attempt, I was doubtful that such extreme despair had resulted from a parental phone call over money. But I still couldn't make sense of the discrepancy between Matthew appearing to be flush with cash on that Friday night — he had even treated a group of friends to a meal at Denny's — and Henson's letters to Aaron and Russell suggesting that Matthew didn't have money when he met them at the Fireside a few nights later.

I also kept wondering why Henson focused on *money* yet he never brought up their reputed hatred of Matthew for being gay.

I questioned Aaron and Russell about Henson again, only to have them repeat that they had no idea who he was. Their response prompted me to write to him myself at the Mississippi post office box he had given as a return address, with a simple explanation of how I had learned about him.

I was intrigued by Henson's straightforwardness but was also puzzled as to why he had waited more than five years to talk openly about his relationship with Matthew. If the two had been as close as Henson said, what else might he know?

In the remainder of his letter to Aaron, he seemed tormented by questions for which he had no answers:

> I am not understanding why you did it. [Matt] was so giving all the time . . . I can tell you that I . . . wanted to see you die . . . But [now] I want you to live and live with what you did to him . . .
>
> I also believe that you don't have that much hate in you . . . I don't think that you intended to kill Matt. But . . . you left him out there in the cold, hurt and bleeding. You could have . . . called someone and told us where he was at. Matt never hurt you and you know it . . .
>
> If you can find it in your heart somewhere please everyday that your [sic] alive, please say to Matt in a prayer that you're sorry . . .
>
> I know what was said in court and I am asking for you to please tell me the truth, please. There is nothing else that anyone can do to hurt me as much as you have done

. . . I just want to know why. Please tell me. I need to know why my Matt? Why him? Thanks for taking the time to read this. T. Henson

Each time I re-read the letters, I was aware of Henson's intense need to understand the murder. But his persistent questions about motive contrasted sharply with the clear-cut logic of media accounts as well as the statements of a couple of key law enforcement officers. Instead Henson offered his own convictions, while giving no clue what they were based on: "you don't have that much hate in you . . . I don't think that you intended to kill Matt . . . Matt never hurt you and you know it."

Henson's words had a surprisingly personal tone considering that he was unacquainted with Aaron McKinney, and that, according to all media reports Henson might have seen, Aaron and Matthew had never met prior to their encounter at the Fireside bar on Tuesday, October 6.

Within days I received an email response from a "Ted" Henson, who said his real name was Tristen but he preferred I call him Ted.

Ted's first few emails were short and guarded. Despite his tentativeness, though, I got the sense that he was relieved to unburden more of his feelings about Matthew and the murder. It also became clear from the abundance of personal details that gradually poured forth that he and Matthew had, indeed, enjoyed a close relationship.

According to Ted, he met Matthew in Dhahran, Saudi Arabia, in the mid-1990s while visiting relatives who lived in the American compound there. Matthew, then sixteen, was attending a boarding school in Switzerland but was home on vacation. Although Ted was twenty-three at the time, he said they grew close quickly and maintained an intimate bond as friends and lovers until the first weekend of October 1998, a few days before Matthew was attacked.

On Friday, October 2 — the same night that Matthew took Tina to the Tornado dance club in a limo — he and Matthew had "a little spat" in Fort Collins. Ted had been "staying with a friend" in the Colorado town, he said, but he declined to elaborate on what his quarrel with

Matthew had been about. As soon as he got word of Matthew's near-fatal beating, however, he rushed to nearby Poudre Valley Hospital, where he spent time at Matthew's bedside until Matthew's parents arrived from Saudi Arabia. Ted later recounted that he had been in such severe shock that a hospital physician prescribed heavy doses of sedatives and anti-depressants for him.

When I began communicating with Ted in spring 2004, I was also in discussions with ABC News *20/20* about producing a story that would reexamine the murder. As our investigation got under way at the network that summer, Ted appeared to grow more trusting and cooperative. He was still reluctant to meet in person but he began to open up about his personal life. He revealed that he was the adoptive father of a three-year-old son and said that he and Matthew had "talked about raising a family together." On several occasions Ted also spoke of the anger and bitterness he felt toward Aaron McKinney and Russell Henderson — "I still am hoping that something happens to them like they did to Matt" — and he repeated more urgently the central question he had posed in his letters to them: "All I am after . . . is the answer to WHY? . . . One way or the other I am going to get it!!!"

Ted offhandedly mentioned "a guy named Bear in Laramie," hinting that he might know more about the murder than he had previously let on. I was aware that "Bear" was the nickname of Aaron's first cousin Adrian McKinney; I had already interviewed him, in fact, but for the moment I kept that to myself. Like Aaron, Bear had acknowledged that he'd been deeply involved with methamphetamine at the time of the murder, both using the drug and selling it.

I found it curious that Ted had brought up Bear's name in three consecutive emails he had written to me in early July. I wondered, of course, what the connection was — if any — between the two men, but I also realized I had to proceed slowly.

When I pushed Ted to tell me more about Bear, he was vague and said he was "a friend of a friend." Yet he was unequivocal regarding any involvement with methamphetamine on Matthew's part, or for that matter his own.

"As for Matt using meth I would have to say no," he wrote, "he never did around me and I am more than sure he would not."

But in his emails that July, Ted passed on other scraps of provocative information that could only mean one thing: He, too, knew a lot more about the personal circumstances surrounding Matthew's murder than he had acknowledged.

"[Aaron] McKinney would sell [himself] to other guys," he stated bluntly, "but I do not believe that Matt would have ever done anything with him like that."

Two days later Ted was more explicit: "McKinney slept with other guys for money to get his drug. There is a guy there in Laramie that was one of McKinney's main guys . . . Matt had told me a while before the murder took place that a guy named Aaron had offered [him] sex for money. But Matt said he did not do it."

I was astonished by Ted's claims. Not only did they lend some credence to what Aaron had told police in his long-sealed confession about a possible drugs-for-sex deal with Matthew, but they also fit with the anonymous letter that had launched my investigation; with Doc's intimations about hustling in Laramie and beyond; and with what I had learned during my underground search in Denver.

Still, I was left with a web of convoluted questions that Ted — and presumably others — would be unwilling, unable, or simply not ready to answer.

For one, how did Ted know so much about Aaron's alleged sex-and-drug activities?

And given his longtime intimacy with Matthew, why had Ted's name never appeared in the public record?

In late June 2004 at ABC News headquarters in New York, Glenn Silber and I made final preparations for filming Aaron McKinney and Russell Henderson's *20/20* interviews at High Desert State Prison in Nevada. All of us involved in producing the report were on edge. At the last minute Wyoming prison officials were trying to prevent us from going forward with the interviews, citing state regulations that prohibit face-to-face interviews with inmates. But the more liberal Nevada Department of Corrections, which was housing a large group of Wyoming prisoners under special contract, insisted the decision on whether to grant interviews was theirs alone.

Elizabeth Vargas, a rising star in TV news who had recently inherited her *20/20* co-anchor chair from Barbara Walters, was stretched thin that summer. Vargas was eager to do the McKinney and Henderson interviews as they represented the kind of exclusive "get" that Walters and other anchors had built their careers on, but she was also nervous that I had been investigating Matthew's murder mostly on my own as an independent journalist. With her reputation on the line and her sights already trained on anchoring the evening news, she was understandably concerned about taking chances with a reporter she didn't know.

Until just a few months before, I had been writing an investigative article about the murder as a freelancer for *The New York Times Magazine*. With the departure of head editor Adam Moss from the magazine, the story had been killed without explanation. Moss, who had commissioned the piece, is widely regarded as a brilliant and somewhat fearless editor; he also happens to be gay. Although his successors at the magazine commended my strong reporting and said they'd like to work with me on "something else," I surmised that the story's politically sensitive content was the problem.

Fortunately for the story, another prominent, openly gay news executive, David Sloan, the executive producer of ABC News *20/20*, was willing to take it on. Sloan, a trusted adviser and friend of Barbara Walters and one of the network's influential gatekeepers, convinced Elizabeth Vargas it was worth a full hour on *20/20*.

Vargas, a savvy, statuesque correspondent with the glamorous presence and sometimes-fussy personality of a movie star, had been filling in frequently that summer for Peter Jennings in the anchor chair on the evening news. Publicly, Jennings was said to be on an extended vacation, but ABC insiders knew he was already ailing with terminal cancer.

The more Glenn Silber and I continued to investigate Matthew's murder on the ground in Wyoming and Colorado — reporting our findings back to Vargas, Sloan, and other network executives — the more aware all of us became of the story's volatility. To his credit,

Sloan believed our investigation was journalistically important and was willing to engage whatever controversy it stirred up. But he would also eventually draw the line at some chilling new information Glenn and I had uncovered about the sinister world of methamphetamine dealing into which Matthew had gotten swept up. No one at ABC News questioned its veracity; they just felt it was too incendiary to put on the air.

During several meetings with Elizabeth Vargas in Jennings's handsomely appointed office, I noticed mementos from Jennings's impressive career as a newsman, amazed that my investigation had found a home in such hallowed surroundings. But I was also walking a tightrope since I had promised *20/20* the interviews with Aaron McKinney and Russell Henderson, but prison authorities had yet to give us a green light.

In the end Nevada prison officials overruled the Wyoming Department of Corrections and cooperated with us fully. Wyoming officials, for their part, settled on having an observer in the room while the interviews were filmed. Were it not for that single turn of events, I would have departed hastily from ABC News in embarrassment. I was certain I would never get another chance with the Wyoming authorities, who would have been content to silence Aaron McKinney and Russell Henderson forever had it been in their legal power to do so. As "the killers" in the most highly publicized murder case in the state's history, Aaron and Russell have the kind of notoriety that prison bureaucrats can live without.

But dealing with state officials was only one of our near-mishaps while producing the report. In July 2004, after shooting an interview at the home of a former Laramie police commander, Dave O'Malley — whom we suspected of concealing or at least ignoring important facts about the murder — Elizabeth Vargas had mistakenly left a confidential memo along with her makeup case in O'Malley's bedroom, where she had been waiting while we set up the cameras. Glenn and I had prepared the memo as background for her interview with O'Malley.

When O'Malley later discovered the items he was livid. He complained vociferously that we at *20/20* had decided prior to the

interview that his version of what motivated the crime was not credible. And to some degree he was right. By then we had examined the
entire case record — including his police reports and those of his
fellow officers — and had already conducted interviews with dozens
of other sources. O'Malley's version simply did not add up. Nor did it
add up in his lengthy interview with Vargas, during which he seemed
to contradict himself.

Nonetheless, I stood by horrified as O'Malley threatened to distribute our confidential memo on the Internet, hoping to discredit and
embarrass us. Vargas's careless mistake had put the whole story in
jeopardy and with it almost five years of my work. I was furious but
did my best to contain myself.

During the *20/20* interview Vargas questioned O'Malley about
Aaron's criminal history, beyond his 1997 burglary of a Kentucky
Fried Chicken.

"What other kinds of crimes?" Vargas asked him.

"You know, just a lot of the petty kind of stuff, and I really
haven't looked at [Aaron's] background in so long I don't remember,"
O'Malley responded, "he was a suspect in a lot of incidents. He was,
uh, one of the people that we, uh, quite frankly, uh, frequently, uh,
received drug-related information about, and, uh, were looking into
at different times, uh, regarding those kinds of issues."

"We keep hearing in this town that methamphetamine use is pretty
common," Vargas stated.

"It's increasing," O'Malley said.

"Why is that?"

"We're playing catch-up, basically, right now. We're educating
on the issue of methamphetamine use *ten years after we should have
started doing that* [italics mine]. We knew in law enforcement it was
going to become an issue and . . . it was going to cause a lot of
problems for us. But it really has started I think in the last few
years . . . to escalate a little bit more. It's cheaper, the high is longer,
[and] we're on Interstate 80 so access coming in off of the interstate makes [Laramie] a little more liable to have that kind of traffic
coming in here. And they were right — the experts were talking

about what kind of an impact methamphetamine was going to have on our country, and I wish we'd have started reacting to it before it got here."

Later in the interview, Vargas asked O'Malley, "At what point did you first learn that Matthew Shepard was gay?"

"Pretty early in the investigation I received a call from one of his friends [who] was at Poudre Valley [Hospital]," O'Malley answered, "and how they got the information early on [that Matthew had been beaten], I don't really know, I don't really recall . . ."

"And did he [Alex Trout] — is he the one who first suggested perhaps that was the motive for this beating?"

"Uh, as I recall, he'd indicated that uh that he thought Matt had used crank uh, or whatever terminology uh — "

"Does that mean methamphetamines?"

"Yeah, I don't know, I think so. But uh you know, we talked to I don't know how many people during the investigation, that never came up again. We searched Matt's apartment, there was no indication of methamphetamine use there, um, you know, I just, I, I thought [Trout] was a flake."

"But while you thought he was a flake," Vargas continued, "you still believed when he said that Matthew was openly gay and that might have something to do with the attack?"

"Yeah, I, I certainly did, yeah."

"Why, if you didn't believe the rest of what he was saying — "

"I didn't say I didn't believe the rest of what he was saying, we couldn't corroborate anything that he said."

Yet later in the interview, O'Malley stated, "I had no indication that Matt was a [drug] user. Is anything possible, you know, certainly. But I don't have any indication of that, and there was nothing that came forward that would make me believe that was the case."

Was O'Malley really ignorant of the information that was present in official police reports, including his own? Trout had been Matthew's friend for four years and Walt Boulden for about six. According to a report by Sergeant Jeff Bury:

Myself, Commander O'MALLEY and Sergeant DEBREE conducted an interview with Alexander TROUT AND Walter BOULDEN . . .

When asked about Matthew SHEPARD'S alcohol and possible drug use, they stated that he smoked marijuana occasionally, however, when he was in Denver, that he had gotten into some cocaine use and had also participated in methamphetamine use.

As I stood in the kitchen of O'Malley's home watching a video monitor of the live interview in the next room, I was aware that there was a substantial amount of evidence — beyond Trout's and Boulden's statements — to indicate that Matthew had struggled with a serious drug problem. As journalists, we were determined to understand the real chain of events behind Matthew's murder.

Surely O'Malley had also seen the same autopsy report I had? Performed five days after the attack, it documents the presence of numerous substances, including phenylpropanolamine, one of the precursor ingredients used in the manufacture of methamphetamine. (In her 2009 memoir Judy Shepard acknowledged candidly that Matthew "self-medicated.")

During the same interview O'Malley said he was "not going to change" his view that Aaron and Russell "did what they did to Matt because [of] hatred towards him for being gay." But O'Malley also admitted, "There's other investigators that worked this case, really good cops, really good investigators, that won't go along with that. [They believe] that there was some other motivation; I don't believe that's true . . . There's some difference of opinion."

If you look back at the massive media coverage of the case, however, you find virtually no suggestion of a difference of opinion among law enforcement officers about the motives behind the attack — until 2004 when we interviewed Cal Rerucha, O'Malley, Ben Fritzen, Flint Waters (a former officer in the Laramie Police Department), and others.

Moreover, when Vargas asked O'Malley if he'd been "surprised at the national reaction" to the crime, he recalled, "The phone kept ringing and it was the media, and I thought, what is going on here? And one person called early [on] and they said, well, do you know the motivation for what happened here? And we said, we're still working on it, we're right in the middle of it, can [you] please just leave us alone? And they said, could this have been a hate crime? And I said, yeah, it could have been a hate crime. And he said, thank you and hung up, and then the phones really started ringing and the human rights groups . . . started calling."

. O'Malley added: "Laramie kind of got a bad rap . . . of being a redneck town and I think the people that spent the time to come here and really spend some time . . . found out that that's not the case. We're a pretty tolerant group of individuals . . . and I think we're good people."

"But getting back to how this wildfire started," Vargas pressed him, " . . . after, 'this could be a hate crime' by a reporter and saying, 'well, yes, it could have been' — "

"Right," O'Malley nodded.

"The next thing you know, it's all over —"

"Right," he agreed again.

" — the media [reports], this is a hate crime."

"Oh, that was the media," he said.

In essence Dave O'Malley concurred with Cal Rerucha about the genesis of the hate crime theory — a theory that defined to a large extent what followed in the police investigation as well as the court case. But it had also taken almost six years since the murder for officials to talk about that aspect on the record.

Near the end of the interview with O'Malley, Vargas touched on the iconic image of Matthew's crucifixion, which remains painfully vivid, even today.

"One of the things you wonder, because massive media coverage can be so distorted and so much can sort of fuzz around the edges in the re-telling," she prefaced her question. "Is it true that Matthew was tied up like he was crucified?"

"No, he was tied with his hands behind him and . . . kind of . . . sitting on his butt on the ground and then [he] had kind of fallen over."

"So where did that story come from?"

"I have no idea," O'Malley said hesitantly.

Then he went on, "I've got an idea that it came from someone in local law enforcement who had never been to the [crime] scene, but I don't know that. That's always been a suspicion of mine."

In this regard, too, O'Malley was all but confirming what Cal Rerucha had told me: The inaccurate, yet highly explosive, crucifixion element of the story had been set in motion inadvertently by a law enforcement colleague during an early press conference with the media.

At *20/20* we were relieved when Dave O'Malley ultimately backed down regarding the confidential story memo he had discovered with Elizabeth Vargas's makeup case. Later, however, O'Malley contributed to tenth- and fifteenth-anniversary "epilogues" to the acclaimed docudrama *The Laramie Project*, in which he (and the show's creators) ridiculed our investigation of the role methamphetamine had played in Matthew's murder. More troubling to us as journalists, however, was learning that O'Malley had tried to convince Cal Rerucha to refuse an interview with us and to avoid discussing certain aspects of the case that had been buried when it ended. O'Malley's argument was a familiar one: to let slumbering truths lie when so much good has been accomplished in Matthew's name. When Cal refused, his twenty-year personal and professional friendship with Dave O'Malley ended.

But this would not be the only consequence that resulted from Cal Rerucha's willingness to tell the truth about Matthew's murder. Other long-term ties were suddenly severed; there were missed career opportunities as well. Several times he was passed over for appointments as a prosecutor or judge — positions for which he was uniquely qualified — when just a few years before he'd been invited to the Clinton White House. He was also later honored with the American Bar Association's prestigious Minister of Justice Award, yet in his home state of Wyoming he had trouble for a time finding a job.

As Glenn Silber and I continued filming the *20/20* story, Ted Henson grew more distant. Worried I might lose him as a source, I foolishly phoned his mother's home in Mississippi and left a message for him. My message was very discreet but it made him angry; he said I had violated his trust.

"It is not that I don't want to talk about Matt, it's just [that] no matter what I can tell you about [him], someone is going to twist it . . ." Ted wrote in one of his sporadic emails. "Yes, there was something going on in [Matt's] life that was bothering him. And I am not going to get into that at this point. It was something that he and I talked about . . . But I am not saying no either. I am thinking on what Matt would want me to do."

As our *20/20* broadcast date approached, it became clear that Ted would not agree to an on-camera interview. While I was disappointed by his decision, I could not shake the sense that he was still withholding important information. This feeling only intensified when I learned that he had been making frequent phone calls to Russell Henderson's grandmother Lucy Thompson.

According to Lucy, Ted introduced himself as "Matt's lover" and confided that he was "certain" Aaron McKinney was "the real culprit" in the murder, though he offered little by way of explanation. He also asked her to call him Tristen, which he said was his "real name."

During their long phone conversations, Lucy said, he reminisced "affectionately" about Matthew and "shared his pain at losing him."

"Tristen also told me on many occasions, 'Russell was in the wrong place at the wrong time,' but he still felt Russell owed him an apology for Matthew's death," she recalled. Thompson said she had assured him that "Russell would welcome the chance to apologize." But she added, "Tristen never really explained all of what he meant by 'the wrong place at the wrong time.'"

Later, when I asked Ted about his calls to Russell's grandmother, he admitted that he had been talking to her as often as he could and said their talks gave him "a lot of comfort." He also informed me that he planned to visit Russell sometime, which baffled me more. Why would a victim of Matthew's murder want to visit one of the men convicted of killing him?

These were a few of the topics Ted didn't want to discuss further. He said he had "personal reasons" and preferred to leave it at that.

SIXTEEN

The Buck

When I first heard rumors that Aaron McKinney and Matthew Shepard had been well acquainted months before Aaron exploded in rage — and that they had an intimate personal relationship — I was incredulous. I assumed it was just that: a local rumor mill churning out gossip. But then several sources who knew both men began to talk about their troubled history together.

On a brisk autumn night in 2004, I made one of several visits to the Buckhorn Bar, a rowdy, Old West–style saloon in downtown Laramie. A block from the historic Union Pacific rail yard, the bar was surrounded at one time by a flourishing network of brothels.

I had been tipped off by a source that I might find a woman named Elaine Baker there, someone I had been trying to track down for weeks. Baker had allegedly spent a long summer night in 1998 partying with Aaron, Matthew, Doc O'Connor, and a group of other locals. I had also been told that she had known Aaron since he was a teenager and might have other useful information.

With the help of a discreet bartender, I finally found her sitting in a darkened window booth having a drink with her boyfriend. But I was wary of approaching her with others around. Time and again I had learned what a tight-knit, somewhat incestuous town Laramie can be. Once people start talking, word travels fast.

All night long I hung out at the Buckhorn waiting for an opportunity and had all but given up when Baker slipped out of the booth to go to the ladies' room. I quickly moved into a corner near the restroom door and waited for her to come out.

An attractive woman with bleached-blond hair and sad, tired eyes, she was startled when I called out her first name. I asked if we could talk for a minute in the back room, which had another full-sized bar but was less crowded. In an instant she measured my intent and was apparently satisfied that I wasn't on the prowl for a pickup.

As we stood talking at the back bar, Baker's relaxed but carefully chosen words gave me the impression of someone who had been waiting a long time to be asked the very questions I was now asking. With little hesitation she acknowledged that she had, indeed, spent an evening socializing with Aaron, Matthew, Doc, a girlfriend of Doc's named Stephanie, and a few others. She said it was the first time she had met Matthew Shepard but "he was someone you wouldn't forget."

"Matthew was just a nice kid, really sweet," she told me. Before I could bring up his murder, she added, "I knew from the beginning the whole thing was a lie and a cover-up. Aaron didn't hate him for being gay. They were friends, for god's sake."

I was eager to continue talking but I knew Baker's boyfriend was waiting in the front room. I asked if it would be okay to call her the next day. Her blue eyes studied me a second longer, then she hastily scribbled her number on a bar napkin. Already she had confirmed a story told to me by Doc's girlfriend, Stephanie Herrington, about the evening the two women spent with Aaron, Matthew, and Doc. According to Herrington, it was not the first time she had met Matthew, nor was it the first time she had seen Aaron and Matthew together. On a different night, she said, she was drinking with Doc at the Buckhorn when both Aaron and Matthew were there as well.

Like other fortuitous encounters I had while investigating Matthew's murder — most of them with strangers — Elaine Baker gave me her confidence sooner than I could have hoped for. The next day we had the first of several long conversations at her dining room table. Elaine's daughter, who had gone to Laramie High with Aaron McKinney and Russell Henderson, and had briefly dated Russell, joined us.

Occasionally tears welled up in Elaine's eyes as she described the hidden relationships among Aaron, Matthew, and Doc O'Connor. When she gestured with her thin hands I noticed she was trembling. "On the totem pole, Matthew was down here, Aaron was here, and Doc was up here," she explained. "Matthew reminded me of the little frail mouse, just no protection, and Aaron the cat, but yet Aaron has Doc the pit bull over him."

Elaine also recalled in explicit detail the night of partying several weeks before the murder. The party began in Doc's limo outside the Buckhorn, she said, and ended at his home in Bosler the following morning.

> In the back of the limo there was me, Stephanie, Doc, Aaron, Matthew Shepard . . .
>
> Doc and Aaron and Matthew were all sitting on the seat in the very back facing the windshield . . .
>
> Aaron was Doc's little whore, his little plaything, that's what he was. And that's what the relationship entailed. Aaron worked for Doc . . . and Doc used Aaron whenever he wanted to . . .
>
> [Aaron and Matthew] were friends. They hung out together . . .
>
> Aaron . . . didn't have any reason to be mad at Matthew for Matthew being gay because Aaron was bisexual . . .

Elaine's memories of that evening coincided almost exactly with Stephanie's. Both women claimed they had witnessed an exchange of money in the limo, which they assumed was for drugs, and said there had been a sexual threesome among Doc, Aaron, and Matthew. According to Elaine and Stephanie, the activities continued at Doc's home, with some variations. Doc invited Stephanie to join him in a bedroom with Aaron (which was later confirmed by both men). Stephanie said that Matthew waited alone in the next room, but eventually Doc and Aaron joined him.

The salacious details of that evening's events did not suddenly shed light on the motives behind Matthew's murder, but they did strongly challenge the widely accepted scenario of a young gay man targeted for robbery and murder by two homophobic "strangers" because he made a pass at them. Interestingly, Russell Henderson was only briefly present in Doc's limo — for a ride of a few blocks from the Buckhorn to the Ranger Motel — when he and his girlfriend Chasity decided to go home. The limo stopped briefly at the motel, where Aaron and Kristen were living at the time.

Everyone I spoke with — Elaine, Stephanie, Doc, Aaron, Russell, Kristen, and Chasity — said that Aaron and Kristen had a squabble because he wanted to go out partying and she had to stay at the motel to care for their infant son. According to Kristen, Aaron was also looking for drugs that night and did not return until the next morning.

SEVENTEEN

Memphis

Nine months after the *20/20* story aired, Ted Henson reappeared out of the blue. I was working on a new writing project when I received a call from Glenn, my producing partner at ABC News. He said he had gotten an "interesting" email from Ted, written to both of us. Dated August 8, 2005, the email stated that everything we reported in the *20/20* program was true, "but I am not going to be quoted on any of it." (Later, Ted would consent to go on the record.)

His email went on: "Matt did know Aaron. Aaron did sell Matt drugs. And sometimes Aaron expected more than money in return. When I found out I confronted Aaron with it. Aaron got very upset . . ."

Ted also explained why he had been calling Russell Henderson's grandmother for nearly a year. "Everyone that knew Matt would know that Matt would not want someone in jail who did not hurt him," he wrote. "Aaron knows the truth [but] he is not going to admit to anything."

In light of the controversy we had generated with the *20/20* story, Glenn and I felt vindicated by these new admissions. Without knowing it, Ted was also confirming information we had gotten from other sources. Some of their revelations had not made it into the televised report, however. They had ended up on the proverbial editing room floor, not because they lacked credibility or couldn't be substantiated, but because the powers-that-be at ABC News decided they were too editorially explosive. It was one thing to report that Aaron McKinney and Matthew Shepard appeared to know each other before Matthew's brutal attack, and another story entirely to examine what their relationship entailed.

Over the next few months I received a steady stream of emails from Ted. Some were disconcertingly graphic, others sentimental but excruciatingly honest. We also spoke on the phone a few times, though Ted, for reasons I didn't understand, was still skittish about meeting in person. Determined not to lose him as a source again, I respected his wishes. Yet privately I held out hope that he would come around.

Ted's emails sometimes had a stream-of-consciousness quality, as if he were speculating about the circumstances behind Matthew's murder rather than speaking from personal knowledge, which reinforced my skepticism. But in addition to answering my written questions, he included other anecdotes and details he had long kept hidden. He said the decision not to talk with the media after the 1998 attack had been his own, "out of respect for Judy and Dennis and [Matthew's brother] Logan," with whom he remained in close contact and occasionally celebrated family holidays.

Yet Ted also volunteered that in the summer of 2004 he had been "pressured" by a New York attorney, Sean Patrick Maloney, not to talk with me or anyone else at *20/20*, and not to provide photos or other documentation of his longtime relationship with Matthew.

I had briefly met Maloney in August 2004 when he accompanied Judy Shepard to ABC News headquarters for an on-camera interview with Elizabeth Vargas. Maloney, who was then acting as counsel for the Matthew Shepard Foundation, had served as a senior assistant to President Bill Clinton in the White House. (In November 2012 Maloney was elected to the US Congress representing District 18 in the Hudson Valley region of New York State.)

Before we rolled the cameras, Maloney, who was seated alongside Matthew's mother, made an odd comment to Vargas and the rest of us on the production team.

"My worst fear is that you're going to tell us Matt was caught up in a drug ring with these guys," he said delicately, his shoulders slightly hunched and hands clasped together in his lap.

Maloney did not specify whom he was referring to by "these guys," though we assumed he meant Aaron McKinney and Russell Henderson.

"We haven't finished our investigation yet, so we haven't come to any conclusions," Vargas answered him.

Maloney's final words before we began filming the interview were to ask us to "please tread lightly." "Matthew Shepard is to gay rights what Emmett Till was to the civil rights movement," he told us.

I could feel anger rising in my throat. I didn't need to be lectured on history or gay rights by a man thirteen years my junior. Before he had reached puberty, I was demonstrating at the First National Gay March on Washington in 1979 and had actively helped pave the way for gay males like him who followed. I realized the most prudent course at the moment was to swallow my anger, but there was something else bothering me.

Prior to his arrival at the network, Maloney had made several phone calls to David Sloan, the executive producer of *20/20* who had hired me to report and produce the story with Glenn Silber. Sloan is also a well-known advocate for gay causes. During one of Maloney's calls, which was played on speakerphone in Sloan's office, other employees from senior management were present when — according to one — Maloney attempted to "smear" and discredit me professionally and personally.

Maloney and others claimed that a Wyoming attorney named Tim Newcomb, who had filed an appeal on behalf of Russell Henderson that year, was responsible for taking the story to *20/20*; they said Newcomb and I were colluding in an attempt to aid Russell's appeal. In reality I had met Newcomb during a trip to Laramie in 2002 while researching the story for *The New York Times Magazine* — long before he became Russell's appellate attorney and about two years before *20/20* took a serious interest in the story. More important, Newcomb had never contacted ABC News, nor was he a source for any aspect of our investigation, on the record or off. Although my colleagues at ABC News didn't buy the allegations that my reporting was biased, it was obvious that Maloney and others had done their best to try to get the story "killed." When that didn't happen, other strategies were adopted.

Tim Newcomb, I discovered upon meeting him, is a longtime friend of prosecutor Cal Rerucha and his wife, Jan. A handsome, sandy-haired native of Nebraska and an expert in constitutional law, it was also Newcomb who, behind closed doors in November 1999, helped Rerucha — in consultation with Matthew Shepard's parents — to craft a last-minute sentencing agreement with Aaron

McKinney's defense lawyers. One of those lawyers, Jason Tangeman, happened to share office space with Newcomb and held him in the same high regard Rerucha did.

True to its "hometown" character, Laramie is a community where more often than not everyone knows everyone else. The sentencing agreement written by Newcomb took the death penalty off the table and guaranteed Aaron McKinney two life terms with no chance of parole. But according to that same agreement, Aaron also pledged that he would not talk to the media about the case. It was I who asked him to disobey that provision in my hope of uncovering the truth behind the murder. Moreover, Newcomb's informal but critical involvement in Aaron's 1999 sentencing agreement did not prevent him legally or ethically from representing Russell Henderson in a 2004 appeal. As Newcomb studied the murder case more carefully, he became convinced that Henderson's original defense team had ignored important evidence and issues in the case.

One thing that may have bothered former Clinton aide Sean Maloney is that several respected gay men had decided to take a more careful look at — or at least reconsider — what appeared to be an open-and-shut case of anti-gay murder, a de facto hate crime. Not just David Sloan and myself, but also celebrated journalist and blogger Andrew Sullivan, who appeared in the *20/20* report. In my interview with Sullivan, he commented on the value of seeking and understanding the truth surrounding the murder, whatever it is or wherever it may lead:

> People really do want to mythologize important events in history . . . And in almost all cases, the mythology, to some extent, takes on a life of its own, and you forget what happened, or what might have been the reality.
>
> It may be that as a culture we don't want to let go of the myth. The myth serves far too many purposes. But myths aren't truth, and however complicated the truth is, I think it's worth finding out. Not to puncture any myth, but simply to find out the truth. I mean, nothing, no context could make this crime less awful . . .

If you're going to base a civil rights movement on one particular incident, and the mythology about a particular incident, you're asking for trouble, because events are more complicated than most politicians or most activists want them to be . . .

So what are we afraid of? Why are we afraid of this thing being more complicated than it may have been to begin with? Is it gonna make the murder seem any less awful? Of course not. No one should be afraid of the truth. Least of all gay people . . . Shouldn't we understand better why and how?

Perhaps Maloney may have also been concerned that I was looking into what his own role may have been — and that of his former boss, Bill Clinton — in helping to shape and "spin" a misleading picture of Matthew's attack from inside the White House. The president's early statements on the case had a powerful and lasting impact on how the crime was perceived at the Justice Department, in the halls of Congress, and by the public at large.

In retrospect Ted Henson's claim that he had been pressured to remain silent no longer seemed dubious or far-fetched. After the attempts to discredit the *20/20* investigation and me failed, at least two national gay organizations, GLAAD (Gay and Lesbian Alliance Against Defamation) and the Human Rights Campaign, contacted ABC News executives in an attempt to intervene editorially. One prominent·activist asked to pre-screen the story and offer feedback on its content before it was broadcast. But *20/20* head David Sloan declined the request.

Unhappy about ABC's decision, GLAAD launched a national email alert in advance of the *20/20* broadcast, advising members of its concern that the program would raise questions about whether or not Matthew's murder was really motivated by anti-gay hate.

In actual fact, no judge or jury found Aaron McKinney or Russell Henderson guilty of a hate crime. Instead it was the national media, special interest groups, and politicians — and hence the court of public opinion — that rendered the decision. Wyoming courts convicted the two men exclusively on felony murder and related charges. Even prosecutor Cal Rerucha, who won their double life sentences, has acknowledged, "I don't think the proof [of a hate crime] was there."

In emails Ted Henson wrote me over a four-day period in August 2005, he stated:

> As I told you many times, Aaron is not telling you the truth. [He] did know Matt . . . Aaron does not want people knowing that he is bisexual . . .
>
> I can tell you I thought I had Matt off meth . . . Matt was going thru [sic] some rough things at the time of his death. He knew that I found out about the meth . . . and that if it didn't stop I was leaving him . . . I believe Matt was worried that I would find out about him and Aaron having sex as well. Matt did [not] like rejections. When Matt loved you, you got him completely. But I think with the meth Matt could not overcome it and did whatever he had to do to get it . . . Aaron did sell meth to Matt. And there was one time Aaron wanted more than just the money . . .
>
> Aaron sold [himself] to be able to keep money for his drugs as well as extra money [in order to] buy and sell them . . . Aaron likes having sex with guys. How [do] I know he sold himself? Thru Matt. And John O.* knows [too] . . . Once when John was with Aaron they [saw] us in town and John walked over and introduced Aaron as his friend. When Aaron walked away to speak to someone else, [John] told me and Matt that Aaron was [an] escort.
>
> Matt owed Aaron money for meth. Matt did tell [him] that I knew about what they were doing. Aaron was scared that it was going to get back to his [girlfriend] . . . [He] was worried that she would leave with his only child . . .
>
> I believe Aaron threatened Matt about the money . . . [Matt wrote,] "I am not sure how I am going to finish

paying this guy I owe some money to, he is coming up to me all the time saying where's my money". . .

I went once in the limo with Doc . . . Matt liked to ride in [the limos] and . . . Doc would not charge Matt . . . Matt and Aaron had sex while doing the drugs in Doc's limo . . .

I know I should have told you a lot before your *20/20* but I got worried . . .

Matt was a very sweet person . . . Have you ever had someone you could never get enough of holding or kissing? If so, you know how I [felt] for Matt. Matt was like a bright light for me . . . But I have to understand that sometimes people do things for drugs that they would not normally do.

Little by little I will give you information, ok?

It was not until five months later — in January 2006 — that Ted Henson finally agreed to meet in person in Memphis, Tennessee.

Our first encounter took place over the Martin Luther King Jr. holiday weekend, at a scruffy gay bar called J-Wags where Ted was working as a bartender. He said someone would fill in for him behind the bar while the two of us talked.

Despite our lengthy email communications, I was anxious about the meeting. I really didn't know what to expect from Ted or what I might be walking into at the bar. He had recently let me know that his older brother, a convicted felon serving a long sentence in California, was a member of "NLR," the Nazi Low Riders, a much-feared prison gang and white supremacist organization. But by then I was more concerned about a network of drug dealers in Wyoming and Colorado — people with whom I was convinced Matthew had become ensnared, and perhaps Ted, too. Glenn Silber and I had already interviewed a few of the dealers for the *20/20* report, but there were others who were not happy about the areas we'd been digging into.

To be on the safe side I hired a former Memphis cop to accompany me undercover to J-Wags, a bar with a reputation for a rough hustler trade and other goings-on in the darkened backyard behind the premises.

As I sat down to talk with Ted in a booth, I was relieved to find that his earlier doubts about me had apparently dissipated. Tall and personable, his short hair streaked with blond highlights much like the style Matthew had worn, he made sardonic remarks in his polite Gulf Coast drawl about his current workplace with its "parade of weirdos" drifting in and out.

A few yards from where we were sitting, the detective I had hired was perched on a bar stool sipping a Coke, pretending he was a patron but keeping an eye on everyone coming through the front door. Earlier that day he had come to check the place out, to avoid any surprises. Just knowing he was there provided a measure of comfort.

Ted was more than willing to share his memories of Matthew, but it would take several more face-to-face interviews before he felt comfortable enough to explain how he had come to know so much. And although he had mentioned previously that his brother was serving serious time, I experienced in Ted's presence the same incomprehension I had felt when I began to realize that Matthew had gotten involved in a hard-core underworld. With his wholesome boyish looks Ted seemed totally out of place at this dingy hole-in-the-wall, yet at the same time cheerfully sheltered there.

Eventually he confided that his brother's conviction was related to methamphetamine and said that Matthew and his brother had met during a trip Matthew took to California. While I found Ted's revelations disturbing, my unease was compounded when he later informed me that his brother would now be serving additional time for stabbing a prison guard with a homemade weapon.

During that first meeting in Memphis, however, I also realized that Ted was more than a source for a "story." He was slowly becoming an ally and a friend — as determined in his own way as I was to unmask the secrets behind Matthew's murder. Soon he agreed to go on the record confirming that Matthew and Aaron had known each other well; that he himself had been together with them several times under less-than-flattering circumstances; and that Russell Henderson had never been present with the three of them. As far as

Ted knew, Matthew had never met Russell before the night of the attack.

Russell had been telling me that right along, but for a long time I didn't believe him. Since he and Aaron had worked together as roofers and constantly hung out as a foursome with their girlfriends, I assumed Russell, too, must have known Matthew, even in passing. But I was wrong.

According to Ted, he and Matthew ran into Doc O'Connor and Aaron at a gay bar in Denver in 1997 — a year before the murder and a year before Aaron and Russell became friends.

"In Denver we [saw] Doc and Aaron a lot . . . they would come to the bar together and leave with someone, in fact many someones," he recalled.

But perhaps the most disquieting piece of information Ted shared during my first trip to Memphis had to do with a conflict that had existed between Aaron and Matthew prior to the attack, including a threat Aaron had made while Ted was present. Ted said that he had driven with Matthew to a Laramie convenience store weeks before the murder when an argument had erupted between the two men. He described the incident further in an email:

> I was waiting in the car while [Matt] went in for some [cigarettes] and some drinks. When he came out, Matt and another guy whom I find out is Aaron [were] in an argument. Aaron was yelling at Matt. I got out of the car and asked if there was a problem and Aaron said no, there's not a problem. While Matt and I [were] walking back to the car Aaron told Matt you better watch your back.

Ted's follow-up communications by email and phone also continued to surprise me, including his eagerness to "help" Russell. He felt strongly that an "injustice" had occurred when Aaron and Russell received the identical sentence of two life terms. Knowing of the personal relationship between Matthew and Aaron, and the escalating tension between them weeks before the crime, Ted said he regretted having kept quiet for so long.

"Matt would never want Russell to get life when he never raised a hand against him and never wanted to hurt him," he wrote me in an email. "Russell has to do some kind of time, but he shouldn't be paying for what Aaron did."

Yet Ted was quick to add that he doesn't have a grain of sympathy for Aaron. "He should've got the death penalty," he said. "It isn't too late if you ask me."

EIGHTEEN

Family Circle

Ted Henson's intimate relationship with Matthew was "on again, off again," as they struggled with their drug use and the competing affections of other guys each of them would occasionally meet. According to Ted, he "wanted to get away from meth" when he realized the destructive impact it was having "on Matt's life and mine." Not only was crystal meth a source of friction between them, he said, but he had also gotten "very worried watching Matt get really sick" from his excessive drug use. In addition, the two men had to deal with the stress of living apart. Though they'd spent a good deal of time in close proximity to each other, including in Denver, "things got harder" once Matthew started attending the University of Wyoming.

From interviews with several of Matthew's friends, it appears that the only other men with whom he was deeply attached emotionally and romantically were Lewis Macenze, who had been his lover at Catawba College in 1995–96; and Carl*, a man a few years older than Matthew who lived in an apartment on 17th and Logan in the Capitol Hill district of Denver. Carl sold crystal meth and other drugs and was also the person who introduced Matthew to heroin — but then frantically struggled to get him off it.

Soon after Matthew died, Carl, who had grown up in Laramie, moved away from Denver and essentially disappeared. However, his identity has been confirmed by multiple sources, including one of the lead detectives that investigated Matthew's murder.

In late May 1997 Lewis, whose feelings for Matthew were still strong, returned to Aurora, Colorado — a Denver suburb — from an assignment with the Red Cross providing emergency relief to flood victims in Minnesota and North Dakota. Lewis had joined AmeriCorps in 1996 shortly after his graduation from Catawba. At the time, Matthew had been living in Raleigh, North Carolina, where he had gone for psychiatric treatment. But now both young men were living in the Denver area and were apparently still trying to sort out their feelings for each other.

According to Lewis, on May 22, the day he arrived back in Aurora, "Matt was waiting for me in front of the compound where I lived . . . [He] apologized to me and asked to get back together [but] I declined . . . I was very upset that he was sleeping with other people. I wrote [in my journal] that the guy who was giving Matt a ride was described [by Matt] as 'just a fuck mate, nothing serious.'"

But looking back on their encounters in Denver, Lewis wrote,

> i still cant help but think how these poorly thought out actions have shaped my life. i see now that these were tough times for him and me. i suppose that i, like so many others, turned my back on him when he most needed someone who truly cared about his well being. i can justify my decisions on being young, still experiencing the world and myself, and of course just not knowing the severity of the situation . . . but i am just as guilty as everyone else who abandoned him.

Without offering specifics, Lewis referred to some of Matthew's difficult experiences "growing up . . . being sent to boarding school and having so many superficial people floating in and out . . . [It] was a recipe for the inevitable," he said.

Over the next several months, despite living in the same trendy gay neighborhood of Capitol Hill, the two didn't see each other. But then on December 15, Lewis wrote in his journal:

> I saw Matt today. It was the most bizarre run-in. We came from opposite directions with the same agenda: to buy a bag of weed at Civic Center Park. A run-in which lasted for 3 hrs or so. It was nice walking down 16th Street, talking, laughing . . . I miss that friendship. But things are

different now. We live only a few blocks apart, but there is so much distance. I miss him.

With [Matt] I truly felt that my being was so vital. I never thought I could love . . . but I do. My attraction isn't merely physical; he's cute but that's not it. That crooked face. His left ear lobe is attached, the right one isn't. And he's so damn skinny . . . but so cute. Damn! And those braces send shivers down my spine! This imperfect boy that I can't seem to get enough of . . .

I wanted tonight to last forever; wanted things to be like they were in [North] Carolina. But it's different now.

Two days after Matthew and Lewis bumped into each other in Denver's Civic Center Park, Aaron McKinney burglarized the Kentucky Fried Chicken restaurant in Laramie with a couple of his friends. Afterward Aaron boarded a plane for Florida with Kristen Price's twin brother, Kevin. Kristen, who was then seventeen and pregnant with Aaron's child, would later say that shortly after he arrived in Florida he told her "he wanted to get his life together." She also said he stopped using meth for a time "and was just smoking weed."

Although Denver is about a two-and-a-half-hour drive from Laramie, Aaron was apparently well acquainted with the Mile High City by 1997. In addition to Duane Powers and Rob Surratt, the former bartenders who had seen Aaron at Mr. Bill's bar, Matthew's friend Ted Henson felt pretty certain that he had met Aaron the first time "around June . . . or the very beginning of July [1997]" while he was at a Denver bar with Matthew. Aaron had come to the bar with Doc, Ted said.

"Aaron introduced himself to me," he recalled. "I know it was before the fishing rodeo in Gulfport, Mississippi, [because] Matt and I went to that in July of '97" — some fifteen months before the Laramie attack.

Coincidentally, it was around that same time, in June 1997, that Kristen was introduced to Aaron by one of her girlfriends. Aaron was then living in a Laramie trailer with David Farris (Russell's half brother); nineteen-year-old Rod Becker (the stepson of Dennis Menefee, who would later be convicted in the rape and death of Russell's mother); and two other friends, "Tex" and Cory — both of whom confirmed the extent of Aaron's meth-related activities at the time and subsequently. Both men also stressed that they had gotten away from those activities a number of years ago.

While Matthew was living in Denver in 1997 and 1998, he struggled with addiction to a mix of prescription and street drugs and became increasingly worried about the amount of alcohol he was drinking. He had first used marijuana and cocaine in high school, but in Denver he was introduced to crystal meth and other hard drugs. He also got swept up in a fast lifestyle in the Capitol Hill area, much of it revolving around bars, dance clubs, and, according to several sources, all-male escort activity. But it was with a network of friends involved in the drug trade, a makeshift "family" of dealers — straight, gay, and bisexual — that Matthew cemented ties that would remain intact after his move to Laramie in the summer of 1998 to begin classes at the University of Wyoming. A couple of the dealers had grown up in Laramie and, like Matthew, traveled back and forth to Denver regularly.

It would not be until six years after his murder, however, that sources close to Matthew began to acknowledge on the record that he had been struggling desperately with drug entanglements in the days before his October 6 attack. His friend and fellow college student Tina Labrie described what was troubling him:

> [Matt] was saying that . . . he just didn't feel safe anymore . . . I thought he was kind of afraid . . . he was in danger . . . I could tell he was really worried about it . . . He said everywhere I move, it seems like I get sucked into the drug scene . . . He just said he left . . . Denver to come up to Laramie to get away from the drugs . . . he sounded really frustrated.

After Labrie's revelation, I learned from other sources that in the year leading up to Matthew's murder the Denver family with whom he was associated was involved in trafficking methamphetamine between Colorado and Wyoming. Occasionally they handled other drugs, but meth was their main business.

A strategic distribution point along the route from Denver to Laramie was Fort Collins, Colorado, another scenic university town and the location of the Tornado dance club, which Matthew and several of his friends frequented. Two of his longtime male friends, Alex Trout and Ted Henson, have verified that crystal meth was becoming a big part of the Colorado club scene then — as well as the lives of all three young men.

Carl, a leader of the Denver dealing circle and someone to whom Matthew grew attached while living in the city, allegedly fled to Europe soon after the murder and hasn't been heard from since. Friends said he was overcome with guilt for the things he'd introduced Matthew to, including heroin.

Two different male friends of Matthew, who were also from Laramie but not, to my knowledge, part of the Denver circle, spoke hesitantly about a party Matthew threw at his Laramie apartment early in the fall semester when both host and guests shot up heroin.

"Matty got hooked very fast" after he used heroin just a few times, I was told by Joan*, a Denver woman who said she developed a "very close" friendship with Matthew in August 1997, more than a year before the murder. According to Joan, who worked part-time as a hairdresser, she always called him "Matty" and "treated him like a little brother." He, in turn, looked up to her as "an older sister" and liked to play with her young son, who was handicapped. Months before Matthew moved to Laramie to attend college, they began meeting for meals on Sunday afternoons at El Conquistador, a Mexican restaurant in town. During those times when he was visiting Laramie, Matthew often stayed at the home of his friend Walt Boulden, a forty-five-year-old lecturer in social work at the university.

With an edge of remorse in her voice, Joan went on to say that the mysterious male friend who had given Matthew heroin "took him back down to Denver and made him get off it." But she also confessed, "I think if it weren't for us taking Matty to Laramie, if it weren't for us introducing him to meth, if it weren't for the drugs — him being who he was . . . Matty would be alive today."

(Since the 1990s, a growing number of meth addicts have turned to heroin in the belief that it will help them "come down" from the ruinous effects of long-term meth use. But the replacement of meth with heroin has also been the result of another development: As the government's efforts to curb the availability of meth began to succeed, many addicts switched first to prescription drugs like Oxycontin, a synthetic opiate. Next they moved on to another opiate that was cheaper to buy: heroin.)

When I probed further into Doc O'Connor's activities, several sources said he was an important figure on the fringes of the Denver family circle, but not a key player. They alleged that he ran an illegal escort service out of his limos, yet successfully concealed it beneath the façade of his legitimate business, "Doc's Class Act Limousine Service."

Two of Doc's regular customers were Aaron McKinney and Matthew Shepard. Aaron began hiring Doc's stretch limos in 1995 after he received a settlement of nearly a hundred thousand dollars for his mother's wrongful death from a botched hysterectomy. Matthew, on the other hand, grew fond of limo rides while living in Denver, where "he had a couple of friends . . . who drove a limousine," his friend Joan said. In the city's Capitol Hill district, he also learned about gay escort services of the kind that proprietors like Doc allegedly offered to high-end customers.

According to other sources in Laramie, Doc negotiated for Aaron's sexual services both locally and in Denver, took a cut of the action, and enjoyed a physical relationship with Aaron as part of the arrangement. Another piece of the bargain apparently allowed Aaron — as well as Matthew and others — to use the limos for transporting, peddling, and using drugs. But Aaron's allegiance was to two or three Laramie suppliers — a different family, so to speak, from Matthew's.

Meanwhile, Doc — much like politicians — could simply hide behind a veil of "plausible deniability." Although he sometimes drove the limos himself, he has steadfastly maintained that he went out of his way to give his customers maximum privacy and "kept [his] eyes alone, "all pissed off at Matt." The purpose of the meeting, two of Matthew's friends said, was for Aaron to sample the product. But he apparently grew angry when Matthew rebuffed a business proposal he had made.

Dealer friends of Aaron said his usual modus operandi was to persuade suppliers to front him drugs with a promise to pay later, after he made some sales. In this instance, Matthew refused to advance Aaron any of the meth without cash up front.

"Matt used his brain," a friend who was present at the Library explained. "He didn't deal with people that only did twenties and thirties" (0.20 or 0.30 of a gram of meth).

With regard to Aaron, however, the same friend stated, "A lot of times if you get too many fronts, you get too much stuff, [then] you end up way behind. And if you still have a habit, then it will get pretty desperate . . . to get more drugs, to get more money."

Aaron McKinney was addicted to methamphetamine for the better part of three years (1995 through 1998), and he was also known to dabble in crack and cocaine.

In 1998, the year Matthew was killed, a single kingpin whom many feared handled most of the cocaine sold in Laramie. The kingpin is now serving a long prison term with slim chances of parole, but to protect confidential sources he will not be named here. One source nonetheless confirmed that "Aaron worked for [the kingpin]" and recounted an instance when Aaron was driven in a stretch limousine to the kingpin's home to make a pickup. Like many dealers' homes, it bristled with surveillance devices.

While there was occasional overlap and even cooperation in the business activities of rival families — and a few members of each group had long-standing friendships — there was also stiff competition around selling meth and cocaine in local bars. The most lucrative sites for quick, clandestine sales were the Library, the Buckhorn, the Fireside, the Ranger, the Cowboy Saloon & Dance Hall, and a newly revamped place called Club Retro. According to numerous bar employees and patrons, as well as friends of Aaron and Matthew, each man regularly visited all of these bars, with the exception of the

and ears out of their business." Often, however, he hired other (
feurs to drive the vehicles and demanded that they, too, follc
procedures to the letter.

Marge Bridges, a former driver for Doc who chauffeured M;
on several occasions, stated in a phone interview that she h;
driven Matthew and Aaron together on a round trip from Lar;
Denver and back, well before the murder.

Doc has repeatedly denied Bridges's allegation, yet acknov
that she worked for him. For Doc to admit otherwise woul
him in serious legal jeopardy if it could be proven that his lim
used to transport drugs across state lines — a federal offense. ,
source, a former roofer who worked with Aaron and Russel
that Doc had personally informed him about the limo trip A;
Matthew took to Denver.

In addition, two former meth dealers who were part of th(
circle and well acquainted with Doc elaborated further.

"Doc was top guy when it came to the cars," one said, v
kingpin of their own group — "who taught Matt how to dea]
"top dog" where dealing was concerned.

On a humid, late-summer night in 1998 — weeks before th(
6 attack — the aforementioned dealers and five other fri
acquaintances of Matthew connected to the Denver circle w
ing at Laramie's Library bar, a popular hangout on Gran
across from the University of Wyoming campus. The Librai
of several bars in town where Aaron McKinney, by his own
to me, sold drugs covertly.

One of the Denver dealers brought a delivery of meth
that night and, according to a pre-arranged plan, left it fo
in a parked car behind the building.

"Me and Duke* went to the Library and dropped the
the vehicle and [Matt and Aaron] went outside [later] to sn
of meth," the dealer recalled.

Matthew and Aaron's encounter in the car, which was
dimly lit area alongside an alley, lasted about forty minute
in the group was surprised when Aaron stormed back i

Cowboy, where Matthew seldom went. A different member of the
Denver circle was responsible for moving product there.

Among Aaron's friends who used and dealt meth, most of them in
their twenties, the bulk of supply that passed through their hands came
from California. Usually it was transported via "the Western route" —
through Nevada, Utah, and across I-80 to Laramie and other destina-
tions to the east. On occasion the meth they purchased came from
Casper, Wyoming, a transshipment point about 150 miles northeast
of Laramie. But in Matthew's circle the flow of drugs ordinarily came
from Denver and sometimes points farther south – Pueblo, Colorado;
border towns and cities like El Paso, Texas; and ultimately Mexico.

Some in the Denver circle were not only involved in transporting and selling meth but also acquired the precursor chemicals to
manufacture it. But at the time of Matthew's murder and during the
prosecutions of Aaron and Russell that followed, their names never
surfaced in official investigations, at least in documents that were
released publicly. A few of the dealers managed to evade apprehension
for their interstate trafficking activities until three or more years after
Matthew was killed. By then the drug underpinnings of the murder
had long since been covered up, often with the help of an unwitting
and credulous media, replaced by a politically expedient version of the
murder and the motives behind it.

One central figure in the Denver circle was Mark Rohrbacher,
known by his cohorts — including Matthew — as Mark K.

Rohrbacher was arrested in Laramie in 2001 for a variety of meth-
trafficking offenses going back to 1997, the year before Matthew's
murder. Although Rohrbacher was incarcerated on the night Matthew
was attacked, sources have identified him as one of the "top dogs"
who taught Matthew how to deal in Denver and later showed him
the ropes in Laramie. In a handwritten letter, a Rohrbacher associate who became a friend of Matthew recalled his first encounters
with Matthew in Denver in 1997 — along with two other family
members, Mason* and Carl:

> I truly hope and pray that none of this falls into the wrong
> hands. It could make me a dead man . . .

That was my job, that's what I did — deal . . . Almost anyone we came in contact with got sucked in — one way or another . . . I was very good at the violence which would later make me a very valuable asset to a certain [organization]. . .

By the end of [a twelve-day period] Matt [had come] around twice . . . Mason said [Matt] was cool and . . . had helped to find the somewhat large amount of stuff we had been looking for . . .

Mason, Carl and Matt all rode to [a Denver bar] . . . and were able to set a deal for two grand within the space of an hour and a half.

The same source also recounted a second Denver incident that involved himself, Mason, Carl, Matthew, and two other members of the circle — Tom* and Suzie*:

Mason said he had to go because this dude [Matt] needed to get to class which really struck me as odd considering all the shit I was standing in at the moment. [Matt] truly looked too innocent and totally out of place to me . . .

Mason had a shotgun of his dad's and I had my automatic and we set out to find Tom and discovered Matt would know where to find the chic [sic] who had gotten the dope from Carl . . .

We go to these apartments and get Matt . . . I was very irritated at this point . . . so I just wanted to get the dope and finish our business . . .

[Later] I saw the chic [sic] we had been looking for and she bolted . . . down a hallway and I raised my pistol and fired into the wall . . .

We went back to Suzie's in Lakewood [Colorado] and got high for a while and [I] remember Matt telling anyone who [would] listen that night about the incident.

At the time of Matthew's October 1998 murder, sources said, Mark K's girlfriend, Jeanne Keenan, then thirty-four, who has a sizable record of meth-related arrests of her own, continued to move the drug while he was in jail. But she did so with the help of other trusted family members. One was Matthew Shepard, who accompanied her to Denver and Fort Collins in the passenger seat — a secondary but critical role that dealers call a ride-along.

"Matt filled in for Mark K, doing the runs from Denver while Mark was away," a former family member stated.

According to the same source, the drug runs were made on a regular biweekly basis. One of the routine runs was scheduled for Tuesday, October 6, the day Matthew was targeted for robbery by Aaron McKinney.

The trip was almost always the same: pickup of twelve ounces in Denver, a stop in Fort Collins for a drop-off of six ounces, then a final delivery to Laramie of the remaining six ounces. But for reasons that remain murky, it was decided at the last minute that Matthew would not go along this time. Whether Keenan or someone else made the trip alone, or with a different companion — or the run was canceled at the eleventh hour or its time changed — are a few of the questions still surrounding the murder.

Nonetheless, a number of previously hidden facts shed new light on the sequence of events leading up to the October 6 attack.

At a friendly sports bar in the Denver suburb of Lakewood, Glenn and I interviewed another member of the Denver circle, Doug*, on the afternoon of October 19, 2004. A darkly handsome, long-haired army veteran who had served in the First Gulf War, Doug said he first met Matthew Shepard in Denver in 1997, but that he had known Aaron McKinney longer, "mainly in passing," since they were both from Laramie.

Doug was not happy about talking to us and made no attempt to hide his displeasure. He had consented to meet with us in the bar's quiet back room as "a favor" to a former girlfriend, yet he appeared just as anxious to find out what we knew as we were to hear anything he might be willing to tell us. Above all, he wanted to be sure that our conversation would not put him back in the penitentiary.

Clutching the neck of a beer bottle tightly in his right hand and slowly peeling away the label with his left fingernails, Doug confirmed much of what we had been told by others: that Matthew began deal-ing for the circle in Denver but then "got into it fairly quickly and successfully when he moved back to Wyoming."

"Some people thought Matt moved too quickly, 'like who the fuck is this guy to be moving into it so fast' in Laramie," he said. "But those people didn't know he'd paid his dues getting into it down here in Denver."

We told Doug that other sources had suggested that when Mark K was jailed in early fall 1998 and therefore "out of the picture in Laramie," Matthew had moved up and helped to fill the void. Doug nodded, nervously tapping the bottom of his beer bottle on the thick wooden table. Once more, he repeated that "some people" didn't take kindly to seeing that happen.

After a long silence, he glared at Glenn and me. "And what have some of these other people you've been talking to had to say about *me?*" he asked.

Worried we had maybe pushed the conversation — and Doug — too far, each of us muttered some pleasantries about the rules and ethics of journalism, and that we were bound to protect all our confi-dential sources, including him. He seemed to accept what we had to say, but we knew it was time to end the interview. The combination of Doug's bulging, bloodshot eyes and his twitchy mood indicated that he had probably been bingeing, and though he was smoothing the rough edges with beer, we thought it best not to ask more questions as he was starting to come down.

NINETEEN

Sleeping Dogs

On a Friday afternoon in late October 2004, a little more than six years after the murder, I drove two hundred miles to meet Kyle*, a former drug cohort of Aaron McKinney, alone at an isolated truck stop off I-80 in western Wyoming.

I had interviewed Kyle twice before in prison and he had been surprisingly cooperative, so I felt more or less safe. Still, I took precautions since he had earlier advised me, "You don't know who you're dealing with," referring to his friends higher up on the drug-dealing food chain.

Kyle worked in the oil fields and had just gotten off a shift. He was still in company overalls, his face and hands stained with crude.

As we sat in the front seat of his parked car talking about Matthew Shepard, whom he had previously claimed to know only in passing, I suggested that Matthew might have gotten in over his head with drugs. Kyle snarled at me like I was an idiot, "Yeah, and he was taking stuff away from the rest of us!"

Without warning two other vehicles suddenly backed into spaces on both sides of us, wedging us in. When I saw what was happening I leapt from the car and ran into the middle of the parking lot, where there were more lights.

Kyle shouted for me to get back in the car but I refused. At that instant a friend of mine, who was planted in a nearby truck monitoring the meeting, called my cell phone. "Get out of there, Steve," he yelled, "they're setting you up!"

"Stay in your car, don't let them see you," I snapped back. Trying not to panic but worried I would get run over or shot, I spun around several times to keep Kyle's car in view as I hustled across the parking lot to a truck stop restaurant. Before I reached the entrance, Kyle's vehicle and the other two tore out of the lot, tires screeching, heading for the ramp to the interstate.

Seconds later my friend picked me up in front of the truck stop, his face a sickly shade of white. In a halting voice he told me how close he thought he had come to losing me there. I knew he was right. With his help I had narrowly managed to escape, but clearly I had been given a message.

Driving away from the truck stop I took my friend's advice and crouched down on the floor of his truck, out of sight. Evidently someone more powerful than Kyle had set me up.

I hardly slept that night in Laramie. Waves of anxiety surged through me till late the next morning. Why had I put myself in danger like that?

The next day, still agitated, I related my roadside experience to Cal Rerucha. He shook his head in disgust. "The methamphetamine trade has made Wyoming revert to the lawless anarchy of the Old West," he remarked pungently. "It's deadly." By then, Cal had been voted out of office in Albany County, after four elected terms. He was now prosecuting state and federal drug cases in the twin cities of Rock Springs and Green River — the epicenter of methamphetamine traffic for the Rocky Mountain West.

After hearing my story Cal told me about a colleague, a Wyoming judge who had recently been surprised by an armed male intruder in the bathroom of his home one morning while shaving. The man was there to relay a message regarding a drug case in which he was awaiting sentencing by the judge. After a few curt words the man quietly slipped away.

I saw no point in asking what the judge decided with a gun staring him in the face. But Cal's reference to the Old West brought back a conversation I'd recently had about Matthew's murder with a veteran cop in the Albany County Sheriff's Office. Friendly, with a studied good-old-boy charm, the cop leaned over his desk toward me, his chiseled, windburned face inches from mine.

"You sure you're not quoting me on this?" he asked.

"It's for background, I won't be using your name," I answered, trying to sound reassuring.

"What happened to Matthew Shepard wasn't a hate crime, not at all," he confided in a low voice. "But why do you want to go digging into all that again? Why not let sleeping dogs lie?"

I wasn't inclined to answer his question candidly. Instead of laying out my suspicions about the involvement of other parties beyond Aaron McKinney and Russell Henderson in events surrounding Matthew's murder, I reminded him that the killing was "a seminal national event, a lot like the civil rights killings of the 1960s," as if he were somehow unfamiliar with the stigma that continued to tarnish his hometown. "The public has a right to know whether the murder was really a hate crime," I said with conviction, "and if not, what was it?"

The cop stared at me as he sank back from his desk, shrugging doubtfully. Almost as an afterthought he flashed me another knowing grin, but again his eyes told me to let sleeping dogs lie.

PART TWO

The Book Of Matt

TWENTY

One Spring Night

Nearly six years after Matthew's murder Glenn Silber and I interviewed Flint Waters, a former officer in the Laramie Police Department. We were interested in talking with Waters because he was the first law enforcement officer to have contact with Aaron and Russell late on the night of October 6, 1998 — only minutes after they'd left Matthew tied to the fence, savagely beaten. Waters was responding to an unrelated report of someone slashing tires when he came upon the two men in Bill McKinney's truck, parked on a quiet residential street. Although Aaron and Russell quickly fled from the scene, Waters chased Russell on foot and caught him.

During the recorded interview in summer 2004, Waters, who had left the police department and gone on to become a leading drug enforcement agent for the Wyoming Division of Criminal Investigation, made a statement that caught our attention.

"Looking back at . . . how this crime impacted Laramie, I think that there was a lot of media attention drawn to this town that was unrelated to anything that happened that night," he said. "What's bothered me about the 'hate crime' title is that I was involved in this the night [it] happened, and I was working security for the court house when all that excitement was going on [during the trials], and none of it appeared to be related."

It was not until several years after that interview, however, that another law enforcement source told me about a separate investigation that Waters had been involved with — an apparently unsolved arson incident five months before Matthew was attacked. The source discreetly handed me a Laramie police record number and told me I'd have to request the report myself, which he indicated had been "buried" with other previously sealed documents. He surmised that Waters had probably not mentioned it earlier because he was still working in law enforcement at the time. (Today Waters is the chief information officer for the state of Wyoming, appointed by the governor.)

A minute or two before 4 AM on May 9, 1998, Flint steered his patrol car onto Park Avenue in Laramie's handsome, tree-lined university neighborhood. Someone in the vicinity had phoned in a report of a car on fire. Heading east, Flint saw a pillar of orange-and-gray smoke billowing into the darkness above the street.

Later that morning, as early sunlight flickered across the prairie, he typed a routine report about the incident near 1115 Park Avenue.

> Upon arrival I saw a station wagon parked in front of the residence . . . fully engulfed in flames. The flames reached . . . about 30 feet in height. I observed an individual who was later found to be the owner of the car, Daniel BALL, standing in the yard with a garden hose spraying water on a nearby pine tree.
>
> . . . While I was talking to BALL one of the tires exploded and shot pieces of the bumper out across the ground . . . I remained in the area awaiting the fire units. I watched . . . for individuals who were wandering through or watching since this is the third fire of this type in a month.
>
> Officer THOMPSON . . . also watched for suspicious individuals . . . I did note that BALL was employed at Mountain Woods [and] I pointed this out also [to] the fire investigator since Mountain Woods has had at least one suspicious fire recently.
>
> I saw individuals standing in a driveway across the street watching the fire department and I walked over and identified one of them. . .
>
> The one that I spoke with was Matthew SHEPARD. SHEPARD said that he was just in the area because he was

walking home. I asked SHEPARD where he had been and he said he was leaving the Cowboy Bar. It was 4:06 A.M., this didn't appear consistent since the bar normally would have all the occupants out by 2:30. I asked SHEPARD if he had come straight to this area and then he paused for a moment and said no, he had been at a party at 14th and Grand on his way home. Since SHEPARD was currently living in the 800 block of south 7th Street this also appeared inconsistent since 14th and Grand is not on the way from the Cowboy Bar to south 7th.

While speaking with SHEPARD I noted that he was very excited. He appeared to be speaking rapidly, his eyes were wide and even when he was talking to me he was watching the firemen and the fire. SHEPARD told me that while walking towards the area he had run into another person who . . . had told him about the fire so he walked over to watch it . . .

I passed this information on to the arson investigator as well. We received a stolen vehicle report [then] and units started searching the area for a vehicle that had just been stolen ten minutes prior so I ended up clearing without further on scene investigation . . .

Nothing further.

Waters later confirmed the story I'd been told by my source as well as his own report. While the arson incident had no discernible connection to Matthew's murder the following October, it seemed curious that the police report had never surfaced before. I only learned of it in 2010, almost a dozen years after the killing.

What continued to perplex me was the concealment and misrepresentation of information about the main participants in one of the most widely reported crimes of the late twentieth century — information about several key figures, Matthew included. Over time I'd come to see a disturbing pattern in how important facts and truths in the murder case were mediated for public consumption, not only by reporters, but also by law enforcement and government officials, and a variety of others with a special interest in how Matthew's story was perceived.

The weathered sheriff's deputy who had advised me to "let sleeping dogs lie" was clearly not alone in his conviction.

TWENTY-ONE

The Tornado

On the first Friday in October 1998, Matthew decided to live it up. He hired Doc that evening to take him in his twenty-five-foot white stretch limo to the Tornado dance club in Fort Collins — a ninety-minute drive from Laramie.

Matthew's moods had recently been up and down, but he hoped that getting out of town for a night would lift his spirits. He also asked his friend Tina to join him. At first she was reluctant.

"I was having a rough week [with] midterms and papers," she later explained. "It was a very stressful week for me with school . . . I was so tired. And [Matt] wanted to go out so bad and he didn't want to go by himself . . . He wanted to take me and I came up with every excuse . . . [but] eventually he exhausted all my excuses."

Before she'd agreed to make the trip, however, "[Matt] called me from his cellphone [while I was still] coming up with all these excuses . . . And he was like, 'Well, I'm right outside your door.' Doc was also outside, waiting in the limo.

"[Matt went] in my closet saying, 'Okay, wear this . . . this will look good.' And so he picks out my outfit. I go and get dressed . . . and I'm still kind of stalling and not sure."

At that point, Doc, whom Tina said she had never met before, knocked on the door — "because he's out there waiting and he's wondering, okay, what's taking so long."

Tina's initial impression of Doc O'Connor as he stood in her door-way reminded me of my first encounter with Doc at his home in Bosler, though he was dressed very differently on this Friday night.

"He didn't look like the type that would be a limo driver," Tina said. "The first thing that came to my mind — even [for her husband] Phil, because later the next day we [wondered], is Doc 'Cowboy

Mafia'? He had a pinstriped suit . . . kind of . . . like Al Capone . . . and a cowboy hat and cowboy boots. And a beard."

I found Tina's phrase *Cowboy Mafia* interesting, as one rumor I'd heard frequently around Laramie related to "the godfathers of Albany County," a group allegedly comprising a few local businessmen and bar owners. I'd even been told that Doc was one of the alleged godfathers, though he laughed dismissively when I asked if it was true.

As soon as the sleek white limo reached the outskirts of Laramie and began coasting down Highway 287 South, Doc and his two passengers in back were surrounded by dark, rugged hills and rolling plains.

Tina was beginning to relax. Doc had already served them cocktails and Brie, and was playing a CD Matthew had brought along — the Squirrel Nut Zippers, one of his favorite bands. Doc had never heard of them before, but he liked the upbeat, swing-style music filling the limo.

"It's *neo*-swing, Doc," Matthew had corrected him earlier with a grin. "That's what I love about it, it's not like regular swing at all."

Stretched out in the back of the limo, Matthew inhaled deeply on a cigarette and turned to Tina. "I don't know what's bothering me tonight," he confided broodingly. "Maybe it's midterms coming up. I'm just feeling all this pressure not to fuck up again."

Tina, who was usually good at consoling her best friend, if not cheering him up completely, squeezed his hand.

"You're always so hard on yourself, Matt," she replied. "You wanted to treat yourself to something special tonight — and me, too — so try to be nice to yourself, *please*? Once you get on the dance floor, you're going to feel a lot better, I promise."

In Tina's opinion, "Matt had everything going for him"; he was smart, handsome, well traveled, and had a terrific fashion sense.

"Oh yeah, right" — he would roll his eyes at her — "the dates are just lining up. I'm a midget, I wear braces, I've got a great build . . . and wait, I almost forgot, I'm amazing in bed."

But Tina was right. When Matthew began dancing at the Tornado, he seemed instantly transformed. Not only was he a good dancer, but his boyish exuberance magnetically drew the attention of others around him.

"Matt liked to show off his own style of trance dancing," Tina recalled with a smile.

Caught in gyrating pools of colored light on the dance floor, he looked like a specter of young Dionysus, surrendering to the ecstasy of the moment.

Later, as Matthew and Tina sat in an outdoor courtyard at the club, they had "another heart-to-heart," something they did often according to Tina.

"I had him over for dinner probably more nights in a week than not," she said. "We saw each other almost every day."

One of her fondest memories was "watching Matt read Shel Silverstein to my kids . . . After dinner he'd be pulling those books off the shelves . . . because he just loved Shel Silverstein."

Tina continued:

> There was a few times we met during the day, like during classes and stuff, when the kids were at daycare. And [we] hung out.
>
> Ironically . . . we had our classes at the same time and our breaks between classes at the same time. So were able to do lunch . . . We were able to catch each other between class for coffee . . . I would stop by his apartment on the way because his place was closer to the campus than mine. And so I'd . . . pick him up and then we'd go grab coffee and then we'd go to class. And then later we'd meet for lunch.

But on the patio at the Tornado as they talked again about their dreams, Tina could sense his emotions beginning to darken again. During the conversation, "Matt brought up death" — his own death.

"He seemed to be having a pretty good time until we were driving home," Tina was later quoted in *Newsweek*. "Then he slumped back into depression. He said he was bummed out about his family and the nightmares [he'd been having]."

Before Doc drove them back to Laramie, however, Matthew

invited a group of friends from the Tornado out for a late-night snack. He also asked Doc to join them.

"The bar closed at 2, 2:15," Doc said. "We end up [sic] going to Denny's restaurant and a bunch of friends went with him in the car . . . I said, 'Well, I'll come in with you, sit with you guys . . . till my sandwich comes and then I'm going to go eat in the car' . . . By this time there was [sic] about 10, 20 people around him. You know, just everybody . . . Matt bought the whole group everything."

It was about 3:30 AM when they left Fort Collins, Doc recalled. He also agreed with Tina about Matthew's sudden mood change during the drive back to Laramie.

"Matt was really upset . . . he was whimpering like a pup," he said.

Doc thought it might've had something to do with a boyfriend "that didn't come up with [Matt] from Fort Collins," but he wasn't sure.

Tina recounted the events of that evening to me over the course of several interviews, but she touched on the subject of crystal meth only once — and only in connection with Matthew's friend Alex Trout, whom Matthew had described to her as "quite a speed freak," she said. I also got the strong impression that Tina was not going to elaborate further and that she felt no obligation to explain why.

But other sources in Laramie, including two former employees of the Library bar, identified a married couple from Casper who were longtime friends of Matthew as regular users of meth. The couple had socialized previously with Matthew and Tina, both at the Tornado and in Laramie.

From all I had learned by then about Laramie's meth underground, as well as the epidemic of meth use at gay bars, clubs, and circuit parties around the nation, it seemed all the more suspicious that the topic had been so thoroughly avoided by nearly everyone associated with the murder case, with the exception of Aaron McKinney's defense team. But even their focus had been on Aaron's personal addiction and not on the thriving criminal networks that had kept these groups of mostly young people supplied — and a growing number of them addicted.

———

As Matthew grew more depressed on the drive back to Laramie, he talked not only about death but also about suicide; he mentioned a possible ultimate escape plan of "taking all his meds."

"There was a couple of times [when] he came to tears," Tina said. What worried her most, though, was his offhanded comment that "if he died no one would even notice until his bills weren't paid, then his parents would call up to bitch and find out he was dead." According to Tina, it was those words that prompted her to sleep on Matthew's couch that night, just so he wouldn't be alone.

The next morning, after Matthew reacted to an upsetting phone conversation with his mother by taking some fifteen Klonopin pills, Tina began to feel that he was having more serious money problems than she'd been aware of.

As I thought about Matthew's anxiety and deepening depression, I was constantly reminded of the threatening remark Aaron had made to Matthew in front of Ted Henson. "Watch your back," Aaron had warned him outside a Laramie convenience store.

But eventually another close friend of Matthew, who insisted on anonymity out of a concern for personal safety, revealed that Aaron was not the only person who had been cornering Matthew.

Late in the afternoon on Saturday, October 3 — hours after his near-overdose in the company of Tina and three days before the attack — Matthew met at the Fireside Lounge with a local businessman to whom Aaron apparently owed money. According to Matthew's friend who was present, there were only a few patrons hanging out in the bar.

"A couple of guys were shooting pool and there was one bartender," the friend said. "The place was dead."

While Matthew and the businessman talked privately in front of the jukebox, his friend noticed that Matt got upset during the conversation. After the businessman left the bar abruptly, Matthew tried to reassure his friend. "Don't worry, I have it under control," he mumbled unconvincingly.

But it was not the first time Matthew had been approached by this same individual, whose suspected criminal ties ran deep.

"I'd tell Matt, 'watch this fucker,'" his friend recalled. "[The businessman] made it known he could take care of someone who crossed him."

Coincidentally, I, too, had been warned by several sources not to cross this individual. I quickly realized that the danger was not being overstated when a highly placed law enforcement officer informed me of threats the businessman had recently delivered at gunpoint, yet unaccountably no charges had been filed against him by local cops.

Matthew's friend who had been at the Fireside that Saturday afternoon offered a blunt explanation: "[For] most of the people in Laramie if you're a dealer, you go to jail. And you serve time. [But] if you're a drug dealer and you talk to the police [as an informant], you don't serve time."

As an afterthought, the friend stated, "Matt definitely knew something that he wasn't supposed to."

Like Mark Rohrbacher (Mark K), Matthew's friend was a member of the Denver dealing circle; and like Rohrbacher, the friend would also later be convicted and serve prison time for an assortment of offenses — but not until years after Matthew's murder case was closed.

For several weeks prior to the October 6 attack, this same friend had met with Matthew frequently for exchanges of methamphetamine, alternating their roles of buyer and seller depending on which of them had product.

"Matt never carried anything [worth] under 120 bucks, he had his rules," the friend said. "And he was taught them by good people."

Yet the friend added pensively, "He had a lot of plans for his future . . . and he was just trying to make extra money and got involved with the wrong people . . . He was a terrific kid [and] he loved [his mother] more than anything."

These words echoed sentiments that had been expressed to me by Doug, another former dealer from the Denver circle.

"[Matt] really was a good dude and the world is less [sic] off without him," Doug wrote in a letter. "I wish I had payed [sic] more attention to him than I did. I just thought he really had it together and was going places that none of us could ever go."

TWENTY-TWO

Friends

Over the remainder of that first weekend in October 1998, Matthew grew more anxious and fearful. On the afternoon of Sunday the fourth, he phoned Tina from Lovejoy's Bar & Grill on 1st and Grand downtown and asked her to join him there.

Situated in the old Johnson Hotel, a handsome red-brick building across from the railroad tracks, Lovejoy's had also been the site of a 1955 fire that killed seven people — the worst blaze in Laramie's history.

When Tina arrived at the bar, Matthew confided that he was still depressed and that he was feeling "paranoid." "He said that he just got off the phone with Walt [Boulden] and Walt was chewing him out for his drinking . . ." Tina recalled. "Walt thought he was drinking too much and that he needed to slow down . . . [Matt] asked me, 'Do you think I'm turning into an alcoholic?'"

Tina said she, too, had noticed that Matthew was "drinking more progressively." "As a friend I just thought it would be best just to support him in coming to terms with that in his own time," she explained.

But Tina also had more to say about his state of mind that weekend:

> He was really worried. A lot of worry . . . I kept getting the feeling there was something he wanted to tell me but he didn't feel like he could. I don't know if he felt he could tell anybody. But it just seemed like there was something bugging him . . . He was more . . . pensive . . . more guarded. He was thinking of getting a roommate or something. Because he didn't feel safe anymore . . . and he thought maybe having a roommate or somebody else in the apartment . . . might give more security.

After a long conversation at Lovejoy's, Tina told Matthew that she had to get home to her kids. Matthew said he wanted to stay at the bar and called Doc O'Connor to invite him down for a drink.

Doc arrived at Lovejoy's a short while later, and, according to his version of events, he and Matthew spent the next several hours talking about every conceivable subject, first at the bar, then at a Subway shop near the university, where Matthew bought him a sandwich.

"That turned out to be approximately a three and a half to four hour conversation with him [at Subway]," Doc said. "I knew more about him than I knew about my own self probably that night . . . It was kind of like, he . . . found somebody that would actually listen to him.

"As time went on, he told me about his first [sexual] experiences" — and before the end of the conversation Matt had allegedly confided, "Doc, I am going to be honest with you . . . I've got HIV."

"He told me he was depressed about it," Doc continued, and he hinted — as he had to Tina — that he was thinking about suicide and "he would just get all his pills together.

"But when we started leaving, Matt really blew me away and this still, today, bothers me a lot . . . He goes, 'You know, I want you to know something. I am going to die real quick here someday, real quick.' And I said, 'What do you mean you are going to die?' And he said, 'Well somebody is going to beat me to death, murder me, and you know, kill me because I am gay.' And I said, 'In Laramie, Wyoming . . . what are you, crazy?'"

In my early interviews with Doc O'Connor, which were spread out over a couple of years, he continued to maintain that he had met Matthew for the first time on the Friday when Matthew hired a limo to take him to Fort Collins with Tina (October 2). Other sources, however, including three close friends of Matthew and a female companion of Doc, insisted that they had been in the company of Doc and Matthew *together* weeks and even months before the murder. But Doc swore they were all lying.

Another aspect of Doc's story that I still had some doubts about concerned his "four-hour conversation with Matt" on Sunday,

October 4. If Doc is to be believed, Matthew poured out the intimate details of his life to a relative stranger, including the disclosure
that he was HIV-positive. While I was able to confirm that the two
had been at Lovejoy's together and I had no reason to disbelieve
that they had a sandwich at Subway, new sources came forward in
2004 and 2005 with pieces of information that Doc appeared to
have purposely left out.

Only gradually, with the passage of more time, did Doc relent and
finally admit that he had known Matthew far longer than he had
originally claimed.

One new source, a female friend of Matthew, said she had seen
Matthew and Doc together on that same Sunday night, October 4 —
not at Lovejoy's or Subway but in the bar at the Eagles club, a Laramie
fraternal lodge in which Doc served as a trustee. Matthew had come
to the club to seek Doc's "advice," the friend stated.

"Matt came in and he was really worried," she recalled. "He was
sweating. He said he was scared to death and was fearful he was going
to get beaten or strangled. He was freaked out . . . [and was] talking
privately to Doc about what he should do."

I couldn't help but notice that Matthew's friend and Doc had used
similar words to describe what Matthew was afraid of: that he was
going to get beaten or killed.

According to the friend, she heard Doc reassure Matthew, "Calm
down, we'll take care of it."

After Matthew left the Eagles club, she said, the name of the businessman with whom Matthew had an upsetting encounter the previous day at the Fireside came up in conversation at the bar. A male
patron who took part in the exchange suggested that the businessman
was the source of Matthew's fear but he also said, "Matt is trying to
straighten out the problem."

Although Doc's version of Sunday's events and that of Matthew's
female friend did not otherwise coincide — and Doc denies to this
day that he saw Matthew at the Eagles club — I kept wondering
if Matthew had, in fact, been threatened with violence several days
before the attack, as his friend now claimed.

What I knew for certain was that Aaron McKinney was well

acquainted with the businessman Matthew had conferred with at the Fireside.

As I continued to reconstruct the events of that first weekend in October 1998, something Tina Labrie had said during her *20/20* interview stuck out.

"Do you think [Matthew] owed money for drugs to anybody?" Elizabeth Vargas asked her.

"He might have," Tina replied. "Or it might have been a case that he knew too much . . . I don't know."

Tina's speculation that Matthew might have known too much was consistent with what I'd been told by Matthew's friend who had been with him at the Fireside the previous afternoon. Despite his anxiety Matthew had tried to reassure the friend, "Don't worry, I have it under control."

Yet according to this same friend, "Matt definitely knew something that he wasn't supposed to."

Every time I went back over the sequence of events on that weekend, I was confronted by the question of whether Matthew had been set up.

If so, by whom?

But there was also something else troubling me: I'd been told that Mark Rohrbacher, a cohort from the Denver circle who was incarcerated on the night Matthew was attacked, had been desperate for Matthew to see some confidential "discovery" documents related to Rohrbacher's drug case. If true, was it that information that made Tina wonder if "[Matt] knew too much"? Or that caused his other friend to say, "Matt definitely knew something that he wasn't supposed to"?

I made multiple attempts to interview Rohrbacher, as I was interested in discussing his later conviction in 2002 on charges related to the interstate trafficking of methamphetamine. Although Matthew's murder occurred in 1998, Rohrbacher admitted as part of his plea agreement that his meth activities went back to 1997, the year before Matthew was killed. It was also in 1997, sources informed me, that Rohrbacher had his first meth dealings with Matthew in Denver.

The last time I spoke with Rohrbacher by phone, he refused to sit down for an interview in person but not before acknowledging that he had, indeed, known Matthew and that Matthew had been part of his meth supply chain. According to Rohrbacher, he "wasn't Matt's direct supplier" but he had "supplied someone else that supplied Matt."

On the same weekend that Matthew was growing more fearful — Friday, October 2 through Sunday, October 4 — Aaron McKinney was in the throes of a methamphetamine binge that had begun with a celebration of Russell Henderson's twenty-first birthday on September 24.

"Aaron and I had been awake for about a week or so prior to this whole thing happening," his friend Ryan Bopp would later say. "We were on a hard-core bender that week."

Ryan and his wife, Katie, were regulars in Aaron's party circle; Ryan also owned a .357 Magnum with a seven-inch barrel that Aaron coveted and hoped to buy.

When Glenn Silber and I finally tracked down Ryan, who had quietly gone into hiding after the 1999 trials, we were surprised to learn he had left his drug activities behind and had settled into a new life far from Wyoming. Once a high-strung meth addict whose scrawny body was plastered with tattoos and amply pierced, he was now living in a pristine Amish farming community.

Sitting alongside his wife, Katie, in the kitchen of their rustic nine-teenth-century farmhouse, Ryan said he had decided to talk because he despised "all the lies you media people put out there about Aaron and Matt." Katie, who had been part of the same druggy underworld in Laramie, nodded in agreement as he divulged some well-kept secrets surrounding the case. He spoke, among other things, of parties he'd been at when both Aaron and Matthew were present as well.

"Aaron McKinney and Matthew Shepard were not strangers," Ryan stated without a trace of hesitation. "They knew each other. Everybody knew Matt Shepard was a partier just like Aaron, just like the rest of us . . . I had seen them at parties . . . I knew Aaron was sell-ing and . . . him and Matt would go off to the side and they'd come back . . . Matt would be doing some meth then."

But in addition to Ryan and Katie Bopp, several other sources eventually acknowledged that they, too, had consumed or exchanged meth and other drugs with Aaron in the week-and-a-half period leading up to the October 6 attack. A few said they had not spoken up earlier because of the stringent gag order that had been in force. But most were afraid of retaliation either by law enforcement officials or by individuals outside the law.

Early on that first weekend in October 1998, Aaron and Russell dropped by Shari's, a twenty-four-hour restaurant on Laramie's North 3rd Street strip where two of Aaron's friends, Shannon Shingleton and Jenny Malmskog, both in their early twenties, were working the graveyard shift. Shingleton was also a casual friend of Matthew's, though he had socialized more frequently with Aaron, beginning in 1997 when Aaron shared a trailer with a group of roommates at a trailer park in West Laramie.

"[The trailer] was essentially a drug haven for McKinney and his buddies and that's pretty much all it was," former Laramie Police Detective Ben Fritzen explained to me. Fritzen had investigated Aaron and his friends on a number of occasions, usually for offenses related to drugs.

According to Shingleton and Malmskog, Aaron and Russell arrived at Shari's in the early-morning hours on Friday, October 2, "sometime after midnight." Soon Aaron began bragging to them about a stash of cocaine he had just gotten his hands on and invited them to come to his place.

"Aaron wanted to go party and came in pretty strung out, talking about drugs," Malmskog said.

From the way he was acting, Malmskog assumed he had been bingeing.

"Aaron said he had all kinds of coke," Shingleton agreed, "an ounce or two," and he wanted to share it with them.

Shingleton and Malmskog declined his offer, but by Monday, October 5 — the day before the attack on Matthew — they had heard from mutual friends that "Aaron had blown through all the coke . . . [it] was gone in four days," Shingleton said.

One of the many questions that remain unresolved is where Aaron got the cocaine. Like Matthew, he was experiencing financial difficulties and was said to owe several people money. According to Kristen Price, Aaron's girlfriend, they didn't have the cash to pay October's rent, yet she was also aware "he was trying to get his hands on some coke."

One of Aaron's creditors was the businessman Matthew had met with at the Fireside on Saturday afternoon, to whom Aaron allegedly owed twelve hundred dollars.

But if Aaron was in possession of an ounce or two of cocaine that weekend, with a street value of a few thousand dollars, what else was going on?

Several sources active in the Laramie drug trade during that period in 1998 said there was not much cocaine in town then. "Meth was cheaper and much more available," one former dealer stated.

However, a dealer who had been part of the Denver circle claimed that Aaron "got into some very deep shit over his meth habit." But the dealer also indicated that Aaron's troubles stemmed from "ripping off another dealer's cocaine" — apparently the same cocaine that Aaron had offered his friends a few days before he robbed and fatally beat Matthew.

Shannon Shingleton and Jenny Malmskog both reminisced without nostalgia about drug parties during which friends from their circle "used to be up for days and days," Malmskog said, mostly on meth. Aaron McKinney was often among them.

When asked whether Matthew had participated, Shingleton responded, "I can confirm that Matt was at these parties . . . In Laramie you were either part of the drug crowd or you weren't."

Not long after Matthew's murder, Shingleton and Malmskog were interviewed extensively by members of New York's Tectonic Theater Project, creators of the docudrama *The Laramie Project*. Both Shingleton and Malmskog were later listed in the on-screen credits of HBO's adaptation of the play.

"We talked to those guys for hours," Malmskog recalled.

"I told people [from the Tectonic] *everything* I knew," Shingleton added, including what he knew firsthand of Aaron's and Matthew's involvement with crystal meth.

Shingleton said he was "angry at how fake [*The Laramie Project*] is" and he couldn't understand why its makers had betrayed the truth to make a political statement.

On the morning of Friday, October 9, 1998, hours after he was arrested for attempted murder, Aaron McKinney gave Detectives Rob DeBree and Ben Fritzen a recorded statement. The complete contents of that statement remained sealed until Aaron's trial a year later, when a recording was played in the courtroom. Not even Russell Henderson, his co-defendant, had been allowed to review the statement while preparing his defense.

The first time I read a transcript of Aaron's thirty-two-page statement, I was startled by several things he'd said, especially his claim that Matthew had offered an exchange of drugs for sex on the night of October 6.

"[Matthew] said he could turn us on to some cocaine or something, some methamphetamines, one of those two, for sex . . ." Aaron told DeBree and Fritzen. "I said I'm not gay, I don't do that stuff."

For a long time I questioned whether there could be any truth to Aaron's allegation, which DeBree and Fritzen had left unexplored. But I initially neglected to pay close attention to the Q & A that followed:

> **Detective DeBree:** You've been involved with metham-
> phetamine before, though, haven't you?
> **Aaron McKinney:** Yeah, in the past.
> **Detective DeBree:** Okay. How long ago in the past . . . a
> month? Two months?
> **Aaron McKinney:** No, it's been longer than that.

Oddly, the subject of drugs in general, and methamphetamine specifically, was dropped for the rest of the recorded interview. Yet it was well known among Laramie cops that Aaron was a chronic meth user and dealer; DeBree and Fritzen had personally investigated him for earlier offenses and knew his history.

While I had repeatedly heard rumors that drugs were behind Matthew's murder — and even whispered talk of an official cover-up — the drug angle only began to preoccupy me when I discovered evidence of a strained personal relationship between Aaron and Matthew prior to the crime. If, indeed, a drug component to the murder had been deliberately concealed, whether by Aaron, Russell, Doc, drug traffickers, law enforcement officers, and/or parties unknown, it once again raises the question: Why?

Did Detective DeBree really take at face value Aaron's statement that he hadn't used meth recently? A careful examination of Aaron's daily activities shows that he lied in his confession. In reality, he had been smoking or snorting a minimum of one to two grams of meth per week, mixing it with other street drugs and large amounts of alcohol. But according to Aaron, "There have been times when I'd use two, three grams a *day*" (italics mine).

At the time, a gram of meth sold for about eighty dollars in Laramie. With his monthly take-home pay of $1,000 or less, and a $370 rent payment, Aaron was spending, at a minimum, the equivalent of $500 a month on his meth habit, excluding cocaine and marijuana.

Aaron himself has also admitted the degree to which he misled police during his recorded statement. "I didn't really want to reveal that I was that into drugs," he stated simply — though he didn't explain why.

It seems equally odd, however, that officials didn't order drug testing for Aaron and Russell, given what they knew of Aaron's activities. Instead DeBree held fast to the opinion he had formulated early in the investigation. In a published interview with author Beth Loffreda for her 2001 book *Losing Matt Shepard: Life and Politics in the Aftermath of Anti-Gay Murder*, DeBree was quoted as follows: "There's just absolutely no involvement with drugs" and "there's no way" the murder was a meth crime.

"From everything that we were able to investigate, the last time [Aaron and Russell] would have done meth would have been up to two to three weeks previous to that night," DeBree said.

In contrast, former homicide detective Fritzen told me in a 2004 interview, "Shepard's sexual preference or sexual orientation certainly wasn't the motive in the homicide . . . What it came down to really is drugs and money."

But Fritzen had something else to say about the police investigation itself. "Anybody who was closely involved in investigating the case . . . pretty much came up with the same consensus . . . that this wasn't a hate crime," he recalled. "Initially everybody agreed . . . [but] as time went on, some [fellow officers] became politically involved in these issues."

Fritzen and prosecutor Cal Rerucha were in agreement about how the case had been exploited politically, even by a few of their law enforcement colleagues who apparently enjoyed being in the national media spotlight. But it wasn't until six years after the murder that Rerucha was willing to speak for the first time on the record about the role of meth.

"If Aaron McKinney had not become involved with methamphetamine, Matthew Shepard would be alive," he stated explicitly. "It was a horrible murder . . . driven by drugs."

TWENTY-THREE

The Ranger

On Monday, October 5, Matthew wasn't feeling well. He had a cold and was still "very agitated," according to Tina Labrie.

Over the course of the day, Matthew spoke on the phone with another friend, Brian Gooden, a thirty-six-year-old Denver optician who was unaware that Matthew had been in a crisis that weekend. The two men had struck up an online friendship several months earlier after Gooden read Matthew's AOL profile ("Matt6926"). According to Gooden, they quickly discovered that they could talk about "anything and everything," from outdoor activities like hiking and camping to fashion or the latest gossip about Madonna.

By late summer the two men had switched from chatting online to talking by phone most of the time. But Gooden also remembered that when they had first started talking, "Matt's mouth was still wired shut" — from the assault he had suffered in Cody, Wyoming, in mid-August.

"You wanted to be around [Matt], he had this energy that wouldn't end," Gooden said. "You just wanted to be part of it . . . One time I spent 45 minutes with him on the phone talking about what clothes he was going to wear."

The more they conversed, however, the more Matthew opened up about his life and some of the issues he'd been struggling with, including depression.

While he was living in Denver and the nearby suburb of Aurora earlier that year, "Matt had a hard time keeping [a] job," Gooden recalled him saying. Matthew also complained about a lesbian roommate who had kicked him out of their Denver apartment "for smoking too much pot."

But according to Gooden, the move to Laramie wasn't proving to be the kind of change Matthew had hoped for, least of all as a gay male. "He said he was an easy target, so he made a conscious effort to dress straight," Gooden mentioned in our first interview more than a decade ago.

"Matt would cry [when he was] insulted for being gay, it would rip him up," he continued. "[But] his world didn't revolve around being gay. He just wanted to meet people. Matt was a worldly person [who] was alone . . . [and] he was reaching out."

During phone conversations with Gooden, Matthew described Tina and Phil Labrie, whom he had just met that summer, as his "best friends." Yet from other things Matthew had confided about their marriage, Gooden got the impression that "Matt was the glue in [their] relationship."

Matthew also slipped another tidbit into one of their long phone chats: He confessed that he had stolen a car when he was a teenager. Gooden couldn't remember the details, but as with most of what Matthew told him he simply took it in stride. It didn't diminish their budding friendship, Gooden said, nor dampen his excitement about driving to Laramie the following Friday, October 9, so they could finally meet in person. Matthew had invited him to homecoming weekend at the University of Wyoming, with plans to attend the Cowboys football game on Saturday and the town parade afterward. Maybe they'd even take a drive out to the Snowy Range on Sunday or to Lake Marie, where the fall colors would be reaching their peak. Matthew didn't like driving too much but he loved taking trips and being outdoors every chance he got.

Since Matthew was still fighting a cold on Monday evening, Tina packed her five-year-old son and two-year-old daughter in the car and drove over to his ground-floor apartment on North 12th Street to see if he needed anything. When she saw he was low on food and out of cold medicine, she took him to the grocery store with the kids. Matthew also asked if they could stop to pick up his Ford Bronco, which he had parked on the street downtown.

Once they arrived back at his apartment, the four watched TV, Tina said. She couldn't recall the exact times that everything had occurred that night, but she remembered that Matthew had been eager to watch

Will and Grace, which had debuted just two weeks before, and that after flipping the channels for a while he'd finally found the show on a Denver station. (A local Wyoming affiliate apparently blocked the broadcast of *Will and Grace* then, due to its gay content.)

Tina estimated that she and the kids had stayed at Matthew's apartment until about 10 PM, when her husband Phil finished a class.

But according to a Laramie police report two days later, Tina told Detective Gwen Smith that the last time she had spoken with Matthew was "Monday evening . . . between the hours of 6:00 and 8:00 PM."

While I had no reason to doubt Tina's honesty or the accuracy of her recollections, I noticed that her versions conflicted with the account that Matthew's friend Alex Trout had given to police — and later to me — regarding Matthew's whereabouts on Monday evening. Trout said he had been with Matthew at the Ranger bar.

"The last time he had seen Matt was Monday in Laramie at the Rancher [sic] at approximately 7:30 PM," Laramie Police Commander Dave O'Malley wrote in his report.

Yet in August 2003, nearly five years after the murder, Tina repeated to me that she had been with Matthew "from 7 to 9 PM, or 7 to 10 PM" on Monday night. Even today, she still believes Matthew stayed at home that evening, with the exception of their short trip to the grocery store and to pick up his Bronco.

Where Matthew really was on Monday night, October 5 — and with whom — would only become relevant in light of other facts that gradually emerged long after the trials had ended. Just as Aaron, Matthew, and some of their respective friends frequented the Library bar, a traditional college pub and restaurant, they also patronized the Ranger bar, a rougher, less upscale establishment on North 3rd Street that includes a motel and package store. Aaron had lived at the Ranger Motel several weeks earlier with Kristen and their infant son. He and a couple of his associates had also sold meth and done "drop-offs" at the bar, which was known to have a more openly gay clientele.

Though Tina told police that Matthew "had become somewhat paranoid . . . and changed the places he used to hang out and was now frequenting Elmer Lovejoy's, the Third Street Bar and Grill and the Fireside," Alex Trout stated that he had gone with Matthew to the Ranger on Monday night. The Ranger and the Library had been Matthew's favorite bars.

Nevertheless, the question of whether Matthew was really at the Ranger on Monday night with Alex Trout is still a mystery. Despite Trout's statement to police that it was the last time he had seen Matt alive, a few days later in Laramie he told an ABC News correspondent that he had not seen Matt on Monday night but had only talked with him.

"I spoke to him on — it was Monday," Trout said. "I was down here that weekend. And I spoke to him and I was trying to get to see him and he . . . said . . . he was studying and that we'd get together, uh, Friday, this last Friday [October 9] and, uh, go out to lunch or dinner and then go to Tornado, a club . . ."

I had already felt uncertain about Trout's credibility, but it didn't stop me from wondering why he would lie about the last time he had seen Matthew in person.

Was Trout aware of Matthew's involvement with the Denver family? Did he decide that the safest course was to remain silent and not incriminate himself due to his own problems with crystal meth? I remembered how positive Trout had been that "Matt was killed because he was gay," while he apparently had no firsthand knowledge of the crime or the motives behind it.

If we set these questions aside briefly, a closer examination of the activities of Aaron McKinney and Russell Henderson on Monday, October 5, and during the day on Tuesday the sixth provides new insight into the sequence of events that exploded in violence on Tuesday night.

If we also simultaneously retrace Matthew's steps on those days, a more complicated scenario begins to emerge — not of two disparate worlds about to collide in a deadly meeting of "strangers" but of three troubled young men whose parallel fates had been on a tragic path to convergence.

On Monday, October 5, during the day, Aaron was still bingeing on meth, but by that evening he had turned to the cocaine left over from the weekend. In interviews with me, he said he "did a bunch of meth" that night with Joe Lemus, the brother of his landlord and roofing boss, Arsenio Lemus.

"We began with meth and ended up with some cocaine," Aaron stated.

In testimony Joe Lemus later gave at Aaron's trial, he confirmed that he had seen Aaron smoke meth on Monday the fifth and snort it the following day, Tuesday the sixth.

Another source, Adrian "Bear" McKinney, a cousin of Aaron, acknowledged to me that he had given Aaron meth on that Monday and also verified that Aaron had been on an extended binge.

But along with his extreme drug use and the compulsive urge to keep feeding his addiction, Aaron was also feeling besieged by other mounting pressures. Sources said that he owed a substantial amount of money to at least two of his regular drug suppliers, who were described to me as co-captains of the local trade. In the meantime his own dealing activities and cash flow were constantly up and down. He was also still awaiting sentencing for his December 1997 burglary of a Kentucky Fried Chicken restaurant.

Aaron's worst fears, however, may have concerned his ability to financially support his girlfriend Kristen and their four-month-old son. According to Kristen, she had told Aaron in no uncertain terms, "We need formula . . . we need diapers . . . we need these things, and you have to pay the rent."

Looking back, she added, "I think he was really torn because it's the desperation of getting your fix or taking care of your family" — a struggle Kristen would come to know even more acutely after the case was over, when she had a second child on the way but was also grappling with her own addiction.

On that same Monday night, October 5, Russell Henderson stopped by to visit his grandmother Lucy Thompson at her home on Laramie's south side. Although Russell had done his share of drinking and using drugs since his birthday on September 24, he was not caught up in the tumult of a nonstop meth binge like Aaron was.

According to Lucy, "Russell showed no signs at all" of being under the influence that evening. Lucy was well practiced at detecting those signs after struggling for years with the alcoholism and drug abuse of her daughter — Russell's mother — Cindy Dixon.

Russell would later say he "didn't even like how [he] felt on meth." His drugs of choice had been "beer and weed," he confessed awkwardly. But he said he began using meth with his girlfriend, Chasity, while they were dating and then "got into it a lot more" when he and Aaron became friends in the summer of 1998.

During that spring and early summer while Aaron was being held in the Albany County Detention Center pending trial on burglary charges, Russell had been spending time with a half brother he'd just gotten to know that year — David Farris. Russell and David shared the same biological father, Gerry Farris, and had been born on the same day one year apart. David, the younger of the two, also happened to be Aaron McKinney's "best friend."

On June 11, after spending two months in jail and pleading no contest, Aaron was released.

"I first met Aaron when David brought him over to my house [and] he mentioned that he needed a job," Russell explained in a letter. "I talked to Arsenio [Lemus] and that's when Aaron started working [at Laramie Valley Roofing]."

Russell had been a close friend of Arsenio's younger brother, Joe Lemus, since high school.

But the friendship between Aaron and Russell did not actually begin until early July, a few weeks after Aaron got out of jail. By early October the two had been friends and co-workers for about three months.

As Russell sat in his grandmother's living room on Monday evening, everything seemed normal, Lucy said. Russell told her that he'd been busy at work but they talked "as openly as we usually did." He spoke of his plans to marry Chasity and mentioned that he was still making installments on a ring for her at Alexander's, a local jewelry store. They also talked about the Christmas party they would have that year.

But Russell was not as forthright with his grandmother as she may have thought, not only about his drug and alcohol use but also about

Chasity and other things. His relationship with Chasity had recently been on shakier ground; both of them were trying to sort out their feelings and decide if they were going to stay together.

Russell had grown more confused in May when he and David Farris dropped by Taco Bell, where Russell had worked while he was in high school. He ran into his old girlfriend and former supervisor, Shaundra Arcuby, with whom he hadn't been in contact since she broke up with him nearly four years earlier. There was still a strong connection between them and Russell promised to give her a call — "but he made it clear it was just a friendship sort of thing because of [his relationship with] Chasity," Shaundra would later recall.

By the end of May there had also been other indications that Russell's life was not quite on track. Whatever it was that was bothering him, he apparently didn't feel comfortable discussing it with Chasity or his grandmother — or anyone else.

Along with his work as a roofer, Russell held a job as an assistant manager at a Conoco gas station in town. According to his boss at the time, Gina Cookson, he also did "a lot of maintenance work . . . on apartment units" on the side, for the former station owner, Dale Poledna. In yet another small-town coincidence, Poledna became Matthew Shepard's landlord that summer.

Cookson, who knew Russell for about four years, described him as "a very kindhearted person" — dependable, ambitious, and someone who always came to work on time, usually opening the station at 6:30 AM. He would even bring her lunch when he was off-duty.

But in early spring Cookson noticed some changes.

"Russell started hanging out with a wild bunch of guys from LVR [Laramie Valley Roofing]," she later told a defense investigator. "They would come to Conoco. David Farris also would come hang around."

On Memorial Day weekend Russell was scheduled to work at the station on Saturday morning. He never showed up for work and didn't call Cookson until late Sunday night. Evidently Russell had gone out drinking with his roofing buddies for the holiday. Although Cookson believed he was afraid to come in and talk with her and that he was "avoiding a confrontation," there was no choice but to fire him.

Later, Cookson would characterize Russell as "a follower" who was easily influenced by others. She also felt "he went downhill" after he stopped working for Conoco.

But almost as a footnote, Cookson mentioned that she had first met Russell through Chasity's mother, Linda Larson. Cookson said he "got along very well" with Linda and her girlfriend Candy Roberts and that he was "okay" with their lesbian relationship.

After he was fired at Conoco, Russell began putting in more hours at Laramie Valley Roofing.

Two weeks later when Aaron was out of jail and desperate for a job, his "homeboy" David Farris knew just the person to turn to: his "new" half brother, Russ Henderson, who would be happy to help out.

In the early-morning hours of Tuesday, October 6, wired from his high-speed cocktails of meth and cocaine but out of money and almost out of drugs, Aaron broke into the Laramie home of his cousin Dean McKinney.

His target wasn't Dean, however. Aaron had heard that a mutual friend, Monty Durand, was staying at Dean's place. Aaron claimed Durand owed him money for drugs. This wasn't the first time Aaron said Durand had cheated him, nor was it the first time Aaron attacked him in a fit of rage. Less than three months before — around July 10 when Laramie held its annual "Jubilee Days" celebrating Wyoming statehood — Aaron had beaten Durand severely while Russell Henderson and Chasity Pasley were present. According to Chasity, the dispute was over "bunk meth" that Durand had given Kristen.

Durand had worked with Russell at Taco Bell a few years earlier — "before Russell was into drugs," Durand told me grudgingly before cutting an interview short in July 2004. I'd been told that Durand's family had a good reputation in town; his grandparents had owned Laramie's roller rink and a mini golf attraction. More important, in the six years since Matthew's murder, Durand had changed his life for the better.

"I just don't want to talk about those things," he said.

But before he warned me to get off his property — a freshly painted, territorial-style bungalow on South 3rd Street, with a tiny front lawn

— he acknowledged that, yes, Aaron McKinney had beaten him up "pretty badly," and "yeah, it was over drugs."

Hours after breaking into his cousin's home and attacking Monty Durand, Aaron went back to work on a roofing job at Bethesda Care Center, a local nursing home. Joining him on the crew with Russell was a thirty-seven-year-old engineering student named Ken Haselhuhn, a native of Rock Springs, Wyoming. Haselhuhn, who had been working alongside them at Laramie Valley Roofing for about a month, was also enrolled at WyoTech, a trade school with several campuses around the United States.

According to Aaron — and subsequently confirmed by other sources — he had used the last of his meth before work that morning. He said he hoped to "score more at a Laramie park" later in the day.

When Aaron first recounted his plan to buy more meth at a town park, I felt sure he was lying again. I knew by then who his key suppliers had been in the summer and early fall of 1998, so I assumed he was protecting them. But the more I spoke with sources close to Aaron, the more I realized how strung out he'd gotten while attempting to keep up with his drug debts. His regular suppliers weren't interested in fronting more meth. What they wanted — and what they were pressing him for — was the money he already owed.

TWENTY-FOUR

Honor Camp

The first time I interviewed Ken Haselhuhn, he was incarcerated at the "Honor Conservation Camp," a minimum-security detention facility in Newcastle, Wyoming. I was interested in Haselhuhn because of the mysterious role he had played as an intermediary in an alleged gun trade on the night Matthew was robbed and beaten. I was also aware that Haselhuhn had been a sequestered witness for the prosecution during Aaron's 1999 trial.

Ultimately, Cal Rerucha had never called Haselhuhn to testify, so it wasn't totally clear what his testimony might have involved. But the fact that officials saw the need to protect Haselhuhn as a witness caught my attention. The only other witness they had guarded that conscientiously was Kristen Price.

When I asked Cal why he hadn't put Haselhuhn on the stand, he said he'd been able "to build a strong case against McKinney without him." That seemed true enough, but I also had a hunch that questioning Haselhuhn might have opened a line of inquiry that a few police officials — if not Cal himself — hoped to avoid.

As I sat at a picnic table in a fenced-in yard with Haselhuhn, a solidly built man then in his early forties, with wavy brown hair and a mustache, I indulged in a little amateur mind reading. It wasn't hard to detect that beneath his courteous, helpful demeanor, Haselhuhn wanted to find out exactly what I knew about Matthew's murder and how I'd gotten the information. I could also see he was being very careful not to tell me much of anything. But if he had nothing to hide, why was he being so cagey?

According to the official story, Haselhuhn's involvement on the night of the crime had been minimal. He had essentially agreed to help Aaron sell his gun, a .357 Magnum, to a friend or neighbor in exchange for cash, drugs, or both. What Haselhuhn would have gotten in return — his cut of the deal — was never specified, however. Was he just doing Aaron a favor?

By the time I left Haselhuhn and started the four-hour drive back to Laramie, I realized I had gotten few, if any, answers to my questions. Yet almost by accident I had picked up a couple of new leads I hadn't been looking for. Whether that had been intentional on Haselhuhn's part or he had deliberately misled me was difficult to know.

But the things he'd conveyed seemed to fit neatly — perhaps too neatly — with other pieces of the puzzle.

In passing, Haselhuhn let me know that Aaron had *definitely* fallen behind in payments to his main drug supplier. I didn't have the gumption to ask how he knew this; I just took it at face value, afraid that he would find me pushy and stop talking. But I had a pretty good idea who that supplier was, without any help from Haselhuhn.

Haselhuhn also agreed with my theory that Aaron's real purpose in trading the gun — if he had intended to trade it at all, which was still a big "if" in my mind — was to get more meth, not to sell the gun for cash. I'd come to that conclusion long before, after Bill McKinney mentioned that he had been interested in buying his son's gun and that he'd offered him two payments of $150, "but Aaron didn't want to do it." Bill had made the offer the weekend before the crime, out of a concern that "Aaron wasn't legally allowed to carry firearms after the KFC felony."

According to Haselhuhn, "Aaron said the gun had belonged to his grandfather," which I knew to be a lie. Was it Aaron's lie or something Haselhuhn had made up for my benefit? In actual fact Aaron had gotten the gun from his friend Ryan Bopp in a trade for meth a few days before he showed the gun to Haselhuhn. (Bopp and Haselhuhn were also acquainted with each other.)

"I had run out of meth myself," Bopp recalled. "I didn't have any. I called Aaron and he said, yeah, I have some. Well I had this gun. I was out of money. So I traded it to him. And he gave me a gram. I did a little bit with him before I left. And I just went on my way."

Bopp's wife, Katie, who accompanied him to Aaron's apartment, and Kristen Price were both present during the exchange of the .357 Magnum for a gram of meth.

During my drive back to Laramie I began to think that the most helpful fragment I'd picked up from Haselhuhn had nothing to do with drugs or with the gun, at least not directly. It had to do with Doc O'Connor. Haselhuhn said he knew Doc fairly well and that Doc had revealed to him, soon after the murder, that "Aaron took a trip in one of the limos with Matt." Haselhuhn went on to say that Kristen, Aaron's girlfriend, "also knew about it."

While I didn't want to push Haselhuhn on how he had come to know so much, I had heard similar things from Matthew's friend Ted Henson. Along with his allegations about Doc, Ted had insisted Kristen "knows a lot more than she's let on."

TWENTY-FIVE

The Library

On Tuesday, October 6, 1998, Tina stayed at home all day with a cold. Something seemed to be going around. Her husband, Phil, had caught a cold on Saturday, Matthew had one on Monday, now it was her turn.

Several times during the day Tina tried to reach Matthew by phone but wasn't having any luck. Phil, who frequently gave Matthew rides around town, would later say he was surprised when "Matt never called on Tuesday."

But one person who did hear from Matthew that afternoon was Doc.

"Matt called me from the Library [bar] at 3:15 PM," Doc told me curtly.

Doc said he knew where Matthew was "because the Library's number showed up on my caller ID."

It was unusual for Doc to be so perfunctory, but on this particular subject he was sticking to just the facts.

According to what Doc told a reporter for *Vanity Fair*, Matthew had been thinking of hiring a limo that night to go someplace with friends but he hadn't said where he wanted to go. Doc explained to Matthew that he had a trustees' meeting at the Eagles club that evening. Since he didn't expect the meeting to get out late, he asked Matthew to call him back later.

Several of Matthew's friends would later say he always carried his cell phone with him, so his call to Doc from a landline at the Library was out of the ordinary.

During my review of the police reports and court files I'd also noticed that there was virtually no mention of Matthew's cell phone. If police had, indeed, checked his phone records — which would be more or less routine in a homicide investigation, especially a case in

which the suspects were facing the possibility of the death penalty —
they had not included that information in their reports.

Apparently Matthew had changed phone numbers often, which
a former member of the Denver circle said was a protective measure
common among their friends. Nonetheless, an examination of
Matthew's cell phone records and a few landlines he had used might
have yielded crucial evidence about the individuals he had been in
touch with in the days leading up to the attack. Had this been an
oversight on the part of investigators or was the information inten-
tionally kept out of the public record?

Patrons who were at the Library bar that evening would later tell
police that Matthew had been there until 6 or 6:30 PM. Police reports
also noted that Matthew had called his friend Walt Boulden at about
6:30 PM to cancel plans they had tentatively made to celebrate Walt's
forty-sixth birthday. When Walt asked where he was, Matt said he
was at a bar.

"We were gonna go to a movie together," Walt later told a reporter.
"And he called and he had gotten behind in his French and he had
to go to classes the next day, so he was gonna study. And so we made
plans to get together later in the week and go to the movies."

But in fact Matthew was still planning to take one of Doc's limos
out that night. Where he intended to go, or with whom, has never
been clarified.

"This conversation [with Boulden] was over SHEPARD's cell
phone," a police report stated, "which was identified by the number
of 761-2673."

At about the same time Matthew was leaving the Library, Aaron and
Russell had just gotten off work. According to police reports, media
accounts, interviews, and other records, Aaron and Russell, still in
their work clothes, drove to 809 Beaufort Street, the home of Ken
Haselhuhn, their co-worker.

The alleged purpose of the visit was that Aaron wanted to show
Haselhuhn his .357 Magnum, which he was carrying in a black case,
in the hope that Haselhuhn knew someone with whom he could trade

the gun for drugs. Some reports suggested that Haselhuhn was a gun collector and that he might've been contemplating buying the gun himself. Haselhuhn would later say he had spoken to some neighbors downstairs, but when they heard a gun was involved they wanted nothing to do with the trade.

Five months after the murder, Priscilla Moree, a respected criminal investigator who was hired by Russell Henderson's defense attorney, interviewed Haselhuhn. She wrote in her report:

> Ken told the police that McKinney and Henderson had wanted to sell the gun for $300 or trade it for crack or meth . . . McKinney and Henderson came back to Ken's house later that evening, again asking him if he could help them get rid of the gun . . . [Then] they again came back to his house later on. He doesn't remember the time that was, but says it was late . . . [he] was in his bathrobe getting ready for bed.

But there was more going on that night than a possible gun trade.

By the time Aaron arrived at Haselhuhn's home, he had already come up with a robbery plan, which he had not yet disclosed to Russell. Part of his plan, Aaron said, was to rob *Haselhuhn*; the business of trading or selling the gun was just a pretext. However, Russell and Haselhuhn did not learn what Aaron had in mind until later.

Earlier that day, while the three men were working together at Bethesda Care Center, Aaron had convinced Haselhuhn to broker a deal for him: He wanted three hundred dollars' worth of meth in exchange for the gun. All three men confirmed to me that Haselhuhn had promised to introduce Aaron and Russell to a friend that evening.

According to Aaron, Haselhuhn boasted to him, "My guy has six ounces of meth, I'll get an eight ball for you."

An eight ball is one-eighth of an ounce. Coincidentally, the six-ounce quantity Aaron planned to rob was also the exact amount that was regularly delivered to Laramie by members of the Denver family. As payment, the two members who made the delivery each received two eight balls, or a quarter of an ounce.

Since Aaron owed his suppliers money and had run out of excuses, the prospect of getting his hands on the whole six ounces was irresistible. If he robbed Haselhuhn's friend, he could satisfy his meth craving and also pay off his debts.

"I was going to rob Ken and the dealer," Aaron told me. "I was carrying two bullets in my back pocket — one for Ken, one for the other guy. I wasn't planning to shoot them, just force them to hand over the meth."

Shortly after six thirty that evening, Haselhuhn used a pay phone near his apartment complex to call his dealer friend, whom he wouldn't identify by name to Aaron and Russell. Afterward, Haselhuhn got into Bill McKinney's truck with the two men and drove with them to the home of a dealer friend, who lived across the street from Washington Park. All three men said that friend was not at home, though Haselhuhn later told defense investigator Moree that only the dealer's wife was at home when he went to the door. They decided they'd try him again later.

According to Haselhuhn, he had asked Aaron to wait in the truck while he went to the door alone. He claimed he "didn't trust McKinney" and felt something wasn't quite right.

"I told him I wasn't taking him up to the guy's front door like that," Haselhuhn stated.

I would later discover that the three men also stopped at another dealer's home — someone with whom Aaron had done business for a couple of years and to whom he owed money. Yet the dealer's name never came up during the murder investigation, at least not in the official records unsealed after the trials were over.

Aaron demanded that I not identify the dealer by name.

"Why would I do that to him?" he snapped at me on the phone.

During a later interview with Aaron in person, when I told him my life had been threatened by one of his former cohorts, I expected him to ask, *Who?* or *Which one?* Instead he shrugged with indifference.

"Maybe it's because you're poking into a hornet's nest," he said.

But beyond his personal loyalties, Aaron may have had other reasons for keeping silent. I'd been told that the unnamed supplier

Matthew Shepard and his father, Dennis Shepard. *Source: ABC News*

Matthew Shepard and his former boyfriend, Lewis Macenze, while they were students at Catawba College in Salisbury, North Carolina. *Courtesy of Lewis Macenze*

This photo of Matthew Shepard, taken at the Shepards' home in Saudi Arabia, was published around the world following the October 1998 attack. *Source: ABC News*

The fence on the outskirts of Laramie where Matthew was beaten and left to die. *Source: ABC News*

Aaron McKinney as a boy. *Courtesy of Bill McKinney*

Aaron McKinney with his mother, Denise McKinney, who died from a botched surgery when Aaron was fifteen. *Courtesy of Bill McKinney*

Russell Henderson receiving his Eagle Scout badge from former Wyoming governor Mike Sullivan. *Courtesy of Lucy Thompson*

Russell Henderson and his grandfather, Bill Thompson. *Courtesy of Lucy Thompson*

Russell Henderson and his former girlfriend, Chasity Pasley, attending a prom. *Courtesy of Lucy Thompson*

Russell Henderson's grandmother, Lucy Thompson. *Source: ABC News*

Aaron McKinney and Kristen Price in Doc O'Connor's limousine. *Courtesy of Kristen Price*

Aaron McKinney, Kristen Price, and their newborn son, summer 1998. *Courtesy of Kristen Price*

Aaron McKinney at a
hearing in the Albany
County Courthouse,
October 1998. *AP Photo/
Ed Andrieski*

Aaron McKinney and
Russell Henderson
at their arraignment,
October 1998. *AP Photo/
Ed Andrieski*

Ryan Bopp, a friend of Aaron McKinney, at a time when they were both hardcore users of methamphetamine, 1998. *Courtesy of Ryan Bopp*

Ted Henson, a longtime friend and lover of Matthew Shepard. *Courtesy of Ted Henson*

Ben Fritzen — former Detective, Laramie Police Department, and current Lieutenant, Albany County Sheriff's Office. *Courtesy of Ben Fritzen*

Dave O'Malley — former Laramie Police Commander and current Albany County Sheriff. *Source: ABC News*

Dennis Shepard talking to the press at his son's funeral, with Judy Shepard at his side. St. Mark's Church, Casper, Wyoming, October 16, 1998. *Source: ABC News*

Protesters associated with the Reverend Fred Phelps at Matthew Shepard's funeral. *Source: ABC News*

Doc O'Connor as a young man. *Courtesy of Doc O'Connor*

Doc O'Connor, 2004. *Source: ABC News*

Wyatt Skaggs and Jane Eakin — Russell Henderson's defense attorneys. *AP Photo/David Zalvbowski*

Jason Tanegman (left) and Dion Custis (right) — two members of Aaron McKinney's defense team — with investigator Frank Rowe. *AP Photo/Ed Andrieski*

Cindy Dixon — Russell Henderson's mother — was found frozen to death in a remote canyon on January 3, 1999, while Russell was awaiting trial for Matthew Shepard's murder. Dixon's killer, who pled guilty to manslaughter and admitted raping her, served four years. *Courtesy of Lucy Thompson*

Cal Rerucha outside the Albany County Courthouse with Judy and Dennis Shepard, after Russell Henderson was sentenced to two life terms, April 1999. *Getty Images/Kevin Moloney*

Aaron McKinney at the Albany County Courthouse on the day he was sentenced, November 1999. *AP Photo/ Ed Andrieski*

Aaron and his father, Bill McKinney, during a prison visit. *Courtesy of D. Harper*

Russell Henderson at Nevada's High Desert State Prison, 2004. *Courtesy of John Sharaf*

had inspired fear in those he supplied with drugs and that he'd always kept a well-trained pit bull nearby.

One friend of Aaron, who had formerly sold drugs himself, said, "When I was in jail, they [agents of the Wyoming Division of Criminal Investigation] offered me a deal if I'd rat [the supplier] out. His arm is very long, long enough to reach me in the pen. I just did my time and shut up."

Russell Henderson, for his part, had used meth frequently with Aaron and their girlfriends yet he wasn't privy to most of Aaron's dealing activities. Similarly, Kristen Price said that Aaron had been "very secretive" about his drug transactions, even with her, and that he was especially guarded when it came to his suppliers. The only thing she knew about the dealer with the pit bull, for example, was his nickname; but "I was never permitted to go into his house" when Aaron went there for pickups. The same was true of Russell — he was always told to wait in the truck.

After Haselhuhn, Aaron, and Russell left the second dealer's home they drove to the residence of their roofing boss, Arsenio Lemus, because Haselhuhn claimed that Lemus owed him some money. Apparently, only Haselhuhn got out of the truck and went to the door; he returned shortly and said Lemus "wasn't there," so they took Haselhuhn home.

According to Aaron, Haselhuhn had no idea he was planning a robbery — nor did Russell. But soon after they dropped Haselhuhn off, Aaron told Russell that what he really wanted to do was steal all the drugs rather than trade the gun.

"It wasn't anything I wanted to do [and] I told Aaron that," Russell recalled. "I was still sober and wouldn't go along with [it] . . . I figured if we just got to the bar and started drinking, he'd forget about it."

As for Haselhuhn, he did not learn of Aaron's plan to rob him until after Aaron was convicted and sent to the Wyoming State Penitentiary for life. Haselhuhn was serving time at the prison for a larceny offense when inmates with ties to Aaron reported back to him what Aaron's real intent had been on the night Matthew was robbed and beaten.

Haselhuhn said it only confirmed what he had suspected all along, "that McKinney was up to no good."

Nonetheless, Aaron and Russell returned to Haselhuhn's home again on that Tuesday evening, shortly after nine o'clock.

"That's why me and Russ went to the Library, to wait for this dude [Haselhuhn's friend] to come home," Aaron explained.

Aaron said he kept calling Haselhuhn from a pay phone in the bar, but Haselhuhn still hadn't been able to reach his friend.

According to Doc O'Connor's version of events, Matthew phoned him at the Eagles club "at about 7:20" that evening. Doc even provided me with the landline number at the Eagles where he had received the call.

Once again, I was surprised at how scrupulous Doc had been about keeping records — or the precision with which he had reconstructed a time line after the fact. Then again, it was still a mystery to me why Doc had retained an attorney after Matthew's attack when no charges had been filed against him.

Doc said Matthew had called him at seven twenty from the University of Wyoming campus where he was attending a meeting. Apparently Matthew still planned to take the limo out, though he had canceled plans with Walt less than an hour earlier and — somewhat improbably – had still not told Doc where he wanted to go.

"I told Matt to call me back [because] this meeting will get out at about 8:45," Doc recounted. "I said, 'I'll go to Bosler, get the limo, and be back about 9:30–10.'"

"Matt promised to call back," Doc said, "but I never heard from him again."

By all accounts, the meeting Matthew attended of the campus LGBTA (Lesbian, Gay, Bisexual & Transgender Association) was uneventful. Fewer than twenty people — a mix of students, university staff, and a couple of other area residents — regularly participated in the gatherings. Since Gay Awareness Week was scheduled to begin the following Monday, the group focused that evening on preparing for the upcoming events, including a lecture by Leslea Newman, author of a book about lesbian families.

One member would later tell police she "could smell alcohol on [Matt's] breath." It was one of the few hints that something wasn't quite right with him that night. Earlier at the Library bar, he had approached two female patrons that he didn't know and asked if he could sit with them at their table.

A week after the attack, Detective Rob DeBree interviewed one of the women — Kim McDougall. "MCDOUGALL stated that they advised SHEPARD that they had friends that were coming to meet with them . . . and SHEPARD graciously pardoned himself and returned to the bar . . ." DeBree wrote in his report. "MCDOUGALL stated that she was under the impression that SHEPARD was slightly intoxicated, but was unsure."

According to an account of that evening's events in the *Los Angeles Times*, "At the [LGBTA] meeting, the group's president [Jim Osborn] told of an incident in which he was harassed near the campus' Fraternity Row and advised students to be careful." The inference of that newspaper — and a large number of other news organizations that reported on the attack — was that Laramie was an unsafe, homophobic environment. But to be fair, that impression was abetted by early interviews with town locals. For example, a manager of the Fireside bar was quoted in *The New York Times* as saying, "If I were a homosexual in Laramie, I would hang low, very low. Openly gay behavior is not only discouraged, it's dangerous."

Yet *The New York Times* also quoted Jim Osborn's comment, "There are always going to be individuals who are narrow-minded and hateful and who are going to cause problems. That happens in any community and is not isolated to Laramie."

At first Osborn was reluctant to talk publicly about Matthew or the violent assault that occurred just a couple of hours after the two men had been together. Following the LGBTA meeting, members of the group had gone to a nearby Village Inn restaurant on East Grand Avenue, where they pushed four tables together and spent time socializing and eating. Several would recall that Matthew had snacked on cherry pie and that he tried to convince them to go to the Fireside bar afterward. But no one seemed to be in the mood.

"What Osborn found impossible to understand was why anyone would want to kill Matthew Shepard, a small, slight man who threatened nobody," an article in *The Denver Post* stated a few days later.

When the gathering of friends at the Village Inn broke up, Kim Nash, a member of the LGBTA group, drove Matthew home to his apartment on North 12th Street at around 9 PM. She told police that she waited for him to go inside and believed he was in for the night.

If we accept Doc O'Connor's statement that as of 7:20 PM Matthew still wanted a limousine later that night, and that Doc told him he'd "go to Bosler [after the Eagles club meeting], get the limo, and be back about 9:30–10" — a round trip of thirty-six miles — the most probable scenario is that Matthew was still considering making the regularly scheduled "run" to Denver, with the usual stop in Fort Collins on the way back.

(Several former dealers who were active in the Laramie drug trade then — and knew Matthew — confirmed this as a well-established delivery route. In addition, numerous case documents involving local, state, and federal investigations support their claims.)

About two and a half hours after he talked with Doc, Matthew would drive his own Ford Bronco to the Fireside bar. The notion that Matthew wanted an expensive stretch limo, with the advance reservation it required, for a five-minute drive across town to the Fireside is utterly implausible. It would have been far easier for him to ask Kim Nash to drop him at the Fireside instead of at home.

If my supposition is correct — and if it's also true that Doc "never heard from [Matt] again" — something happened between their phone call at 7:20 PM and Matthew's arrival at the Fireside at approximately 10 PM that convinced him not to leave Laramie that night.

Again, a diligent examination of phone records by police might well have yielded concrete evidence about where Matthew intended to go in Doc's limo.

But my suppositions only raise more questions:

Why did Aaron and Russell follow in Matthew's tracks so methodically that evening, first to the Library and then to the Fireside? Did Aaron (and Ken Haselhuhn?) know about the routine run scheduled for that night?

Is it possible the run was canceled altogether?

———

More than a decade after the murder, Ted Henson, who had quar-
reled with Matthew a few days before the attack, offered another
opaque clue.

"I know [Matt] was mad about not being able to go to Denver to
pick up some meth," he said. "It could have been [because he told]
someone he was going to get [the meth] and it did not happen . . . I
do not care what Tracy* or any [of Matt's] other friends say, they kept
him on meth. I blame them some for Matt's habit."

At nine o'clock on Tuesday evening, Russell and Aaron picked up
Russell's girlfriend, Chasity, at the University of Wyoming student
union, where she had just gotten off work. The three drove together
to Ken Haselhuhn's home for a second attempt to connect with his
dealer friend. This time Aaron went inside to talk with Haselhuhn
alone while Russell and Chasity waited in the truck.

After Aaron left Haselhuhn's residence and got back in the truck,
he instructed Russell to drive to the home of one of the dealers they
had visited earlier, with no explanation of what Haselhuhn had to say.
Once again Russell and Chasity waited in the truck while Aaron went
to the dealer's door, leaving his gun behind. But apparently the dealer
still hadn't come home.

If Aaron's real interest had been selling or trading the gun, it makes
no sense that he left it in the truck instead of taking it along to show
a potential buyer. Haselhuhn had also told Aaron earlier that he
wouldn't take him to the dealer's front door, but this time Aaron went
to the door unaccompanied while Haselhuhn stayed at home.

In truth, Aaron knew both dealers whose homes they visited that
evening quite well. One was thirty-eight-year-old John Earl Baker
Jr., a well-known auto mechanic and reputedly a leading player in
Laramie's secretive methamphetamine underground.

From a review of previously undisclosed documents I'd learned
that in March 1999, shortly before Russell's trial was set to begin,
defense investigator Priscilla Moree had interviewed more than a
dozen of Aaron and Russell's fellow inmates at the Albany County
Detention Center — including Baker. Baker, who had known Aaron
prior to their incarceration, spoke of conversations he had with Aaron

at the jail. Initially Baker seemed to confirm Haselhuhn's story about a gun sale, but he also added something more.

"There is something about a drug deal and McKinney was supposed to trade the gun for drugs," Baker told Moree. "A guy named Ken [Haselhuhn] . . . had something to do with the drugs. They were getting dope from Shepard."

In May 2003 I met with John Earl Baker Jr., then forty-two, and several other sources familiar with the local meth scene for a group interview at Laramie's Village Inn restaurant, coincidentally the same restaurant Matthew had visited with a group of college friends on the evening of October 6, 1998, hours before he was attacked.

By the end of the interview Baker confirmed what he had told Moree at the county jail four years earlier: that Aaron had mentioned something to him about a drug deal and "getting dope from Shepard," and that Haselhuhn had functioned as an intermediary on the night of the crime.

Prior to Matthew's murder and in the years since, Baker has accumulated a record of meth-related crimes that — if nothing else — demonstrates an exceptional personal knowledge of the drug trade. While his credibility deserves careful scrutiny, his position as a key figure in the Laramie meth scene was confirmed by numerous sources on both sides of the law.

I was also fascinated to discover that several other inmates interviewed by Moree seemed to echo what a close friend of Matthew from the Denver circle had confided about Russell's participation in Aaron's scheme.

"It's possible [Russell] knew something was going to go down, but not the extent of it," Matthew's friend told me.

Ron Golas, who was Aaron's cellmate during part of the time he was incarcerated, told Moree, "Russell did not have anything to do with it at all. He was like a bystander. McKinney was the man who hit him [Shepard]."

A second inmate, John Paul Baker (not to be confused with the aforementioned John Earl Baker Jr.), stated, "Russell did not do anything . . . If it wasn't for McKinney, Russell would not have been arrested. Russell did nothing."

And according to a third inmate interviewed by Moree, named Dan O'Connell, "[Henderson] did not have anything to do with it."

While I'd ordinarily be very skeptical of jailhouse sources, I was aware that Cal Rerucha had also relied on one of Aaron's fellow inmates as a confidential informant, to learn about Aaron's conversations at the jail. In addition, two other inmates incarcerated with Aaron and Russell when Moree conducted her interviews in March 1999 were Monty Durand and Chris Baker; both Durand and Baker were friends of Aaron and had extensive knowledge of his meth-dealing activities. In Durand's case, Aaron had attacked him in a fit of anger the night before he attacked Matthew — also over drugs.

Another inmate interviewed by Moree at the Albany County Detention Center (known locally as "ACDC") was Albert Castaneda. Moree's written report on her interview with Castaneda suggests a view of Aaron McKinney at odds with depictions of him as rabidly anti-gay.

"Albert is gay and when McKinney was his cell mate, they talked openly about homosexuality," Moree noted. "McKinney gave him no problems at all . . . and they got along fine."

Moreover, a high-ranking officer in the Albany County Sheriff's Office, who requested anonymity on the subject of Aaron's sexual orientation, stated that at least two other law enforcement officers had witnessed Aaron engaged in homosexual activity while he was under surveillance. One incident occurred at the jail while he was awaiting trial for Matthew's murder. But on a different occasion long before his arrest, police grew suspicious when they surprised Aaron and a male companion in a parked car one night. The two men were in a deserted "lovers-lane-type area in town" and the vehicle's lights were out.

Did officials write routine reports on those episodes, much as they had documented Matthew's presence at the scene of a mysterious fire several months before he was murdered? If such reports ever existed, were they deliberately expunged from the public record? And why had officials kept silent regarding Aaron's known homosexual activities?

When I posed these questions to several longtime sources, I heard a variety of stories in response. According to a female acquaintance of Aaron's, he had "regular appointments" with a former athletic coach in town, who was not only very popular but also closeted. In addition, she said, the coach's brother was a cop in town, so efforts were made to spare the family any embarrassment following Aaron's arrest.

Ted Henson claimed that he and Matthew had run into Aaron in Laramie one day while Aaron was in the company of a gay male friend of Matthew's from the University of Wyoming — John*. Like Matthew, John was active in the gay student group on campus. Ted said that after Aaron and John walked away, "Matt told me, 'They're not boyfriends. Aaron's getting paid for it.'"

But according to Ted, John later became very outspoken about the crime's anti-gay motives, while concealing his personal association with Aaron.

After trying unsuccessfully to contact John by phone and email, I approached him in person at his Laramie office to request an interview. I offered to protect his privacy and not use his name or otherwise identify him, but he politely declined. I had no interest whatsoever in exposing his personal life; I just wanted to know if Ted's allegations were true and whether John had played a part, however small, in covering up the truth about Aaron — and hence the complex truths about Matthew's murder. (A former co-worker of John at the University of Wyoming suggested unconvincingly to me that John may have refused to talk to protect the reputation of the school, which was his alma mater.)

I also noticed other discrepancies that were intriguing. For instance, how many times had Aaron and Russell actually visited Haselhuhn's home that night?

Russell was convinced he had been to Haselhuhn's only *twice*. "The second and last time we went there was with Chasity, before we took her home, and I didn't go in that time," he said.

In a statement five months after the murder, however, Haselhuhn claimed that Aaron and Russell had visited him *three times* that night. According to Haselhuhn, Laramie police had questioned him at length a couple of weeks after the attack and had shown him two guns to have him identify the one that belonged to Aaron. Yet I was unable to find a record of that interview in the unsealed police reports. It also seemed strange that police had chosen not to investigate Haselhuhn immediately after they arrested Aaron and Russell.

Aaron, whose recollections I often found to be the least credible of the three men— due, in part, to his prolonged drug use — told me in a 2003 interview that he and Russell had gone back to Haselhuhn's home "maybe even four times," but then he corrected himself and said "three to four times." On the other hand, Aaron confirmed that Russell and Chasity had waited in the truck while he went inside to talk with Haselhuhn alone during the second visit.

One possibility I had to consider was that Aaron had gone back to Haselhuhn's home a third or even a fourth time that night without Russell. By then I'd come to appreciate how thoroughly Aaron had lied to protect his drug cohorts; and that Haselhuhn and Doc had also given misleading statements — though perhaps to a lesser degree — in order not to incriminate themselves or their friends and associates.

After Aaron, Russell, and Chasity drove to the home of Haselhuhn's dealer friend, they went to Aaron's apartment on North 4th Street. According to Kristen's later statement to Detective Ben Fritzen, "Me and Aaron sat down and he told me what he was doing that night and he was supposed to be home within 20 minutes . . . He was going to go sell the gun and . . . bring the money home." Kristen said Aaron had told her earlier, "I am going to sell it and get our rent money."

When Aaron and Russell left the apartment, they got into Bill McKinney's truck and followed Chasity in her car to the trailer where she and Russell lived in Fort Sanders. Russell showered, changed his clothes, and before leaving again with Aaron collected some change to buy beer.

Aaron wanted to go to the Library bar and wait there until Ken Haselhuhn was able to reach his friend. Aaron's choice of the Library seemed telling, since Matthew had spent several hours drinking there that afternoon, on a school day while classes were in session and he was concerned about midterms. The bar had also been the site of a previous encounter between them that hadn't gone well. And although Aaron liked to sell drugs there, mostly to students, it wasn't his favorite place in town to drink.

According to a reliable confidential source, Haselhuhn had also been at the Library "very recently" while Matthew was there and "he definitely knew who Matthew was" prior to the attack. This was not a trivial piece of information insofar as Haselhuhn, like Aaron, had stated that he "didn't know Shepard."

On Tuesday night Aaron and Russell arrived at the Library between ten and ten thirty. They ordered a pitcher of beer and began drinking; Aaron also got up repeatedly and went to a pay phone to make calls — to Haselhuhn, he claimed.

"I'm not sure how long we were [at the bar] but we drank a couple of pitchers of beer while we were there," according to Russell. He said they "decided to go to — somewhere else besides there" and "we ended up at the Fireside."

But when asked, "Why did you go to the Fireside that night?" Russell answered, "I don't know exactly why."

Aaron, on the other hand, admitted it was he who picked the bars they went to — and the dealers' homes they visited.

In Aaron's extensive interview for *20/20*, only a small portion of which was broadcast, he explained what was really on his mind that Tuesday and retraced the steps he and Russell took before they went to the Fireside.

> **Aaron McKinney:** I was supposed to get some more
>   [meth] that afternoon, but that fell through. That's
>   when I was supposed to trade the gun in. So when
>   that fell through, that's when I started to explore other
>   options.

Elizabeth Vargas: What other options?

Aaron McKinney: Well, I had something brought to my attention . . . a guy that had a lot of it, so I decided I would go over there and rob him for it.

Elizabeth Vargas: This was on Tuesday?

Aaron McKinney: Yeah.

Elizabeth Vargas: Your friend Ken at work told you that there was a dealer in town that had how much meth?

Aaron McKinney: He said he had about six ounces in his house.

Elizabeth Vargas: Did you tell Russell about your plan?

Aaron McKinney: Uh, yeah.

Elizabeth Vargas: What'd he think?

Aaron McKinney: Uh, he didn't like it at all.

Elizabeth Vargas: What'd he say?

Aaron McKinney: Uh, he didn't want to be a part of that.

Elizabeth Vargas: Was it after work that you [came] up with this plan to rob this drug dealer?

Aaron McKinney: No, during work.

Elizabeth Vargas: It was during work?

Aaron McKinney: Yes.

Elizabeth Vargas: And you told Russell at that point?

Aaron McKinney: No, sometime on the way there . . .

Elizabeth Vargas: So you went to the drug dealer's house, or you went to Ken's house?

Aaron McKinney: I think we picked Ken up first, and then we went to the dealer's house.

Elizabeth Vargas: Nobody home?

Aaron McKinney: No, oh, yeah, he was home, but he didn't have nothing [sic].

Elizabeth Vargas: So then what'd you do?

Aaron McKinney: Oh, well, we were supposed to wait, because he was supposed to get it. Supposively [sic] it was supposed to be there any minute, so . . . uh, we went to a bar [the Library] and waited for awhile.

Elizabeth Vargas: Did you go back to the house?

Aaron McKinney: Uh, I think so. We went back to Ken's house.

Elizabeth Vargas: And a second time you tried, and the dealer still didn't have any drugs?

Aaron McKinney: Yeah.

Elizabeth Vargas: How many times did you call the dealer?

Aaron McKinney: Well, probably four or five.

TWENTY-SIX

The Fireside Lounge

Sometime between 9:30 and 10:30 PM Matthew drove his Ford Bronco to the Fireside Lounge downtown and parked on the street out front. Bar employees later questioned by police had slightly different recollections regarding the time of his arrival.

Doug Ferguson, a bouncer at the door who had started his shift at 9 PM, felt pretty certain that Matthew had walked in between 10 and 10:30. Ferguson had seen Matthew at the Fireside many times previously but didn't know his name, he said. He also noticed nothing out of the ordinary after Matthew's arrival.

It was karaoke night, so the bar was a little livelier than on a typical weeknight, with about thirty-five to forty patrons. Matthew simply ordered a drink and sat by himself at the bar, next to the wait-station, Ferguson recalled.

Matt Galloway, a bartender who started work at 10 PM, would later say that he'd seen Matthew in the bar approximately five times in the past and had spoken to him on a few occasions. A junior at the University of Wyoming, Galloway would also come to realize that he had attended grade school and part of high school with Matthew in Casper, though he was unaware of it on the night of October 6 when Matthew sat down at the bar.

Within a couple of days, media stories would offer a remarkably detailed picture of that evening's bizarre sequence of events. Nearly all of them advanced the premise that Matthew had been quietly "lured" from the Fireside because — in so many words — he was the perfect target: He was well dressed, he was obviously gay, and he may have had the temerity to show a sexual interest in Aaron McKinney and Russell Henderson. Repelled by his homosexuality, the two "rednecks" decided not only to rob him but also to beat him with the barrel of a gun and hang him on a fence for having only thirty dollars in his wallet. Or in the words of Kristen Price, "Aaron and Russ . . . wanted to teach him a lesson not to come on to straight people."

According to *The Denver Post*, which cited bartender Matt Galloway, Matthew sat at the bar as he usually did and had three or four different kinds of beer over the two hours or so he was there. Similarly *Newsweek* reported: Matthew "kept to himself, nursing his drinks — a Heineken, a cocktail, a Corona — alone for two hours." The general consensus was that Matthew hadn't been intoxicated; at most he was "buzzed."

Galloway believed there were fewer people in the bar than Ferguson had estimated — "20 to 25," he thought.

Inevitably, there were also different recollections regarding the time that Aaron and Russell arrived at the Fireside. Doug Ferguson thought they had gotten there between 11 and 11:30 PM; others placed the time at about 11:45.

But before they drove to the Fireside, Aaron and Russell did two things: They went to the home of Ken Haselhuhn again. Haselhuhn stated that they were there around 11:30 PM. They also stopped briefly at the Cowboy bar downtown, where there was "not enough going on," according to a statement by one of Aaron's attorneys at his trial the following year.

Aaron and Russell said that when they arrived at the Fireside they ordered a pitcher of beer and sat on stools at the end of the bar, with two young women sitting next to them. It was their third pitcher of the evening, as they had already consumed two at the Library.

Matt Galloway was pretty sure Russell had ordered the pitcher, but it was Aaron who poured a bunch of change on the counter to pay for it. Galloway later described the two men to police as "not clean cut by any means. One of them had . . . extremely dirty hands . . . I just remember [their clothing] being just grungy."

Galloway's speculations regarding a motive for the crime were repeated frequently in media stories. "Here's this little kid, dressed very nice," he told a reporter for *Vanity Fair*. "Maybe they've seen him before and thought he was gay."

Ferguson recalled that Aaron and Russell "were at the short end of the bar" when they got their beer, about four to five chairs from where Matthew was sitting. Ferguson didn't hear their conversation and didn't know how long they talked. Galloway agreed with him: He couldn't hear what Aaron and Russell were saying, but they talked for "about 15 to 20 minutes" and it seemed like a regular conversation.

Ferguson said he had seen Aaron and Russell in the Fireside a number of times previously — "10 to 15 times," with more frequent visits over the past month. He had also seen Matthew, Aaron, and Russell in the bar at the same time, though he didn't remember them associating with one another.

Since Russell had just turned twenty-one two weeks earlier, on September 24, it seems unlikely that he would've been allowed into the Fireside before that date. He and Aaron readily acknowledged that they had been to the bar together on other nights, yet Aaron stressed that the drug sales he had conducted there were his alone. Aaron's admission was later confirmed by sources familiar with his dealing activities at local bars.

While Fireside employees were quick to distance themselves from any association with Aaron and Russell, sources also stated that Aaron regularly sold meth to a couple of people who worked at the bar.

Russell remembered that Aaron had tried talking with the two girls sitting on the stools next to them but "he wasn't getting anywhere." Russell said he began to pay more attention to the TV over the bar, hoping that by the time they finished drinking Aaron would have forgotten his earlier idea of robbing Ken Haselhuhn and his friend.

According to an Associated Press report, "The two friends [Aaron and Russell] shot pool" at the Fireside. Matt Galloway also claimed that the two men had played pool and that they had remained in that area of the bar for twenty minutes to half an hour. Aaron and Russell, on the other hand, insisted that they never shot pool that night. I was also unable to find any other bar patrons or employees who had seen them playing pool.

However, the Fireside DJ named "Shadow" said he had seen Matthew and one of the two men — Aaron or Russell — talking near the pool table.

"They were standing, talking for a little bit, for like two, three minutes . . ." Shadow recalled. "I can't remember which one it was, he's the one that had the sideburns . . . I remember the sideburns, like Elvis Presley sideburns. And he was the one actually talking to Matthew for a little bit down by the pool table. But then after Matthew came back, he just walked off."

Photos taken a couple of days later, after Aaron and Russell were arrested, leave no doubt that the person with "Elvis Presley sideburns" — who spoke with Matthew at the pool table — was Aaron.

According to Shadow, he met Matthew for the first time "about two and a half, three weeks prior to that," on the same night that he went to a party at Matthew's apartment.

"I had met him with a group of people that came in here [to the Fireside] and partied," he said. "And they invited me over to this party after our party and that's how I met him."

By all accounts it was the same party that three other friends of Matthew had told me about — during which hard drugs, including heroin, were used.

When I asked Shadow if he'd seen "more serious drugs" (heroin, meth, cocaine) at the party, he replied, "Not really. Okay, everybody was just trying to have a good time . . . I was trying to talk to a young lady, too, that I was kind of interested in, so I wasn't paying attention to the surroundings around me."

But earlier in the same interview, he stated, "I know when we went to the party at his house, there was a lot of alcohol. I mean, *lots of alcohol*" (emphasis in original).

Shadow also remembered what Matthew was drinking on the night he left the bar with Aaron and Russell: "He had a Heineken and a Jack and Coke if I'm not . . . mistaken. That was his last drink that he had."

There were conflicting accounts as well about how Aaron and Russell "met" Matthew at the Fireside. Some speculated that Matthew had offered to help pay their bar tab, which was not substantiated by Galloway, who had served all three. Other reports said Aaron and Russell went into the bathroom together to plan their robbery of Matthew, though there is eyewitness evidence indicating that Aaron went into the bathroom with *Matthew*, not with Russell.

Even prosecutor Cal Rerucha theorized — based on the evidence available at the time — that Aaron and Russell had lured Matthew out of the bar with some promise of sex. But what Matthew may have promised was not made public until Aaron's trial, more than a year after the murder.

Within a few days of the crime, however, Rerucha and other officials were aware of Aaron's allegation that Matthew had offered cocaine or methamphetamine in exchange for sex. But as a matter of legal strategy, they worked hard to keep any mention of drugs out of the record.

Moreover, despite his initial lies and misrepresentations, and those of Kristen Price — which formed the basis of his "gay panic" defense — Aaron has admitted that Matthew never made a sexual advance on him or on Russell at the Fireside. Instead, Aaron now acknowledges that it was he who approached Matthew first. He said he went over to Matthew, who had moved to a table, and "bummed a cigarette" while Russell was watching TV at the bar.

But before Matthew got up from the bar, Aaron quietly pointed him out to Russell. The slight, well-dressed young man Aaron indicated was not someone Russell knew or had met before.

"That's when Aaron mentioned robbing Matthew," Russell said. "I told him 'No, I don't want to do that.'"

Russell still hoped that if they kept drinking, Aaron would settle down and the night would come to an end. But according to both men, Aaron persisted.

"[He] explained how we should take [Matthew] out by Wal-Mart, that he would do everything and I didn't have to do anything," Russell continued. "I still said no."

By then, Matthew had gotten up from the stool where he'd been sitting and was walking around the bar.

The contradictory accounts of what happened on the night of October 6 were not conclusively resolved by the police investigation, media stories, trial proceedings, or eventual convictions of Aaron and Russell. In numerous instances law enforcement officials, news organizations, and other parties reported significant facts and details erroneously — not only about events at the Fireside, but also with regard to the attack on Matthew and the motives behind it.

After a concerted examination of the trial testimony of witnesses who were at the bar, case records, formerly sealed documents, and some files that remain confidential — as well as my extensive interviews with Fireside patrons and employees, principals on both the prosecution and defense sides of the case, and numerous other sources — I will offer here what I believe to be a more accurate account of the violent events set in motion at the Fireside — events that had been simmering for weeks, if not longer.

Soon after Matthew left his stool at the bar, he stopped at the table of another patron, Mike St. Clair, then a twenty-two-year-old geology student at the University of Wyoming. According to St. Clair, who testified at Aaron's trial and whom I interviewed, Matthew asked if he could sit down with him and muttered that he "didn't want to talk to the assholes at the bar anymore."

It was later assumed that Matthew had been referring to both Aaron and Russell, though I found no evidence that Russell and Matthew had spoken with each other.

Since Aaron had not approached Matthew directly yet, I wondered whether Matthew's remark had to do with the preexisting discord between them. It was also not inconceivable that the two men had spoken by phone earlier in the day or had some contact over the preceding weekend, or even at the Library, where both had been earlier that evening. It was also possible that hostile communications had been relayed through an intermediary.

Lest we forget: Matthew had confided in a few different people about how frightened he was; he was "scared to death," he said.

As I began to understand the brutally competitive meth-trafficking activities taking hold in Wyoming and Colorado at the time, none of those possibilities seemed out of the question.

I also remembered what I'd been told by a couple of sources who had been close to Aaron McKinney.

"We had a little syndicate going," one of Aaron's cohorts explained before he moved permanently from Laramie to take a job in the Pacific Northwest.

Kyle, the formerly trusted source who had set me up in a parking lot off the Wyoming interstate, had sneered, "[Matt] was trying to take stuff away from the rest of us."

I'd also discovered by then that Kyle himself had played a part in the tangled web of events on the night of October 6.

Mike St. Clair, who is six feet tall and weighed 230 pounds at the time, was at the Fireside with two friends, Keith and Jay Staley. St. Clair would later testify at Aaron's trial that when Matthew walked over to his table near the dance floor, he made a provocative, off-color remark.

"It set off something inside me," St. Clair said. "It made me angry . . .

"[Matthew] leaned down and said something about 'head,' which at the time was really offensive to me . . ." he elaborated. "He also licked his lips like . . . it was him trying to be sexy . . . showing he was interested in me, hitting on me . . . but I think he got the idea that I was really mad when he did that."

After re-reading St. Clair's testimony several times and interviewing him at a Mexican restaurant he'd opened in Laramie, it occurred to me that the so-called gay panic aspect of the murder case had really begun with this little-understood incident that had occurred between Matthew and St. Clair, not between Matthew and Aaron. It was also evident as I talked with St. Clair that he was neither homophobic nor suggesting that Matthew was somehow responsible for, or "deserved," the violence that was inflicted on him that night. St. Clair had simply felt uncomfortable and angry with the way Matthew had come on to him, which I suspected had partly been a consequence of the amount of alcohol Matthew had consumed, beginning that afternoon at the Library.

Before news of the attack had spread, however, the notion of blaming the aggressive behavior of the victim held certain logic, albeit twisted. Aaron, for one, was desperate for a cover story that would protect his drug associates as well as himself — and he was apparently desperate to stay in the closet as well. His solution was to concoct a claim not unlike Mike St. Clair's and allege that Matthew had made an unwanted sexual advance, which set off his rage.

Nearly six years later, after I'd questioned Aaron about his gay panic alibi innumerable times, he stated, "At the time, that seemed like . . . the best way to prove that I didn't mean to kill him." Aaron said the decision to use that strategy in court was "a little mine . . . a little of the lawyers . . . [but] it was mostly me."

Once he and Russell arrived at the Fireside, the thing that was still foremost in Aaron's mind was robbing the six ounces of meth that Ken Haselhuhn's dealer friend was supposed to have.

"We went to the Fireside to wait and there was still no ounces," Aaron said.

Since Haselhuhn had not been able to reach his friend yet, Aaron was privately seething. All he could think about was getting his hands on the meth.

But this is where Aaron's story falls apart again. I don't doubt that he was gradually slipping into a full-throttle meth rage; but there are also many reasons to believe that the six ounces Haselhuhn had bragged about and the six ounces Matthew was slated to deliver to Laramie that night were one and the same. And Aaron surely knew that. His suggestion that he randomly shifted plans from robbing Haselhuhn and his "friend" — whom he'd been plotting to rob since Haselhuhn told him about the six ounces early in the day — to robbing Matthew is another fabrication.

Whomever Aaron intended to rob, he was undoubtedly aware that robbing six ounces of meth that had come from an organized crime network in Denver was a serious offense and that someone had better have his back, whether on the street, in prison, or both. He was shrewd enough to know that without protection he didn't stand a chance.

From the estimates of several individuals who were at the Fireside that night, Aaron and Russell were in the bar for roughly an hour before they left with Matthew.

Mike St. Clair's recollection was that Aaron and Russell sat at the bar from thirty minutes to an hour. Yet according to Russell, during the hour or so he and Aaron were in the Fireside "we were separated for about 20 minutes." Aaron said the same thing: that he and Russell had separated for a while.

Assuming the latter statements are true — and I have found Russell's version of events at the bar to be credible in light of all the available evidence, including Aaron's belated admission that it was he who had approached Matthew first — their remaining time in the Fireside went like this:

Aaron and Russell got up from the bar and walked over to the dance floor. Aaron wanted to ask Shadow to play his favorite song — "Gettin' It" by the rapper Too Short. As they made their way across the floor, Russell ran into an old friend, Nicole Cappellen, who was celebrating her birthday. Cappellen, whom I interviewed by phone at her home in Los Angeles in October 2004, said she and Russell had known each other "as kids and in high school."

According to Cappellen, she danced a little with Aaron and Russell, though other witnesses — and Aaron himself — also recalled that Aaron had acted "a little crazy" on the dance floor.

"I talked to Nicole for a little while," Russell later recounted in a letter, "then I went back and sat down alone at the bar, where we were originally sitting."

In the meantime Aaron went to the DJ booth.

(It's unclear whether Cappellen ever spoke to the police, as she left the following morning for a week's vacation in Las Vegas. But both she and the DJ confirmed the above sequence of events.)

After Aaron requested the song, he made his way over to the table where Matthew was sitting with Mike St. Clair.

As Aaron leaned down to Matthew, St. Clair heard Aaron say,

"Hey buddy." Aaron claimed he also "bummed a cigarette" from Matthew.

Although St. Clair did not hear the rest of their conversation, he noticed that Matthew listened, nodded yes, put out his cigarette, and got up.

When police first questioned St. Clair, however, there was some confusion about whether it was Aaron or Russell who had approached Matthew at the table. The confusion involved a crucial piece of evidence that would be misconstrued throughout the homicide investigation and the court cases that followed.

Russell owned a silver Boss jacket that Aaron had borrowed from him, which, according to several witnesses, Aaron was wearing that night. St. Clair could only recall, "It was the guy with the silver jacket" that had come over to talk with Matthew.

But more important, St. Clair saw that same individual — Aaron — enter the Fireside bathroom with Matthew. St. Clair was certain that he'd seen only one of the men go into the bathroom with Matthew, not both. This fits with Aaron's admission to me that only he spoke with Matthew in the bar. It also coincides with what Russell has always maintained — that he never talked with Matthew.

In addition, I found no other firsthand witnesses to corroborate the widely reported fallacy that Aaron and Russell had gone into the bathroom together to plan the robbery. That rumor began with the false story Aaron allegedly gave Kristen when he arrived home that night, shortly after he and Russell left Matthew at the fence.

What Aaron and Matthew discussed in the Fireside bathroom will never be known, though it most certainly clinched Aaron's decision to proceed with robbing him. And despite Aaron's persistent lie that he'd never met Matthew before that night, his familiar, laid-back manner when he approached Matthew at St. Clair's table ("Hey buddy") — and Matthew's decision to join him in the bathroom — do not suggest a meeting of strangers.

But regardless, a preponderance of sources have established not only that Aaron and Matthew knew each other before their October 6 encounter at the Fireside but also that their relationship had taken a bad turn.

Witnesses at the Fireside agreed that the three men left the bar together on what appeared to be friendly terms, sometime around or shortly after midnight. Doug Ferguson thought it was close to 12:30 AM; Matt Galloway estimated that they left between 12:20 and 12:45. The only indication of any hostility was the remark Matthew had made earlier to Mike St. Clair about "the assholes at the bar."

According to Russell (whose version was confirmed by Aaron), "I was finishing the last mug of beer and watching TV when Aaron came over to me with Matthew. They sat down for 20 to 30 seconds, at the most a minute, and [Aaron] said, 'Let's go.'"

Russell admitted that he went along knowing that robbery was what Aaron had in mind, but he said that he and Matthew never exchanged a single word. Russell also stated that he was completely unaware then of any personal relationship between Aaron and Matthew.

Aaron and Russell walked out of the bar first, followed by Matthew, who bumped into Shadow near the door.

"I was walking up by the door to catch some fresh air," Shadow recalled. "I lit up a cigarette and [Matthew] was walking past . . . And I looked up and he said, hey Shadow, what are you doing? I was like . . . you getting ready to leave?

"He's like, yeah, I'm getting a ride with those two guys right there. And I looked over and I saw them standing [next] to a truck . . . [Matthew] stopped and talked to me but he was, like looking over to see if the guys were actually waiting on him . . . looking to see if they were telling him to hurry . . . something like that."

According to Shadow, he spoke with Matthew "give or take . . . thirty-five [to] forty-five seconds . . . He asked me for a cigarette . . . and I was like okay, here you go . . . I lit it for him . . . He took one drag . . . and after that he just walked off. And I told [him], well give me a call."

When asked if he thought methamphetamine was involved in the violent episode that began minutes later, Shadow said he had no personal knowledge of that. But he added, "Meth is a big thing around this town . . . You just got to know the right people and it's not hard to find it . . . it's right there under your nose . . . You could find that anywhere in Laramie. Anywhere, I mean, the cops even know where to find it. They know exactly who to go to and stuff like that. But every time they knock one person down, two, three more pops up."

One enduring mystery of that night, which can never be adequately resolved or reconstructed, is the conversation that took place once Aaron, Russell, and Matthew left the Fireside in the black Ford pickup owned by Aaron's father. Aaron said that he and Matthew engaged in small talk at first, and Russell has consistently maintained that he couldn't hear exactly what was said between the two men. For that matter, Russell hadn't been privy to the words they exchanged earlier near the pool table or in the bathroom, which apparently prompted Matthew to leave with them.

But both men have also told me unequivocally on numerous occasions that it was the other robbery Aaron was planning — the one involving Ken Haselhuhn, Haselhuhn's friend, and six ounces of meth — that drove the night's events.

While Aaron continues to say that he abruptly shifted plans from robbing Haselhuhn and his friend to robbing Matthew, his patchwork of stories doesn't add up. Moreover, in light of new information and evidence I discovered about the meth-trafficking activities of both Aaron's associates and Matthew's during the time period leading up to the attack (and afterward), there are compelling reasons to conclude that Aaron's two planned robberies were not only connected but one and the same.

For a long time I was confused about why Aaron would spin such a complicated web of lies. Why didn't he simply confess that he and Matthew had been friends and that they'd bought and sold drugs from each other?

I could even comprehend why Aaron might lie about their hidden sexual relationship, given the likelihood that he'd spend the rest of his life in prison. Standing all of five foot six and weighing about 130 pounds, for him to admit otherwise would have been an open invitation to predators.

But it was a couple of Aaron's former drug cohorts who helped me understand that Aaron had no choice but to protect the suppliers that he — and they — had worked for. One particular supplier had a lot to lose if his name surfaced during the Shepard case, as he was in Laramie awaiting sentencing on federal drug charges on the night Matthew was attacked. For Aaron to implicate him in the sequence of events involving Haselhuhn, Matthew, and an attempted robbery of six ounces of meth, which exploded in murder and became a national event, would have been disastrous for the supplier — and also for Aaron. His life in prison would have been perilous at best.

TWENTY-SEVEN

Sounds of Silence

In his opening statement at Aaron's trial the following year, Cal Rerucha gave jurors a summary of what occurred after Matthew left the Fireside with Aaron and Russell:

> The next part of this story, this journey, will be told by the defendants themselves. Mr. McKinney and Mr. Henderson. You will get to look at their statements. You will observe what was said . . .
>
> After they got Matthew Shepard out of the bar, they took kind of a strange route, if you're familiar with Laramie. Normally you go to Grand Avenue, because it's a through street, but neither one had driver's licenses that were valid, so they took kind of a different route . . . They go to Garfield . . . until it deadends into 15th Street. Then they go to Grand Avenue . . . and go east . . . and it takes them past the Wal-Mart store.
>
> . . . Of course this is late at night; traffic is light, perhaps four or five minutes to get from the Fireside Lounge to the area of Wal-Mart.
>
> And then begins the three-part ordeal of Matthew Shepard. Matthew Shepard sits between Mr. Henderson, who is driving the vehicle, and Mr. McKinney. At the approximate location of the Wal-Mart, Mr. McKinney says these words, "We are not gay, and you're getting jacked."
>
> Now, Mr. McKinney can't remember if the first blows that were struck were with fists or with a .357 Magnum with an eight-inch barrel, but [Matthew] was hit in the vehicle. And the reason for that was that he would produce his wallet . . . Mr. McKinney said he produced it with

ease. Unfortunately the contents of that wallet yielded only $20 [sic].

They proceeded further and the beating continued, perhaps three, six more times in the vehicle, all at the hand of Mr. McKinney. They drove to an area that was familiar to Mr. McKinney and to Mr. Henderson . . .

Nowhere in his opening statement did Cal Rerucha mention methamphetamine or any of the convoluted events and circumstances that had been building, bit by bit, in the hours and days leading up to Matthew's encounter with Aaron and Russell at the Fireside. Although Cal was not aware of *all* of those circumstances at the time, his reasoning as a prosecutor was simple: He expected Aaron's defense team to rely heavily on meth as a contributing factor and, therefore, he did everything he could to keep mention of meth out of the record.

He turned out to be right. Aaron's attorneys did include meth as a key element of their defense strategy, but their focus was almost exclusively on Aaron's personal addiction. They stayed away from the complexities of his dealing activities — and they apparently knew nothing of Matthew's. Instead they stuck with Aaron's cover story: that he hadn't known Matthew before that night.

According to the opening statement of Jason Tangeman, one of Aaron's defense attorneys, "When they get ready to leave for the bars, Aaron and Russell haven't talked about robbing anybody. They haven't talked about beating anybody. And they haven't talked about hatred of homosexuals or anything of that nature. *In fact, Aaron and Russell . . . have never even heard the name Matthew Shepard*" (italics mine).

With regard to the latter claim, both the defense and the prosecution sides of the case appeared to be in complete agreement, which served to advance further the media-driven perception that a pair of strangers had targeted Matthew because he was gay.

In a June 2004 interview, Russell gave an account of their drive to the fence, which essentially corresponded with Cal Rerucha's summary.

"How long were [the three of you] in the truck together before Aaron pulled out the gun and began to hit Matthew?" Russell was asked.

"Just a matter of minutes," he said. "As long at it takes to get there [to Imperial Heights]. Two or three minutes, five minutes at the most."

"Where were you when the beating started?"

" . . . It happened right before we turned into the residential area," Russell continued. "And that's when [Aaron] pulled the gun out . . . he said that, 'You're getting robbed,' basically . . . Then it was after we had went [sic] into the residential area that he hit him."

"Why did he then begin to hit him if Matthew gave him his wallet?"

"I don't know. I don't know why he decided to hit him . . . I was surprised, shocked. Because I didn't expect it to go the way that it did . . . I guess I didn't know what to expect but I really didn't want Matthew to get hurt out of the whole thing."

The sequence of events that Cal outlined in Aaron's trial — insofar as when and where the crime began and how Aaron, Russell, and Matthew ended up minutes later in an orgy of violence at a remote prairie fence — matches for the most part the versions recounted by Aaron and Russell, with a few crucial differences. But significantly, neither the prosecution nor the defense ever offered a complete or accurate explanation of the crime's underlying motives. Both sides also failed to distinguish sufficiently between Aaron's role and Russell's, including the hidden personal factors that came into play.

In his 2004 interview with Elizabeth Vargas, Aaron provided the most complete — and the only videotaped — account of his brutal attack on Matthew since his rambling confession to police six years earlier. (To my knowledge, the only other recorded interviews with Aaron are those that I conducted and a brief interview with a Wyoming radio station.)

> **Elizabeth Vargas:** You had told police that at some point
>   Matthew reached over and grabbed your leg.
> **Aaron McKinney:** Yeah.

Elizabeth Vargas: And that you thought he was coming
   on to you.

Aaron McKinney: Yeah.

Elizabeth Vargas: Is that true?

Aaron McKinney: Yeah.

Elizabeth Vargas: When did that happen?

Aaron McKinney: On the way out. On the way out of
   town.

Elizabeth Vargas: What did he say? What did you do?

Aaron McKinney: I don't think he said anything. He just
   did it.

Elizabeth Vargas: And what did you do when he grabbed
   your leg?

Aaron McKinney: I hit him.

Elizabeth Vargas: You hit him?

Aaron McKinney: Yeah . . .

Elizabeth Vargas: So that's what triggered the robbery
   attempt?

Aaron McKinney: No, I was already going to rob him. I
   guess that just gave me a jump, an off-cue [sic], to get
   it started . . .

Elizabeth Vargas: So you pulled out the gun and hit him.

Aaron McKinney: I had my arm behind the seat with it
   . . . [he demonstrates] like that. I was getting ready to
   do it, to pull it on him anyways.

Elizabeth Vargas: And what did he do when you hit him?

Aaron McKinney: Not a whole lot. He became pretty
   cooperative after that . . .

According to Aaron, he told Matthew, "'Give me your wallet' . . .
something along those lines." He said Matthew immediately handed
over the wallet.

Elizabeth Vargas: How much money was in there?

Aaron McKinney: Thirty bucks.

Elizabeth Vargas: Thirty bucks?

Aaron McKinney: Yeah, that's it . . .

Elizabeth Vargas: So if he gave you the wallet and money, did you stop beating him?

Aaron McKinney: No.

Elizabeth Vargas: Why not?

Aaron McKinney: I don't know. I'm not sure. I was pushed past my point — my tolerance.

Elizabeth Vargas: Well, why were you so angry? What made you go off?

Aaron McKinney: Well, a lot of things altogether. My financial situation — and drugs I was on. That anger and violence, I already had building up with everything, and then, you know, the drugs just make that a lot worse.

Seconds after Aaron pulled out his gun, Russell followed his instructions and took a left off Grand Avenue into the Imperial Heights subdivision. Aaron told him to drive to the last street with houses, bordering the edge of the prairie.

"It dead-ended there," Cal later explained to the jury, "and they travel on a dirt road four hundred yards."

"I told [Russ] to take an old dirt road," Aaron agreed, years after his trial. "It was in a rocky field. I figured that would be a good place — "

It was also an area Aaron knew well because he had grown up in the subdivision and had often played in the fields of dry grass and sagebrush. As a boy it had been his backyard.

But now, in the front seat of the truck, Matthew continued to shield himself from Aaron's blows.

"I hit him probably five or six times altogether," Aaron told Elizabeth Vargas.

"How badly was he hurt?" she asked.

"He was bleeding pretty good," he responded vacantly.

"Did he say anything to you?"

"Yeah, he was still talking — mostly, you know, 'Don't hit me.' And he's being real apologetic, real cooperative."

"So if he was being apologetic and cooperative, and he gave you all of his money, why did you continue to beat him?"

"Sometimes when you have that kind of rage going through you, there's no stopping it. I've attacked my best friends coming off of meth binges . . . Any little type of thing when you've been up for that long can set you off and make you snap right away."

Aaron also described the physical sensations he was experiencing at the time, much as he had to police during his confession.

"I was hallucinating pretty bad," he said. "I wasn't in any condition to be driving . . . It was almost like an out-of-body experience, I guess, or what they tell you. Felt more like I was watching the whole thing."

Although Aaron initially lied to police about his weeklong meth binge, he admitted in 2004 that he'd also been in the midst of "coming down" on the day and night of the crime.

"You're still wide awake, but you . . . can feel your body is really tired, and that you want to sleep, but you can't," he stated. "You want to stop doing [meth], [yet] you want more . . ."

As the lights from nearby homes receded behind the truck carrying Aaron, Russell, and Matthew, the road grew more bumpy and desolate.

According to Cal Rerucha's summary,

> They stop in an area that borders the old Warren Livestock land . . . To make it a little more aesthetic, instead of just "No Trespassing" signs, the owner of the property erected a rail fence . . . It is secluded. It is in a depression. This is where phase two of the ordeal of Matthew Shepard takes place.
>
> Mr. McKinney pulled Matthew Shepard from the vehicle. This is probably the only time he fights back. Mr. McKinney said it was a frail attempt. He tried to kick at my chest, but I was soon able to pull him out of the vehicle, and the beating continues . . . As each blow is stuck, there is the pain and the screams that come forth when he is struck. There is also the begging for some type of mercy.

Actually begs for his life, and there is negotiation going on at the same time. Matthew Shepard negotiates with McKinney for his own life.

He tells them, there is only $20 [sic] in the wallet, but in my home I have $150. Take what you will, but give me mercy. The beating continues. Blow after blow.

Finally when McKinney is satisfied that he has extracted the information needed so he can burglarize Mr. Shepard's house, there is a pause. He tells Henderson to go get some rope in the back of his truck. Mr. Henderson dutifully responds, and it's a white clothesline, and Mr. Henderson lashes Matthew Shepard to the fence.

Later, when asked why he told Russell to drive to that particular spot, Aaron said,

"It seemed like a good secluded spot to drop [Matthew] off. And it would take him a while to get out of there, with no shoes. I took his shoes . . . That whole field is rocky, riddled with cactus. It would take a guy a long time to walk across it barefoot."

Aaron added, "Well, he's going to call the cops on me when he's done. I'm out on bail for another felony [the KFC burglary]. I got to have time to get away . . . I decided it probably be even better idea [sic] to go ahead and tie him up while I was at it . . . It would give us more time. I decided at some point — I was going to rob his house while I was at it."

Russell admitted that it was he who tied Matthew to the fence, but the sequence of events he described was somewhat different from Cal Rerucha's account to the jury. When I first noticed the differences, they appeared subtle and almost irrelevant.

According to Russell, after Aaron pulled Matthew out of the truck,

I got up and came around from the truck and then, at that time, at that point, [Aaron] said, Get some rope so we can tie him up. And so I went and got the rope out of the back seat of the truck. And ended up tying his hands . . . behind

his back . . . I didn't even, I didn't even really tie it. I just
wrapped the rope around so he could eventually get away
. . . It wasn't very tight. I just — cause it was a real long
rope. And I just wrapped it around a bunch of times and
that was it. And I just didn't even tie it.

When asked if he tied the rope to the fence, Russell said, "It wasn't
even to the fence. It was just, his arms were around the pole of the
fence."

It was hard to believe Russell's statement, as the police officer who
untied Matthew from the fence the following day noted that the rope
was extremely tight.

"So how did it get tight?" Russell was pressed further.

"I don't know," he answered. "I don't know. The only thing I could
think of is, is cause it was wrapped a few times around and it just . . .
cause they said his [wrists], that he had swelled. And when it swelled
it seemed like it was tight on there, I guess."

According to the narrative Cal Rerucha presented to the jury, Aaron
asked Russell to get the rope and tie Matthew *after* most of the beating
had occurred, "blow after blow." Yet Russell stated that he had gotten
the rope and tied Matthew moments after he got out of the truck.

"At first Mr. Henderson laughed," Cal said, "and as the beating
continued, he became afraid, and he asked his friend, Mr. McKinney,
for mercy for Matthew Shepard."

The assertion that Russell laughed during the beating is easily
traced back to the secondhand statements of Kristen Price, who
claimed Aaron had told her that after the crime. But Kristen, who
also helped fabricate Aaron's gay panic alibi and concealed his dealing
activities, has since admitted the degree to which she lied; she "would
have said or done anything at that point to get him out."

Aaron himself, in his interview with Elizabeth Vargas, was asked to
clarify Russell's involvement:

Elizabeth Vargas: What was Russell doing during all this
    time?

Aaron McKinney: He didn't want to [be] any part of it.
   He wasn't happy with what was going on at all.
Elizabeth Vargas: What did he say to you?
Aaron McKinney: He was telling me to quit it. You know,
   cut it out. Quit hitting [Matthew]. Quit pushing him
   around. Just leave him alone.

Aaron said Russell was also saying those words "on the way to the fence," then "once we got there . . . it all happened pretty quick."

But it would not be until six months after Matthew was killed that Russell spoke for the first time about his attempt to stop Aaron from beating Matthew at the fence. Russell had already accepted a plea bargain for two life terms by then, to avoid a possible death sentence.

"[Aaron] was still hitting—" Russell stated tentatively at his sentencing on April 5, 1999, "— he hit Matthew a few times with the gun, and Matthew looked really bad, so I told him to stop hitting him, that I think he's had enough. And at that time, he hit me with the gun."

Cal Rerucha apparently believed that Russell had, indeed, tried to stop the beating but failed. "Mr. McKinney took his attention away from Mr. Shepard, turned to his friend, Mr. Henderson, and struck him in the lip with the .357," he told the jury at Aaron's trial in November 1999. "Mr. Henderson went back to the truck to lick his wounds."

Several years later, when asked what Matthew's condition was at the time he tried to stop the beating, Russell stated, "He still seemed coherent . . . he was still conscious . . . but I mean, he was bloody and looked like he had been beaten up pretty bad . . . When I went and got into the truck, he was still conscious at that time . . . I know that when I left, that Matthew was still . . . talking."

After Russell returned to the truck, according to Cal's opening statement,

Mr. McKinney went to the buck fence where [Mr. Shepard]
is tied, his hands behind his back, to the bottom part of

the fence, unable to defend himself, and this is the third part of this saga.

. . . As Matthew Shepard is lying there . . . he is asked a question,

"Can you read my license plate?" For whatever reason, Matthew Shepard said, "Yes, I can read your license plate." And reads it to Mr. McKinney. With that information and the knowledge that he can be identified, Mr. McKinney once again raises the .357 Magnum pistol, looks down at Matthew Shepard, defenseless, who cannot raise his hands even in his own defense, and strikes him as hard as he can in the head, once. He strikes him again in the head as hard as he can, twice. He strikes him as hard as he can in the head three times.

As Mr. McKinney turns away from Matthew Shepard, there are no screams of pain; there is no negotiating; there is no nothing. There is [sic] the sounds of silence, because he knows Matthew Shepard is dead or will soon be dead.

Over the past fourteen years, each time that I've read Cal's description of the pain and suffering Matthew endured that night, I have felt a sickening sense of sadness and despair. But those feelings have also left me with a moral imperative to understand, to the very best of my ability, what really happened that night — and why.

Just as the media missed or left out essential components of this multifaceted tragedy, there were important elements missing from the case Cal Rerucha presented to the jury — and also from the defenses raised by Aaron's lawyers as well as Russell's.

In his description of those final moments at the fence, when Aaron asked Matthew if he could read his license plate, Cal assumed a motive or purpose that can no longer be substantiated by the facts.

"With that . . . knowledge that he can be identified," Cal said, "Mr. McKinney once again raises the .357 Magnum pistol . . . and strikes him as hard as he can in the head . . ."

In light of the personal relationship between Aaron and Matthew and their ongoing conflict, there was never a question of Matthew's ability to identify Aaron. (Ten different sources have acknowledged that they were in the company of both men together, or that they learned from Matthew himself about his relationship with Aaron.)

I'm not questioning whether Aaron asked Matthew if he could read the license plate. But what was really driving Aaron's rage?

According to Cal's narrative, Aaron asked Matthew about the license plate after he'd struck Russell with the gun, causing him to retreat to the truck.

But Russell said the exchange about the license plate took place *first*, after he had tied Matthew to the fence.

"The only thing I can remember that was being said is that [Aaron] did ask him if he could recognize the license plates on our truck," Russell stated. "And Matthew — Matthew said, Yeah, that he did. And then [Aaron] hit him a few more times . . ."

It was then — when Aaron continued beating Matthew — that Russell tried to stop him and was struck across the face with the gun.

"It didn't do any good cause it didn't help Matthew any . . ." Russell added dismally. "After that I went and got in the truck."

When asked why he got back in the truck, Russell said, "I was scared . . . of the situation. At how far it had got [sic] out of hand . . . Just cause . . . [Aaron] had lost control."

But in April 1999, shortly after he was sentenced to two life terms and long before my own interviews with him, Russell was questioned extensively by Detective Rob DeBree, who was still trying to piece together the real sequence of events at the fence.

"Do you think it was an accident that [Aaron] hit you?" DeBree asked.

"No, I'd say it was intentional," Russell answered unequivocally. "Actually I was pretty scared. Scared of the same thing [sic] would happen to me, that was happening to Matthew."

Beyond Matthew's ability to read the license plate on Bill McKinney's truck, Aaron revealed some things in a 2004 interview — perhaps unwittingly — that serve as a further indicator of what was really driving him that night.

He described his final moments with Matthew at the fence, after Russell had returned to the truck but as his own rage intensified:

> I just got done telling [Matt] . . . you know, "Don't tell on me or there'll be consequences." Letting him know I took his ID's and told him that certain people would have his ID's. So it would be in his best interest not to tell on me. I felt like I finally got the point across to him, not to tell on me. Then when I'm leaving, he says he's going to tell on me.
>
> It's almost like he mouthed off . . . I went back and hit him one more time. But I hit him real hard that time — in the truck it wasn't so hard. The last time I hit him I held [the] gun like a baseball bat. It had a really long barrel on it. And a full swing.
>
> . . . He was [talking] until I hit him, but once I hit him that was it. He went out.

Aaron's threat that "certain people" would have Matthew's IDs almost slipped by me unnoticed. Aaron had always been deliberately evasive about naming those people, yet his words implied that Matthew knew who they were. His statement also seemed to belie his persistent claims that he hadn't known Matthew before that night.

According to Aaron, after he inflicted that final crushing blow, "In the back of my mind there was some concern with the last hit [because] he made some kind of a weird noise, and the way he slumped over . . . I still . . . hoped that he would come out of it. That was the . . . original plan . . . I never meant to kill him. But you get kind of a — a feeling in the pit of my stomach the last time I got him."

Looking back, he said, "The thing that's the most eerie to me is . . . that he wasn't scared. You know, I wondered what was going through his mind. What was going through mine . . . It was kind of surreal, really . . . A lot of it's a blur."

But Aaron did remember getting back into his father's truck and telling Russell to drive back into town.

"So they drove away in silence, retracing the steps," Cal would tell the jury. "The silence in the car was probably deafening."

Russell felt numb as he tried to stanch the blood over his upper lip with his sleeve. "I didn't really say anything," he recalled. "I was scared partially. And then partially I was in denial of what had just happened . . . I didn't know how to accept it."

Next to him Aaron stared listlessly out the passenger window at neon signs along the strip.

"Mr. McKinney's purpose at this time was to burglarize Mr. Shepard's home, get that $150, and get rid of the .357 Magnum pistol," Cal continued.

Aaron more or less agreed. "I had his ID's and I was looking to find his house," he said.

"Take a right on 7th," he mumbled to Russell, "just go up there a ways."

Russell followed Aaron's instructions once more. He drove them past several blocks of university buildings, then turned north onto a darkened residential street. As they moved slowly up North 7th Street, Aaron rifled through Matthew's wallet. When he came upon an ATM card, he swore angrily and tossed it on the dash.

At the intersection of 7th and Harney Streets, Aaron pointed to a large empty parking space on the northeast corner of 7th Street and told Russell to park there. Russell pulled into the space but kept the engine running, while Aaron continued to look over the contents of Matthew's wallet.

Later, there would a good deal of speculation as to why Aaron and Russell ended up parking on the 800 block of North 7th Street. It was even suggested that Aaron wanted to dispose of his gun in a nearby lake.

In fact, Matthew had often stayed with his friend Walt Boulden at 807 *South* 7th Street before getting his own apartment that summer and had used Boulden's address on his driver's license. It was also the same address that Matthew had given to police officer Flint Waters at the site of the unsolved arson incident the previous May.

But Aaron offered his own reasons for ending up at the wrong end of 7th Street:

> I had his I.D. and I was on the right street but . . . I remem-
> ber I couldn't read the numbers. I had a spotlight and
> everything. But when you're hallucinating that bad and
> you look at the numbers . . . they just change right on you.
> Your vision is just gone.
>   . . . Mostly, stuff is real out of focus at this point . . .
> you see things move that aren't there. You see people that
> aren't there. Shadow people. You know, I try to look at the
> numbers on the house. I couldn't read them. They'd go in
> and out of focus. It's almost like they — they melt around.

His plan to rob Matthew's apartment notwithstanding, the notion that what was foremost in Aaron's mind was stealing $150 is highly improbable. All day long, Aaron had been thinking about the six ounces of meth that Ken Haselhuhn's dealer friend was supposed to have that night. With a value of more than ten thousand dollars, Aaron saw the six ounces as a solution to his problems.

Aaron also had good reason to believe that Matt was one of the two couriers from Denver and Fort Collins that night. Or at the very least, Matt would know who had done the pickup and where the meth was.

(If you take into account Aaron's KFC burglary the previous December, which yielded twenty-five hundred dollars, the idea that he was driven to murderous rage over a small fraction of that amount becomes even more implausible.)

Considering how threatened Matthew had felt for several days and the apprehension he'd expressed to Tina Labrie about being "sucked . . . back into [the drug scene]," it seems very likely that he found himself caught between rival operators. As she and others surmised, he may also have known too much.

At the last minute on Tuesday evening, something or someone persuaded Matthew not to take Doc's limo out and to steer clear of the six ounces scheduled for delivery to Laramie that night. How clued in was Aaron about the delivery? Was it Matthew's sudden change in plans that Aaron discussed privately with him in the bathroom at the Fireside?

Typically, the two people who made a meth run to Denver would each receive a quarter of an ounce as compensation, worth around four hundred dollars. But the "top dog" in Denver, whom Matthew knew well from his time living there, usually advanced a total amount of twelve ounces, with a street value of over twenty thousand. Six ounces were delivered first to Fort Collins, and then the remaining six ounces were distributed in Laramie.

"Matt would be getting the quarter ounce . . . he'd be getting the two eight balls," one of his friends from the Denver circle confirmed.

While there's no doubt that Aaron was hell-bent on robbing the entire six ounces, it's also possible that his cohorts led him to believe that Matthew had gone ahead and made the run to Denver that evening, as planned. The two had taken limo rides together previously and Aaron knew what the routine was when it came to moving drugs. It would also help explain why Aaron went to the Library with Russell and waited there for more than an hour; and then to the Fireside, where Aaron continued to wait for news about the six ounces — allegedly from Ken Haselhuhn. Not only had Aaron and Matthew met at the Library for a previous drug exchange, but both men were also known to do drop-offs and pickups there and at the Fireside.

After Matthew was fatally beaten and the national media descended on Laramie, both Aaron's drug associates and Matthew's scurried for cover. But a few of them say they still don't know what happened to the six ounces of meth that night. They have reason to believe that the total delivery of twelve ounces made it as far as Fort Collins, where it was customary to drop off half the load. But did the other six ounces ever arrive in Laramie? If so, who delivered it — and perhaps more important, to whom?

"This is the one time Matt didn't go to Denver," a key source told me. "He was supposed to go but didn't."

After extensive interviews with former members of the Denver circle and a few of their associates, some of whom expressed bitterness as well as a sense of guilt and remorse over the murder, I found no evidence that the six ounces actually passed through Matthew's hands that night — or through Aaron's. One key player stated that the two men were pawns who were manipulated by two co-captains in Laramie.

Sources from the Denver circle also believe an unforgivable betrayal occurred: that "someone set Matt up" by passing on misleading information to individuals close to Aaron — people to whom Aaron owed money. This only served to intensify an existing rivalry, they said.

One thing is certain, however: Aaron was not the only person who was angry with Matthew or felt he had "moved too quickly" after he arrived in Laramie that summer. However, the same source who characterized Aaron and Matthew as pawns said that if Aaron had snitched on his suppliers to law enforcement, he would've been killed "in a flash."

"A very interesting thing happens at this time that has nothing to do with the Sherman Hills incident," Cal later informed the jury. (Sherman Hills was the actual location of the fence where Matthew was beaten.)

". . . At 12:43 in the approximate location of 660½ North 6th Street, a vandalism was called in . . . Two individuals, Mr. Morales and Mr. Herrera, were on the streets . . . What they were doing was petty vandalism . . . They had taken a sharp object and punctured an individual's tire.

". . . Flint Waters will tell you that in such a location . . . what [police] do is try to surround a general area and work in, and that is what they did . . . As the police were looking for vandals, Mr. Morales and Mr. Herrera are walking . . . and who should they come upon? Mr. Henderson and Mr. McKinney."

According to Aaron and Russell, they had just gotten out of the truck and walked to the corner. As they turned west on Harney Street, they began searching for a street address. But right after they made the turn, they surprised two young Mexican men puncturing a tire.

"What the hell are you doin' that for?" Russell apparently challenged them.

One of the men, Emiliano Morales, then nineteen, was wielding a knife. The other, Jeremy Herrera, eighteen, attempted to conceal a small wooden club up his sleeve.

"For shits and giggles," Morales replied. "You got a problem?"

Aaron was already in his face. "Yeah, we got a problem. I guess you wetbacks don't have nothin' better to do."

"Go to hell, man!" Herrera said, closing ranks with his friend.

Russell looked Aaron's way for some signal.

"Real bitches, these two," Aaron snickered.

Herrera defiantly showed his weapon. A whittled-down piece of wood, maybe sixteen inches long, rounded like a miniature base-ball bat.

As Aaron ran to the pickup, Morales shot back at him, "Who are you, calling us bitches now?"

Out of the corner of his eye, Herrera saw Aaron racing back toward Morales with the .357 pointed at him.

"Emiliano! He's got a gun, man, let's go!" Herrera shouted.

The warning was too late. Aaron attacked Morales from behind, slamming the gun into the top of his head. Morales staggered across the pavement, hunched over in pain.

With nothing to lose, Herrera charged Aaron, swinging the club into the side of his head. Aaron fell back, dazed by the blow.

Herrera quickly grabbed Morales, whose head was spitting blood, and dragged him down the street. (Cal Rerucha would tell the jury that Morales's wound looked "like a zipper on a bad sleeping bag.")

Cussing from the pain, Aaron stumbled back to the truck with Russell at his side.

Moments later Flint Waters pulled up behind the truck in his Laramie Police Department vehicle. Once again, Russell was at the wheel and Aaron was on the passenger side.

"The [police] have no idea what has happened in . . . Sherman Hills," Cal explained. "What they think is that they have the people who have committed the vandalism . . . [Mr. Waters] tries not to get too close to the vehicle until help and back-up can arrive, but he watches the individuals . . .

"There is a rearview mirror on the truck. He can see that the driver . . . can see him in the rearview mirror. At the same time, both doors fly open. In one direction flies Mr. Henderson, running as fast as he

can. And on the other side . . . Mr. McKinney exits as fast as he can
. . . and they go in opposite directions."

Immediately Flint Waters jumped out of his vehicle and took off
after the driver.

"He turned south through a yard," Waters recalled. "Fortunately
for me there was a bit of a shrub in the back of the yard, and he slowed
down. That gave me the chance to catch up . . . I caught him [and]
took him to the ground.

"I cuffed him up; told him why I was there; said I wanted to make
sure I understood what was going on . . . and he told me that I knew
who he was. And I stood him up and turned him around, and sure
enough I did — it was Russell Henderson . . . I saw that he had a
pretty good cut on his face . . . it was a gash and it was open [and]
there was a lot of blood . . . Soon as I saw that . . . I called for an EMS
unit."

Waters escorted Russell back to his police vehicle and, minutes
later, turned him over to the EMS crew, who had arrived with an
ambulance. As they began treating Russell, Waters walked over to the
passenger side of the black Ford truck.

"I saw something laying on the ground," he said. "I looked at it,
and it was a large gun rug . . . for a large target pistol. I looked in the
back of the truck and laying [sic] in the back . . . was a large frame
revolver. The thing was huge. Like an 8-inch barrel that had blood all
over it . . . Seeing that gun covered in blood, I assumed that there was
a lot more going on than what we'd stumbled onto so far."

TWENTY-EIGHT

Witnesses

Kristen Price would later tell police she was curled up on the sofa watching late-night TV when Aaron burst into their apartment, clutching a wound on the side of his head.

"Shut the door!" he yelled.

Kristen was shocked by the blood on his clothes. "What the hell happened to you, Aaron?"

"Just turn off the lights," he instructed her. "Everything — "

As she quickly switched off the lamp and TV, he grabbed a towel in the bathroom to soak up the blood.

According to Aaron,

> I couldn't really talk. I was trying to tell her what happened . . . I knew what I wanted to say but it wouldn't come out. It was just a bunch of mumbling. But she was obviously real concerned. My head's bleeding — I'm covered in blood. Babbling on . . . You know, I was scared to death at that point.

But when Cal Rerucha sketched out that part of the crime to the jury, he stuck to the facts; he wasn't buying the proposition that Aaron was a victim that night.

"[Mr. McKinney] is hurt from the blow on the head," he stated bluntly. "He talks about the incident to his girlfriend . . . Kristen realizes there is a man either dead or badly hurt on the plains of Laramie, Wyoming. They do nothing."

In a media interview a few days after the crime, Kristen described Aaron's actions after he arrived home:

> He went straight to the bathroom. He was cleaning himself off and . . . I told him to take off his dirty clothes

and I helped him get undressed because he was stumbling. And I went and found some clean clothes and put that [sic] on him.

. . . He told me everything that happened. But he was stuttering. And he kept on telling me, "Look out the window, the cops are going to show up any minute, I know they are."

During the same interview, Kristen was asked, "Now, why do you think they decided to rob Matthew?"

"I don't know," she answered. "I really don't know."

"What do you think happened in that bar?" the same reporter questioned her a minute or so later.

"I don't know what exactly happened because I was not there," she said. "And Aaron was too — his speech was too messed up to be able to really tell what was going on . . . Aaron said, 'I was not myself. I don't know who that was who did that.'"

It would not be until early evening on Wednesday, October 7 that Matthew was found at the fence, some eighteen hours after being abandoned there by Aaron and Russell. Around 6 PM, while cycling in Sherman Hills, Aaron Kreifels, a University of Wyoming freshman, hit a patch of prairie scrub and fell off his mountain bike. As he got up, he saw something about fifteen feet away — what looked like blood shining off a face, probably a scarecrow.

"Halloween was coming up, so I thought it was just a Halloween gag," he later told a TV reporter.

But as he got closer, he heard heavy breathing sounds and realized it was a person, injured and unconscious.

"[Matthew] was breathing very heavily through his nose . . . [it] was sounding terrible," Kreifels would remember.

Immediately he ran for help, to the home of a university professor a couple of hundred yards away.

First to respond to the scene — at 6:22 PM — was Reggie Fluty, a deputy with the Albany County Sheriff's Department. Fluty's unsettling account of how she untied Matthew's battered figure from the fence would soon become known worldwide, especially her initial impression that he was a boy of thirteen or so.

"Baby, I'm so sorry this happened," she consoled him.

Horrified by Matthew's massive head injuries and overcome by the pale tracks on his face where blood had been washed away by tears, she cradled him in her arms.

"Little boy, don't die, please don't die," she pleaded.

At Cal Rerucha's suburban-style ranch home on Duna Drive, his wife, Jan, was helping their two sons with homework when Rob DeBree phoned him around 7 PM with word that a badly beaten young man had been found.

"We've got a potential homicide, Cal, we're at the hospital," DeBree informed him. "Dr. Cantway doesn't think the boy's gonna make it. We may need search warrants."

Cal was startled by the news — his home was just a few minutes from where the victim had been found, in an area where his eleven- and twelve-year-old sons liked to ride their mountain bikes. Cal's immediate concern, however, was being sure the crime scene was secure and none of the physical evidence got lost.

"The first 24 hours are critical," he later explained. "You can't lose any of the evidence. Fast is important. If you lose stuff, you don't get it back."

He also asked DeBree, "Does the young man have family here?"

DeBree said he was working on that and would call him back with an update. But before he hung up, he added, "Cal, he's gonna die. We're gonna have a homicide."

At about the same time, Tina Labrie phoned Laramie police to ask them to check on her friend Matt Shepard. She said she'd been trying to reach him since that morning but had gotten no answer and was worried about him. Tina was surprised when they told her they were sending an officer over to her home to talk to her. Phil, her husband, thought that Matt might have committed suicide, because of his intense depression lately.

Doc O'Connor claimed that he, too, had tried calling Matt numerous times during the day but Matt's cell phone just rang and rang.

Dr. Cantway, who treated Matthew in the emergency room at Laramie's Ivinson Memorial Hospital, would later say, "I've never seen anyone with such massive head wounds live."

When Cantway phoned Matthew's parents in Saudi Arabia and awakened them with the news — it was about 5 AM there, due to an eleven-hour time difference — there was little he could offer them in the way of hope. He explained that Matthew had a severe spinal-stem injury from the horrific beating inflicted on him. He was comatose and was also suffering from hypothermia, as he had lost blood when the temperature dropped. The only thing Cantway could do was move Matthew by ambulance to Poudre Valley Hospital in Fort Collins, where they had more advanced equipment.

Shortly after the ambulance transporting Matthew departed from Laramie, Rob DeBree arrived at Ivinson Hospital. Fellow officers had informed DeBree that Aaron was at the hospital. Kristen had driven him there to be treated for the injury he'd gotten during the previous night's street fight.

But upon arriving at the hospital, DeBree later explained on the witness stand at Aaron's trial, "The first thing . . . I noticed [was] the pickup in question, that I had seen at 7th and Harney that same morning. I walked up to the truck, and without doubt at that point I knew this vehicle had been at that scene [at the fence] . . . All of the botanical evidence located on the hitch was more than apparent to me that [sic] was going to be an immediate match . . . I immediately wanted that vehicle seized . . . until we could obtain search warrants."

Police also saw a pair of black shoes inside the pickup that would turn out to be Matthew's.

Inside the hospital DeBree proceeded with his plan "to initiate an interview with Aaron McKinney, who was in a room off to the side that they used to refer to as a suture room . . . Sitting in this same room was Kristen Price as well as Aaron."

After verbally advising Aaron of his Miranda rights, DeBree said, "the first statement out of his mouth was whether or not I had caught the people that had done this to him."

Aaron's head injury notwithstanding, DeBree noted, "He knew his name, knew his whereabouts. He seemed coherent. Speech was not slurred . . . He did seem a little bit depressed but alert."

DeBree continued to describe his interview with Aaron:

> I asked him generally where he had been that day . . . especially that night previous . . . He told me that he as well as Russell Henderson had gone to . . . the Library Bar, and had some beers, and then he went into a story . . . that this unknown individual walked up and took his car keys from the bar and walked out and didn't come back for over an hour. Obviously I considered that somewhat suspicious . . . I asked for the description of the individual. He was unable to give me one.
>
> . . . [I] asked him why he didn't call the police if somebody just took off with his vehicle. He stated he didn't know, and the individual apparently showed back up again . . . [and] wanted to take them to a party . . . He stated he and Russell went with this individual, drove to the area of 7th and Harney where this individual got out, went to check and see where the party was at, and then Aaron said that the next thing, "we got jumped by these people," allegedly.

After DeBree questioned him, Aaron was transferred to Poudre Valley Hospital as well, for twenty-four-hour observation of his subdural hematoma. While the wound to his left ear was minor compared with Matthew's near-fatal injuries, Aaron — weirdly — seemed to be trailing in Matthew's footsteps again. That night at the hospital the two men lay in beds just down the hall from each another.

"[Matthew's] most serious wound, a crushing blow behind his right ear, caused a 2-inch depression to his skull," *The Denver Post* reported a couple of days later.

Also at the hospital that night was Emiliano Morales, whose injury from Aaron's gun required twenty-one staples in his scalp.

"Later on at night," Cal Rerucha summarized, "stories are put in place so they can tell police a concocted story. This was done in advance by Kristen Price, by Chasity Pasley, by Mr. Henderson and Mr. McKinney. It was also at that time where [sic] Price, Henderson, and [Pasley] take bloodied clothes belonging to Mr. Henderson over to Cheyenne where . . . evidence of the crime can be hidden.

" . . . Officers from the Laramie Police Department will also tell you . . . that they recovered Adidas athletic shoes from Pasley's mother's residence, from where Henderson and Pasley had hidden them."

Cal's narrative regarding the attempts of Russell, Aaron, and their girlfriends to conceal evidence was meticulously accurate. But there was a critical element he left out, of which he was apparently unaware at the time (though he later said it didn't surprise him at all). After Kristen left Aaron at Ivinson Hospital and was picked up there by Russell and Chasity, the three — on Aaron's previous instruction — gathered all their drug paraphernalia together, including meth pipes and other items, and disposed of them in the trash at a Laramie fast-food restaurant. (All four confirmed this to me in separate interviews.) Since police barely touched on drugs during their investigation, Aaron's plan to hide that part of the evidence succeeded perfectly.

Early in the morning on Thursday, October 8, police rounded up Russell, Chasity, and Kristen at the Fort Sanders trailer where Russell and Chasity lived. They took them downtown to the county sheriff's office where each was questioned individually.

At a table in one of the three interview rooms, Kristen held her four-month-old son, Cameron, in her arms as she tried to convince Ben Fritzen that Aaron had fallen asleep in a Laundromat after the street fight he and Russell had with the two Mexican men.

"When he woke up he tried to figure out where he was," she said. "I asked him why he didn't come straight home and he said he was afraid those guys would follow him. He was worried about me and Cameron."

Fritzen conducted an extended interview with Kristen that lasted more than three and a half hours. Her interview statements, which were made a few days before she remarked notoriously to a reporter, "[Aaron and Russ] just wanted to beat [Matthew] up bad enough to teach him a lesson, not to come on to straight people," would also become the foundation on which Cal Rerucha built his case for first-degree murder.

During the first part of her interview, Kristen spilled out the long-winded alibi she and Aaron had made up with Russell and Chasity's help. She said that late on Tuesday night Aaron and Russell were at the Library bar and had met a guy, an apparent stranger, who told them about a party and offered to drive them there.

"He had a driver's license . . . and neither one of them were supposed to be driving," Kristen stated. " . . . They said, 'This guy is going to drive the truck over there and we'll call you [and Chasity] later on tonight whenever we get at the party if you want to meet us there, or if it's an okay party then we'll call you and let you know.'"

Fritzen didn't believe most of her story and reminded her of how much she had to lose, including her four-month-old son, who was by her side during the interview.

"What are we leaving out here?" he asked.

"You see, I can't change my story now because then I go to jail," Kristen answered.

"Listen to me," he warned her in a firm but quiet voice. " . . . If I have to sit here for another two hours, drag information out of you, find out that you're lying to me, [then] all bets are off and I am not going to work with you."

"I can't," she said.

"My dear, you don't have a choice."

"I know I can't — I've already gotten everybody in trouble . . ."

"Do you understand how serious this is, Kristen?"

"Yeah I do."

"Do you understand what life in prison means?"

"Yeah. You better start the tape all over again then," she told Fritzen. " . . . It's also going to be my word against everybody else's."

"It sounds like you guys' stories are pretty well rehearsed."

"Yeah they are."

In the second part of the interview Kristen made several statements that cast further doubt on the crime narrative that was soon to be solidified in official accounts and by the media.

Regarding Aaron's plan to rob Matthew's home, Fritzen inquired, "Did [Aaron] say where the money was hidden in the house?"

"No," she said.

"But the guy [Matthew] did tell him where it was?"

"[Aaron] said that he told either him or Russ — I forget which one he said. He said he had told them where he had kept his money at and that they were going to go there and take the money."

"Okay. Was that just in casual conversation that [Matthew] mentioned it or did he say that like, to get them to stop beating him, or . . .?"

"No," she said, "*it was at the bar he had told them*" (italics mine).

"Where he kept his money."

"*Mmm hmm* [yes]. I guess."

"Okay."

"That's what I think Aaron and [Russ] said."

If Kristen's statement is true, that the three men were at the Fireside when Matthew revealed where he kept his money, that suggests a very different purpose behind the meeting at the bar — and a different set of conclusions.

Since the evidence shows that Aaron and Matthew had a conversation in the bathroom, and that Russell and Matthew never spoke at the bar, one possibility is that Aaron was trying to collect a debt from Matthew — just as he'd done the previous night when he went looking for Monty Durand.

This might explain why Matthew was severely depressed over money and almost suicidal a few days earlier, and also why he'd told at least three friends that he feared for his life.

Lastly, on this particular Tuesday night when Matthew's Denver group was scheduled to deliver the usual six ounces to Laramie (including compensation of two eight balls for Matthew), Aaron, who owed his own suppliers money, may have seen the perfect opportunity to collect.

Detective Fritzen also wanted to know what Aaron had told Kristen about the actual beating.

" . . . How many times did they hit [Matt]?" he asked.

"I don't know," she said. "'Cause I asked him how many times he had hit him and he says he doesn't remember, all he knows is he just started hitting him."

"With the pistol."

"Yeah. And he says he doesn't know how many times Russ hit him or not [sic], so he said they both just hit him."

"They were both hitting him? Do you know what Russ was hitting him with?"

"I don't know . . . I don't understand that part because *I don't know if they were taking turns*" (italics mine).

During Chasity Pasley's two interviews with police that morning and early afternoon, she cried so much that her eyes were bloodshot and swollen. In her first interview, which began shortly before 9 AM, Chasity repeatedly told Detective Gwen Smith of the Laramie Police Department that she didn't recognize the silver Boss jacket that police had found in Bill McKinney's truck.

"Does [Russell] usually wear a coat?" Smith asked.

"No, he never wears a coat," Chasity replied. "It'd be freezing outside and he won't wear a coat."

Smith broached the subject again a few minutes later. "And you said he never wears a coat . . . He wouldn't have like a silver Boss coat?"

"No."

"Does Aaron have — "

"No, not that I know of."

" — Silver Boss — or you or Kristen?"

"No."

"Okay . . . It looks like that new stuff . . . that's really, really silver."

"No, not that I know of."

"Okay. So you haven't ever seen that at your house?"

"Huh-uh." (No.)

At about the same time in a neighboring office, however, Kristen insisted the silver Boss jacket belonged to Russell.

"I know Russ loves that coat . . ." she told Detective Fritzen. "I've seen that coat over their house ten million times. I saw him wear it a couple of days ago."

Detectives Smith and DeBree conducted a second interview with Chasity that began just before noon.

"Do you know of Russ or Aaron using any illegal drugs?" Smith asked her.

"No, I know they were drunk and that's all I know," Chasity replied.

"Have you ever seen them or heard them talking about using any illegal drugs?"

"No."

"Okay," Smith said. "Rob, do you have some questions?"

"You said . . . that they met this guy at where [sic]?" he asked Chasity.

"The bar. This guy was hitting on Russ and Aaron."

"Which bar?" DeBree continued.

"I don't know. I think the Ranger or the Library."

"Does the Fireside ring a bell to you?" he pressed.

Chasity answered, "It may. I don't know. That's what they told me, [the] Ranger . . ."

But minutes later, Smith posed the question again, "What about the Boss jacket?"

"It's Russ's," Chasity admitted.

"Is it new?" Smith asked. "Does he wear it a lot?"

"He never wears a coat," Chasity repeated. "I don't know why he wore one that night."

At regular intervals during the police interviews with Kristen, Chasity, and Russell, Cal conferred privately in his office with DeBree to be sure they were covering all the necessary ground. Already it

was becoming apparent to Cal that Kristen would be his most valuable trial witness and that he and the police investigators "needed to
tread very carefully in order not to lose her." Indeed, it was Kristen
who would shortly lead them to Matthew's wallet, hidden in a soiled
diaper at her apartment.

But in the meantime, the county attorney's office was being
swamped by calls from the media asking for information about the
suspects. When Cal declined to comment, "a few reporters got nasty,"
he recalled.

Just as he was putting the phone down after one such query, DeBree
walked in.

"He hung up on me, the rude s.o.b.," Cal griped. "I guess I should
spill my guts to him so we can have a mistrial before anyone's even
been arraigned."

DeBree was feeling a little more optimistic since Kristen and
Chasity were beginning to change their stories. But Cal, who was still
piqued, was less forgiving.

"That's great that these young ladies are turning into Mother
Teresas right before our eyes," he said. "I still want them booked as
accessories after the fact."

More often than not, DeBree could tell you exactly what Cal was
going to say before the words tumbled out.

True to form, Cal reminded him for the third or fourth time, "Just
guard that silver coat with your life, Rob. I don't want any surprises
like tainted evidence."

Apart from the questions surrounding Russell's jacket, Chasity's
statements intrigued me for several reasons. She, too, had lied about
drugs, yet she later admitted to me that she had used meth regularly
herself; that she had helped get rid of all their drug paraphernalia
to conceal it from police; and that she'd been aware on the night of
the crime that one of the homes she drove to with Aaron and Russell
belonged to one of Aaron's suppliers. It also seemed curious that she
mentioned the Ranger and Library bars, where Matthew had been,
respectively, on Monday night and for several hours on Tuesday.

More important, by the time Chasity took the witness stand in Aaron's trial a year later she told a different story:

"During that summer [of 1998], did you ever see Aaron McKinney using drugs?" Jason Tangeman, Aaron's attorney, asked while cross-examining her.

"Yes, sir," she said.

"What drugs?"

"Methamphetamines and marijuana."

"Did you ever see how often he used drugs?"

"Yes, sir."

"How often did he use methamphetamine?"

"At first it was not very often, and then it got really often."

"Did you ever see Russell use methamphetamine?"

"Yes, sir."

"About how often?"

"Same as Aaron."

"Where was Russell getting his methamphetamine?"

"From Aaron."

Later in his cross-examination, Tangeman asked, "Up to that point — that evening [of the crime] — you hadn't ever heard Russell or Aaron talk about robbing anyone, had you?"

"No," Chasity said.

"And they hadn't talked about hating homosexuals?"

"No, sir."

Similarly, during the redirect examination that followed, Cal Rerucha inquired, "The question was asked about like or dislike of homosexuals; do you remember that line of questioning?"

"Yes, sir."

"At that specific time frame, did Mr. Henderson make any reference to homosexuals?"

"What do you mean?"

"The individual involved in this," Cal responded opaquely, yet obviously referring to Matthew.

"He just said that he was gay."

Although Tangeman raised the objection that Chasity's answer was beyond the scope of the question — and the presiding judge sustained it — Cal immediately raised the subject again.

"Anything else, generally, about homosexuals that [Russell] had stated at that time?"

"No, sir."

Interestingly, while Cal was eliciting Chasity's admission that she knew a person had been seriously hurt yet she proceeded to help hide evidence, he asked her, "And did you know that person's name?"

"I knew it was 'Matt' from Kristen," she said.

It seemed strange that Kristen — like Aaron — would refer to Matthew by the more familiar "Matt," especially since the driver's license, bank card, and other items in his stolen wallet identified him as *Matthew* Shepard. But this was not the only indication that Kristen knew a lot more about the real purpose of Aaron's meeting with Matthew than she ever let on.

During a recorded interview in 2004, while talking about his plan to rob six ounces of meth that night, Aaron said, "I'm not going to take Kristen with me on K [methamphetamine], somebody's got to stay home with the kid, you know? And I'm not going to take her on something like that anyways."

"And she had no idea what you were planning?" Aaron was asked.

"Uh, no," he said first. But then he promptly added, "Somewhat."

However, according to a different source — a close male associate of Aaron who requested anonymity — he visited Aaron's apartment on Wednesday afternoon, October 7, shortly before Kristen drove Aaron to the hospital and before Matthew was discovered at the fence. During his conversation with Kristen then, the source said, "she mentioned that Matt was into drugs." If true, how did Kristen know that?

The extent to which Aaron personally covered up his relationship with Matthew (apparently with Kristen's help) became even more evident when I gained access to Aaron's "black book" — a small address book in which he kept the phone numbers of his friends, drug cohorts, and a few former girlfriends. The book is organized alphabetically according to first names. Not surprisingly, the page of listings under the letter M is the only one missing.

———

At one point during his second interview with Kristen, Detective Ben Fritzen turned the tape recorder off, left the room briefly, and then returned with Laramie Police Commander Dave O'Malley. O'Malley did his best to reassure Kristen that he found her highly credible.

"We're going to go all the way to the wall for you," he promised. "We do not want you to go to jail . . . We thank you for sticking with your guns because it takes a lot of guts to do what you did . . . I've got the utmost respect for you. I can see in your eyes . . . you're not a criminal and you don't have criminal eyes and you don't have a criminal face, and anybody that looks at their child the way you did is got [sic], in my book, a lot going for them, okay."

Kristen, who had gotten teary several times during the long interrogation, began to cry again.

O'Malley offered her a Kleenex. "[You're] like me, I get crap in my hair and got snot running down my mustache and everything," he said. "Just do good, okay."

"I will," she responded. "Thank you."

"You betcha."

By Thursday afternoon Kristen and Chasity had given detailed statements implicating themselves as accessories. But Russell, who had lied to Detectives Mark Beck and Rob DeBree when questioned early that morning, stuck to the alibi about meeting a guy at the Library who offered to take them to a party, refused to continue talking, and asked for a lawyer.

About 8:40 AM, just before placing Russell under arrest for attempted murder, DeBree asked him if he knew who Matthew Shepard was.

"No, I don't . . . no one by that name," Russell answered.

A few hours later DeBree asked Chasity if Matthew had ever been in her home.

"I've never seen him before in my life," she said. "I know Russ didn't know him either. That's why I don't understand it."

In Russell's brief and incomplete statement to police — his only statement until he was sentenced six months later — there is no suggestion of anti-gay feelings or motives of any kind. All of the allegations and inferences that the attack on Matthew resulted from an unwanted sexual advance would come from Kristen and Aaron, and to a lesser degree Chasity.

During her interview with Detectives Smith and DeBree, Chasity described how the four of them had gradually pieced their stories together in the early-morning hours on Wednesday and again later in the day:

"Kristen told me when I got there that night [after 1:30 AM on Wednesday] . . . that Aaron had killed somebody. Aaron had beat somebody real bad . . . I go, 'We have to go to the hospital, Russ is in the hospital' . . . And she's, 'I know. I know what's going on,' and she told me that Aaron had beat some gay guy to death."

"And so when did you guys get your stories straight?" Smith asked.

"Wednesday day after I got off of [sic] work . . . I went and got Russ and we went over to Aaron's."

"Okay," Smith probed a few minutes later. "And . . . what did [Aaron and Russell] say to . . . the victim in this case?'

"Russ told me Aaron said, 'You are getting jacked; it's gay awareness week,' and he hit him in the truck once . . . and the guy asked him to stop, and Aaron wouldn't stop."

"The guy begged [him] to stop?"

"The guy asked Aaron, 'Please don't hurt me anymore. I'm sorry for hitting on you guys,' and Aaron didn't stop."

"What was Aaron's demeanor when he's telling you this story?" DeBree asked Chasity.

"I don't know," she replied. "What do you mean by demeanor?"

"Well, is he kind of laughing about it 'cause the guy's — "

"No, he was so scared," Chasity said.

"He was scared?"

"Yes. He doesn't know what came over him . . ."

"What was Russell like?'

"He was scared."

TWENTY-NINE

The Consensus

Upon his release from Poudre Valley Hospital at about 11:30 PM on Thursday, October 8, Aaron was arrested and charged with attempted first-degree murder before police escorted him back to Laramie. DeBree thought it would be best to allow him to have a good night's sleep — and also give him time to think.

"I'm not real tired," Aaron stated when he arrived at the Albany County Detention Center around 1 AM.

After he was advised of his rights, he said he still wanted to tell his story.

Aaron's recorded statement to DeBree and Fritzen the following morning — before he had sought the advice of an attorney — would become the basis of the state's case against both him and Russell Henderson. The sometimes-muddled confession, which was rife with inconsistencies and lies, was made less than two days after he'd been admitted to the hospital with a hairline fracture to his skull (or what some described as a subdural hematoma). But later attempts by Aaron's defense lawyers to have the confession deemed inadmissible would ultimately fail.

The complete tape and transcript were said to contain strong evidence of Aaron's homophobic motives for the attack on Matthew, but the court immediately sealed the statement and prevented it from being examined until more than a year later. That didn't stop the media, however — and hence the public at large — from quickly concluding that an anti-gay hate crime had occurred, based almost exclusively on the hearsay statements of Kristen Price, Alex Trout, Walt Boulden, and a couple of others.

Six days after the crime, Boulden, then forty-six, and Trout, twenty-one, were interviewed on *Larry King Live*, with CNN's Wolf Blitzer acting as the guest host ("The Death of Matthew Shepard: Examining

Anti-Gay Violence in America"). Blitzer introduced the report by stating, "Authorities in Laramie, Wyoming, still say robbery was the main motive but that Shepard may have been targeted because he was gay."

Blitzer asked Boulden, "Tell us what, in your opinion, was the motive. What happened to Matthew Shepard?"

"Well, the way I understand — " Boulden said, "Matt made the mistake of basically just telling these guys that he was gay, and for Matt, that would have been . . . He had to feel incredibly safe around somebody to let them know he was gay, and the way I understand it is . . . in the course of a conversation with these two gentlemen, he revealed that he was gay, and then they told him that they were also gay, and that's how they got him to go with them."

Boulden was quoted similarly in *The New York Times*, but in essence he was repeating Kristen's story — which she had allegedly heard from Aaron.

"[Matt] was sitting at the bar, having a beer, when two men came up and talked to him," Boulden said. "He indicated he was gay, and they said they were gay, too."

The New York Times also noted, "Mr. Shepard's friends say he did not know his alleged tormentors."

In the early-morning hours of Friday, October 9, Cal Rerucha couldn't sleep. He got up around 4 AM and turned on the TV, "hoping to catch a Three Stooges rerun."

Aaron McKinney would be questioned in just a few hours. Cal was eager to hear what he had to say, but from the conflicting stories of Russell, Kristen, and Chasity, he and his investigative team were already beginning to construct a theory of what had happened on the night Matthew left the Fireside with the two men.

As Cal flipped the channels, he landed on a news show and saw the Albany County sheriff, Gary Puls, talking to reporters outside the county courthouse the previous day. According to Cal, he had carefully gone over the press release the sheriff had written, which they planned to distribute.

"It had basic information — the charges, who's been caught, things like that," Cal explained. "Then Puls went out back [of the courthouse] and gave a press conference." (This was the same press release that Matthew's friend, Jason Marsden, remembered coming over the fax machine in the newsroom at the *Casper Star-Tribune*. It didn't mention that Matthew was gay; nor did it suggest any possibility of a hate crime.)

While watching TV at that hour, "I saw what the case was about to become, it was going to be a huge media event," Cal said.

During the press conference it had somehow slipped out that, yes, the attack might have been a gay bashing — and it might even be accurate to describe it as a crucifixion.

"I like to be very careful about publicity and stay close to the code of ethics," Cal added. "But the fence and where we are [geographically] also had a lot to do with how people viewed this . . . It would be the worst case we've ever had. Never [had] one like this before."

Cal was right: News of the appalling crime on the Wyoming prairie spread nationally and internationally in a matter of hours. People everywhere were stunned by reports that a boyish-looking, "all-American" college student had been beaten savagely and hung on a fence because he was gay. More significantly, an outraged gay community mobilized immediately.

At the time many — myself included — agreed with Walt Boulden's reasoning. "If you're going to rob somebody, you go knock them in the head, take their money, and dump them somewhere," he told Wolf Blitzer. " . . . They hung [Matt] to that fence as a very clear message for the rest of us that this isn't a place that you're supposed to be if you're gay . . . They displayed him like some kind of a trophy. You don't do that to a robbery victim."

In the wake of reports that Matthew had been not only beaten mercilessly but also tortured, burned with cigarettes, crucified, and left to die on a freezing prairie, an array of interests seized on this graphic image and began to embellish it further.

One major newspaper published an illustration of a Christ-like Matthew with his arms spread out, bound to a crossbeam.

A front-page headline in *The Washington Post* read, "Gay Man Near Death After Beating, Burning . . . Hate Crime Suspected." The story began, "Matthew Shepard, slight of stature, gentle of demeanor and passionate about human rights and foreign relations, lived a relatively open gay life in [Laramie] . . . This week, he paid a terrible price." The article went on to report "burn marks on his body" and stated he was "tied to a fence like a dead coyote."

But embedded in these and other media accounts were a surprising number of inaccuracies and distortions, both large and small. Although it was reported that Aaron and Russell burned Matthew with cigarettes, no such burning took place. *Time* magazine described the two assailants as "tall, muscular men" when both are below average in height — only a few inches taller than Matthew, who was barely five foot two. In just a single paragraph of that magazine's coverage, I found half a dozen factual errors.

"Everything happened so fast [that] all we could do is try to stay one step ahead of the blaze," according to Cal Rerucha. "We'd never had a case that big in Wyoming before, with the whole world watching us."

But it was not only the media who were to blame, he said. "We never intended to misrepresent the facts, but a reporter would shove a camera in the sheriff's face and ask if Matthew was crucified, and the next thing you know the sheriff is kind of agreeing, 'Well, I guess from the way he was tied to the fence you might say that.'

"Now that time has passed we might look back and see things differently, but all we could see then was what was right in front of us."

Cal emphasized again that words like *might* came into play often in the rapidly unfolding story of the attack — and the motives behind it.

Matthew's friends Walt Boulden and Alex Trout rushed to his side at Poudre Valley Hospital after Boulden received a call from Dennis Shepard in Saudi Arabia with the news that Matthew had been severely beaten. Along with contacting Jason Marsden, Matthew's friend at the *Casper Star-Tribune*, Boulden and Trout contacted gay organizations in Wyoming and Colorado to report that Matthew had been the victim of an anti-gay attack. Trout said that Marsden, who is gay but had yet to come out publicly, was instrumental in helping to disseminate the story nationally through the Associated Press.

(Today Marsden is the executive director of the Matthew Shepard Foundation.)

Boulden and Trout would later state that the first time they heard talk of a hate crime was at Poudre Valley Hospital when an unidentified police officer had mentioned in passing that the attack on Matthew "might have had something to do with him being gay." The two men said the remark confirmed their worst fears and prompted them to act.

But Tina Labrie told a somewhat different story when Elizabeth Vargas interviewed her in 2004. The following excerpt from that interview was not broadcast at the time:

> **Elizabeth Vargas:** When did you first hear that Aaron and Russell may have attacked Matthew because he was gay?
>
> **Tina Labrie:** That day [Thursday, October 8] while we were down at Poudre Valley Hospital . . . when Walt and Alex showed up that evening, and that was pretty much their take on the situation.
>
> **Elizabeth Vargas:** They just assumed that he was beaten up because he was gay?
>
> **Tina Labrie:** Well, they were pretty sure about it.
>
> **Elizabeth Vargas:** But you don't know why they were sure?
>
> **Tina Labrie:** No.
>
> **Elizabeth Vargas:** And told the media that this was a hate crime.
>
> **Tina Labrie:** . . . I just know that's what they talked about a lot.
>
> **Elizabeth Vargas:** How soon after Walt and Alex arrived at the hospital . . . did they begin to feel that this beating happened only because Matthew was gay?
>
> **Tina Labrie:** That was pretty much the consensus every time I saw them.
>
> **Elizabeth Vargas:** But they never told you what proof they had for that.

Tina Labrie: Right. They never told me what led them to
that conclusion . . .

Elizabeth Vargas: How quickly did they begin to call the
media and gay rights groups?

Tina Labrie: That day. We were up at the hospital — and
then media showed up that evening . . .

Elizabeth Vargas: All asking questions about whether this
was a hate crime?

Tina Labrie: Yeah . . . it was pretty weird . . . that frenzy
of media attention. This very quickly became an enormous issue about being gay and about homophobia
. . . Like they wanted to make [Matt] a poster child or
something for their cause or their anti-cause . . . they
either wanted to make him a saint or they wanted to
say he was burning in hell . . . I think when you go to
[those] extremes, you lose the truth.

As Cal Rerucha prepared for the arraignments of Aaron, Russell,
Kristen, and Chasity on the afternoon of Friday, October 9, the case
got off to an uncommonly chaotic start.

"The media stormed the walls for the arraignment," Cal recalled.
"It was as close to a riot as I've ever seen."

Reporters and television crews crammed into the district courtroom
on the second floor of the Albany County Courthouse, surrounding
the judge's bench with cameras and boom mikes, with barely an inch
to spare. Cal found one reporter squatting under his desk and another
perched on top.

Unable to handle the pressure, Circuit Court Judge Robert Castor
began to hyperventilate, forcing Cal to take charge in the frenzied
courtroom. Castor had been a mentor and boss to Cal at the start
of his legal career, which made his sudden loss of confidence in the
judge's ability to deal with the media presence all the more difficult.

"I grabbed a couple of officers in back and we pushed all the press
people back behind the communion rail," Cal said, shaking his head
in disbelief long after the murder case had ended.

But even with a semblance of order restored in the courtroom, "television cameras lined one wall," according to a newspaper account. "Friends of Matthew Shepard, reporters and curious citizens filled the chairs, knelt on the carpet and spilled into the hallway outside." Several gay activists from Denver and Fort Collins had also traveled to Laramie for the arraignment.

The following day, *The Denver Post* reported:

> The judge read aloud from investigative reports that show prosecutors believe [Matthew Shepard] did nothing to provoke the attack except let his eventual assailants know he is gay.
>
> . . . For Shepard's friends, several of whom attended Friday's hearing, Castor's reading of the official allegations sounded like confirmation of what they had suspected all along — that Shepard was beaten because he is gay.

That afternoon Castor ordered that Aaron and Russell be held in the Albany County Detention Center on a one-hundred-thousand-dollar cash bond.

Kristen had already been released earlier in the day on a thirty-thousand-dollar bond. But Chasity, who had been less cooperative with police — at least initially — didn't fare as well. She was arraigned on the charge of being an accessory to attempted first-degree murder and held in lieu of a thirty-thousand-dollar bond. According to *The Denver Post*, she "sobbed throughout the hearing, dabbing at her face with a tissue."

Cal also filed an official notice that day under the ominous caption, "Potential of the Death Sentence," and requested that Judge Castor seal the case records. Castor agreed to take the latter under consideration.

For Matthew's parents, Dennis and Judy Shepard, the ordeal of traveling home to the United States from Saudi Arabia was agonizing — first a wait of eighteen hours for visas, then a twenty-eight-hour journey with several layovers. On the way to Colorado, they stopped in Minnesota to pick up Matthew's younger brother, Logan, who was attending boarding school there. Logan accompanied them on the flight to Denver and, lastly, the one-hour drive to Poudre Valley Hospital in Fort Collins where Matthew lay in a coma.

When the Shepards arrived at the hospital on Friday evening, October 9, they were startled to find not only the media waiting but also dozens of flower arrangements lining their path to the elevator.

But nothing had prepared Dennis and Judy to see Matthew in such a lifeless state.

"I wasn't even sure this was Matt," Judy would later say.

They found him propped up slightly in bed, with his head shaved and wrapped in bandages — comatose and motionless. His swollen face was covered with stitched wounds; there were tubes everywhere; and just one of his blue eyes was partially open.

"To walk into his hospital room and see him lying there, not moving . . . made me want to just sit down and cry," Dennis recalled.

Beyond the family's muffled sobs, the only sound in the room was the rhythmic contraction of the respirator that was allowing Matthew to breathe.

A full day would pass before Logan could muster the strength to go into the room and face his brother. The two had talked of rooming together the following year when Logan enrolled at the University of Wyoming as a freshman.

Ted Henson said he, too, was at the hospital when the Shepard family arrived. He remembered feeling lost in a haze of grief, not only from "seeing how bad Matt looked," but also from realizing "Matt isn't going to make it."

Tina, who had visited Matthew the previous night with her husband Phil and two other friends of Matthew — newlyweds who had just returned from their honeymoon and gotten the news — remembered feeling "like I was in some surrealist environment."

"It's something nobody wants to see," Tina said, " . . . it [was] pretty overwhelming. And then on the other hand it was kind of bizarrely comforting.

". . . I had a chance to say good-bye to Matt. And that's something I feel fortunate about. Because I think on some level, even though he was brain dead and not really connected with his body . . . his spirit was able to hear me say good-bye . . . There was so much I wanted to still tell him and there was so much he would have been able to tell me.

". . . I felt like . . . nothing was really real."

On Cal's instructions, Rob DeBree met the Shepards at Poudre Valley Hospital on Friday night and remained at their side for the next couple of days, serving as a buffer between the family and a growing number of reporters and camera crews outside.

Over that weekend, spontaneous candlelight vigils were held outside the hospital and began to crop up at locations around the country.

President Bill Clinton also phoned the hospital to express his sympathy and support to the Shepard family, and to promise his administration's assistance in bringing Matthew's assailants to justice.

As Matthew lay in a coma and it was all but certain that he wouldn't survive his injuries, the president made an impassioned statement urging Americans to support the federal hate crime bill then stalled in Congress. He likened Matthew's beating to the racially motivated lynching of James Byrd Jr. in Jasper, Texas, four months earlier.

"There is nothing more important to the future of this country than our standing together against intolerance, prejudice, and violent bigotry," Clinton said. "We cannot surrender to those on the fringe of our society who lash out at those who are different."

However well-intentioned the president may have been, he spoke up prematurely, before law enforcement agents on the ground in Laramie had completed a thorough investigation of the crime and its circumstances.

News of the alleged hate crime also became an instant flashpoint that further polarized liberals and conservatives, who were already pitted against each other in so-called culture wars.

During the previous summer, then Senate Majority Leader Trent Lott had made comments on national television suggesting that gays are "sinners," according to his reading of the Bible.

"You should try to show them a way to deal with [homosexuality] just like alcohol . . . or sex addiction . . . or kleptomaniacs," Lott said.

Pat Robertson of the Christian Broadcasting Network had warned, "The acceptance of homosexuality is the last step in the decline of Gentile civilization."

Now, in the aftermath of the attack on Matthew, each side took turns pointing the finger at the other about who was to blame for the violence, and why hate crime legislation was either desperately needed or altogether unnecessary.

As soon as Lewis Macenze, Matthew's lover and friend from North Carolina, received word of the almost-fatal beating, he immediately booked a flight to Denver and then drove to Fort Collins, desperate to see Matthew while he was still alive. Unbeknownst to many, he and Matthew had been in close contact recently, and according to Lewis had talked seriously of getting back together. Their plan was to live in Denver, where both of them could go to school, Lewis said.

But an official at Poudre Valley Hospital wouldn't allow him to see Matthew, presumably due to a stricter visiting policy for non-family-members and despite Lewis's explanation of his close relationship to Matthew. Lewis said he tried not to take it personally, yet suddenly he found himself adrift in a large crowd of strangers outside the hospital. The majority of those who had come to pay tribute to Matthew and demonstrate their anger and grief over the attack had learned about him on TV.

By the time Matthew died at 12:53 AM on Monday, October 12, the Laramie attack had already become the most widely publicized event in Wyoming's 108-year history as a state. But despite the outpouring of public interest and media attention, Cal Rerucha sat quietly in his living room and wept for several minutes after DeBree called him with the news.

He thought about the repeated blows Matthew had endured; of his lonely suffering and his family's anguish and the pain that Cal knew would always be with them. He was also overcome by the same incomprehension he'd experienced when fifteen-year-old

Daphne Sulk had been found, her fragile body riddled with stab wounds.

But mostly he kept thinking about his sons Luke and Max, safely asleep in their beds down the hall. Cal was reminded that Matthew's parents had also raised two boys. He prayed silently for all of them.

Later that morning Cal's phone began to ring incessantly. At the courthouse and at home, the phones wouldn't stop ringing.

Within less than a week the political stakes had been raised immensely in a case that continued to grip the nation. Memorial gatherings were organized in New York, Denver, Seattle, Los Angeles, Chicago, and Atlanta. In San Francisco one demonstration turned violent when protesters clashed with police. Dozens of other vigils and protests were being planned in cities and towns nationwide, while in Laramie, a thousand people held candles aloft and sang "We Shall Overcome" outside the University of Wyoming.

Hours after Matthew's death, Cal changed the attempted murder charges he had filed against Aaron and Russell to three new counts: kidnapping, aggravated robbery, and murder in the first degree. Kristen and Chasity were also facing more serious charges now as accessories after the fact.

Sworn to before Judge Robert Castor on October 12 and filed on October 13, Count I of the new charges against Aaron and Russell stated:

> After Mr. Shepard confided he was gay, the subjects deceived Mr. Shepard into leaving with them in their vehicle to a remote area near Sherman Hills Subdivision in Albany County, Wyoming. En-route to said location, the Defendant(s) struck Mr. Shepard in the head with a pistol, and upon arrival at said area, both subjects tied their victim to a buck fence and continued to beat and terrorize him while he was begging for his life.

Initially, as the Clinton administration conducted its own discreet inquiry into the case under the direction of Attorney General Janet

Reno in Washington and the local supervision of the US attorney for Wyoming, Dave Freudenthal, it was unclear whether Cal would actually prosecute the case or a federal prosecutor in Cheyenne would take over those duties. But in the meantime Cal's role as county attorney was instantly — and unofficially — redefined to include crisis management around the clock.

A couple of days after Matthew died, President Clinton made another statement about the presumed motives behind the crime.

"The public outrage in Laramie and all across America echoes what we heard at the White House Conference on Hate Crimes last year," he told reporters before boarding a helicopter for a fund-raising trip. "There is something we can do about this. Congress needs to pass our tough hate crimes legislation. It can do so even before it adjourns, and it should do so . . . One thing must remain clear: Hate and prejudice are not American values."

Judging from the turnout of five thousand people at a candlelight vigil on the steps of the US Capitol on Wednesday evening that week, many shared the president's view that the Laramie attack was an unqualified hate crime. Gay activists, human rights advocates, and politicians expressed their outrage and sorrow over Matthew's killing and demanded stronger protection against hate crimes. But no one expected the large number of senators and members of the House that showed up — from both sides of the aisle.

Senator Ted Kennedy spoke eloquently. "The crime against Matthew Shepard has shocked the conscience of the country, and a powerful response is clearly required," he said. " . . . Hate crimes are on the rise, and we need to send the strongest possible signal as a nation that these crimes will not be tolerated in the United States of America."

Actresses Ellen DeGeneres and Anne Heche were also among the speakers, as were Matthew's friends Walt Boulden and Alex Trout.

"I can't stop crying," Ellen confessed to the crowd. "You know, I just — I think — I mean, I know we all feel the same way, and I'm here . . . he's got his two close friends here — I don't even know him, and I'm thinking this is just really selfish of me . . . And then it just hit me why I am so devastated by it. It's because this is what I was trying to stop. This is exactly why I did what I did [came out publicly]."

The words of Anne Heche, Ellen's girlfriend at the time, were more pointedly political. "Mr. Trent Lott, Mr. Newt Gingrich, Mr. Jerry Falwell, how many Christs must bear the crosses until we learn that we are all children of God?" she stated. "You have witnessed a demonstration of what your ignorant teachings about gays and lesbians breed. You preach in support [of] groups that encourage me to change who I am, to become more like you. I do not want to be like you."

Just as quickly, however, forces on the Religious Right were mobilizing to defend their anti-gay positions, while insisting they had done nothing to create an atmosphere in America that encouraged hatred or condoned violence.

When Bill Clinton later compared Matthew's murder to genocide in Bosnia, I admired him for telling what I thought was an unvarnished truth. At the time, I never gave it a second thought that Matthew's accused assailants had already been found guilty of a hate crime in the court of public opinion — even before they were arraigned for the murder. The president also let it be known that he favored the death penalty for both men.

Furthermore, I had no reason to question the hate crime theory then, nor did I take notice of the timing of Clinton's statements.

A few days before the October 6 attack on Matthew, the House Judiciary Committee had released thousands of pages of material from special prosecutor Kenneth Starr's investigation, including damaging grand jury testimony and transcripts of the Monica Lewinsky–Linda Tripp tapes. Then, on October 8 — the day after Matthew was found at the fence — the House of Representatives authorized a wide-ranging impeachment inquiry on the president on a 258–176 vote. Thirty-one Democrats joined Republicans in supporting the move toward impeachment.

Surely it isn't difficult to imagine Bill Clinton, a consummate political strategist, doing everything in his power to save his presidency, including shoring up key constituencies in his hour of crisis. Clinton also has a peerless gift for plucking our collective heartstrings at just the right moment. Symbolically if nothing else, the apparently random attack on Matthew revived, however briefly, a mythic

American innocence that may have been preferable to the tawdry sex scandal threatening to bring down the president.

On the weekend before Matthew died, gay activist Cathy Renna, then the director of community relations for GLAAD (Gay and Lesbian Alliance Against Defamation), was quoted in the *Laramie Boomerang*:

> [Matthew] seemed kind of defenseless. He presented a very safe image of gay people. That's what affected people," she said. "He could have been the boy next door. He looked like Leonardo DiCaprio, and the media jumped all over that.

But this safe image of "the boy next door" was also more politically expedient than coming to terms with the troubled young man that Matthew really was and the complexities surrounding the crime, including his well-hidden relationship with Aaron.

Years after Matthew was killed, Judy Shepard was asked by a reporter why there had been such a huge media frenzy following the attack on her son.

"There are probably a dozen reasons why the story got so big," she said. "Maybe people were sick of Clinton and Monica."

In truth, however, Bill Clinton may have had several reasons of his own for making the Shepard case a personal cause célèbre. According to Cal Rerucha, the Clinton administration and Attorney General Janet Reno were worried that the Laramie situation was volatile and "could turn into another catastrophe like the 1995 Oklahoma City bombing," which claimed 168 lives. (During the 1993 siege at the Branch Davidian compound in Waco, Texas, which also occurred during the Clinton administration, seventy-six lives were lost.)

Another factor that apparently worried government officials was Matthew's HIV infection. At the time of the 1998 attack, it was potentially explosive news and they did their best to conceal it — especially since it wasn't totally clear what had triggered Aaron's violent outburst.

———

When it leaked out in a March 1999 *Vanity Fair* article that Matthew had AIDS, his parents stated that he had been unaware of it. But others who had been close to Matthew knew differently, yet they refrained from discussing it with the media.

According to Ronnie Gustafson, who briefly dated Matthew in Laramie, Alex Trout had introduced him to Matthew but had also cautioned him to "be careful" if they became sexually involved, as Matthew was HIV-positive. Doc O'Connor also later acknowledged, "Matt told me he had AIDS." In his early interviews with the media, however, Doc had never broached the subject.

Whether or not Aaron learned prior to the attack that Matthew was HIV-positive will, in all likelihood, never be known. (Doc said he kept Matthew's confidence about this until months after the murder.) But in retrospect, it's easy to understand why the Clinton administration feared that more violence could erupt in Laramie. Since Aaron was instantly depicted in the media as a homophobic "redneck" — his friend Travis Brin, then thirty-four, told a reporter, "One time [Aaron] said we ought to get all these people with AIDS, stick them in an airplane and blow it up" — the idea that he could've exploded in rage after realizing he'd been exposed didn't seem far-fetched.

It's also not inconceivable that Aaron and Matthew might've had unprotected sex.

According to Russell, however, he "never heard any mention of AIDS" on the night of the crime. Nor did a single patron or employee of the Fireside Lounge notice any kind of animosity as the three men left the bar.

Nevertheless, in the fifteen years since Matthew's murder, several reliable studies have found that users of crystal meth engage more frequently in unprotected sex than non-users do. Studies have also linked meth addiction in the gay community to higher rates of HIV transmission.

In February 2005, more than six years after the murder, journalist Andrew Sullivan posted the following on his website, under the heading "Meth Is the Issue":

The real problem in the gay male epidemic right now is the use of crystal meth (it is hurting the health of people already HIV-positive just as much as it is contributing to the infections of people who are HIV-negative). This drug has rampaged and is coursing through straight rural America and parts of gay urban America. As many of you know, I'm a libertarian when it comes to recreational drug use (and what consenting adults do in private). But I draw the line at this drug. It's evil, potent beyond belief, it's destroying people's minds, careers, lives and souls. If we don't get a grip on it, it may undo all the progress we have made against HIV in the gay world . . . We should start insisting on zero tolerance of this drug among our friends and loved ones. We should do this . . . out of love and concern for one another. We should encourage every addict to get treatment . . . We have risen to the occasion before and we can do so again. Not by stigmatizing, blaming or ostracizing, but by confronting, persuading, begging one another to overcome this menace.

At 10 AM on Friday, October 16 — a cold, snowy morning — a funeral service for Matthew was held at St. Mark's Episcopal Church in the Shepards' hometown of Casper, Wyoming.

Cal had been advised by federal officials not to attend the funeral, due to security concerns. As another precaution, armed SWAT teams were deployed on nearby rooftops to monitor a small band of angry demonstrators and to quell threats of violence. But perhaps most ominously, Matthew's father wore a bulletproof vest when he came outside to address the media.

Inside the church, law enforcement agents had combed the pews searching for explosives before an overflow crowd of mourners was allowed inside.

In a park across the street from St. Mark's, a notorious preacher from Kansas, the Reverend Fred Phelps, marched with members of his congregation, chanting venomous slogans like "No Tears for

Queers" and "No Fags in Heaven." Phelps, a defrocked Baptist whose website address was godhatesfags.com, had come to the funeral not only to protest but also to celebrate Matthew's death.

"We want to inject a little sanity and gospel truth into what's shaping up to be an orgy of homosexual propaganda," he said.

In Phelps's ideal world, civil law would be based on biblical code, and the government would execute homosexuals.

To many, Reverend Phelps — with his hateful ranting and oversized cowboy hat — came across as a pathetic caricature. Yet the previous weekend in Fort Collins, while Matthew was still alive on a respirator, a group of college students from Colorado State mocked Matthew's suffering in a homecoming parade. For laughs, they decorated a float with a scarecrow and the words "Up My Ass," then paraded it a few blocks from Poudre Valley Hospital where Matthew lay dying.

As if the trauma of Matthew's murder and all that followed weren't enough pain for the Shepard family, Dennis's uncle suffered a fatal heart attack in the kitchen at St. Mark's Church while waiting for the funeral service to begin. Then, within less than a month's time, Dennis's father — Matthew's grandfather — would also die suddenly.

"The stress of losing Matt would also cost me my father," Dennis later recalled.

About two weeks after the attack, Cal finally received a clear directive from US Attorney Freudenthal to proceed with prosecuting the case under Wyoming state law, which had no hate crime provisions. Freudenthal also relayed once more the Clinton administration's promise to help with the case in any way they could. (Although President Barack Obama signed the Matthew Shepard Act into federal law in 2009, Wyoming legislators have yet to amend the state's laws to include hate crimes.)

However, it could later be argued that the Clinton administration's pledge of assistance was more symbolic than actually fulfilled. When news of Matthew's beating first made headlines, federal officials signaled that they would play a central role in the case and would be there to offer whatever support was needed. But thirteen months later when the trials were over, Albany County, Wyoming, would be left to foot the bill. The county's financial deficit would also result in the elimination of several deputies' jobs in the sheriff's office. It was an ironic outcome, given that a prominent feature of the hate crime bill pushed by the Clinton administration was more police enforcement.

At times, the federal government's behind-the-scenes coaching of Cal bordered on the ridiculous.

"Always wear a blue shirt, otherwise you'll look like a corpse," he was advised, courtesy of Attorney General Janet Reno.

Another pearl of wisdom from the feds was, "Don't let the media lights shine on your bald head."

Lastly, he was instructed, "Don't beat up on a public defender again." Apparently, word of Cal's sometimes-steamy temper had made the rounds all the way to Washington.

Soon Cal began to receive death threats. Anonymous callers to his home in the middle of the night warned that they would take justice into their own hands if they had to. On one occasion a drive-by shooter fired a bullet through his living room window, but luckily no one was hurt.

The FBI quickly stepped in with special security measures to protect the Rerucha family. Cal's wife, Jan, and their two sons, Luke and Max, were forced to curb their usual daily activities. The boys were no longer allowed to ride their school bus and were under constant surveillance. Cal had to restrict his movements to just a few places: the courthouse, the gym, church, and home.

His conduct as a prosecutor was also being watched carefully, not only in Wyoming but in Washington as well. Early in the case, he and Rob DeBree realized that unidentified federal agents were looking over their shoulder, keeping track of every move they made. Both the US attorney's office in Wyoming and the FBI also kept abreast of the latest developments in the case.

Cal's decision to seek the death penalty for Aaron and Russell didn't come until he'd consulted at length with Matthew's parents. It was his first death penalty case — and "not a decision I took lightly," he said. Instead he would find himself wrestling with his conscience every step of the way.

For advice and guidance he turned to the same seasoned defense attorney who had once been Wyatt Skaggs's boss — Leonard Munker. Munker cautioned him about the heavy emotional toll of a death penalty case and told him to read Norman Mailer's epic book *The Executioner's Song,* about the Gary Gilmore case in the 1970s. (Gilmore was executed by firing squad in Utah in 1977, after a ten-year moratorium on executions in the United States.)

To keep his personal motives in check, Cal also made frequent visits to his parish church of St. Laurence O'Toole for confession, often several times a week. He struggled to adhere to "my duty as a prosecutor but not to thoughts of revenge," he later explained.

An intensely moral man and a lifelong Catholic, Cal felt his higher duty was to the law he had sworn to uphold and to ensure that justice was done. But by his own reckoning, he also struggled constantly with the less noble urge to exact revenge for Matthew's killing. Succumbing to vengeance was a sin, he believed, and a temptation to be monitored vigilantly.

At the same time, Cal's conflicts were compounded by his personal ambivalence regarding capital punishment, and the equally difficult question of whether the death penalty was morally compatible with Catholic doctrine.

As he pondered the atrocious violence inflicted on Matthew, he also had to contend with the knowledge that Aaron and Russell were not strangers to him, or to the courthouse. Aaron, who belonged to the parish of St. Laurence as well, had committed a string of earlier offenses, both as a juvenile and as an adult. Aaron had also been "known to abuse animals for the fun of it," according to Cal.

Nonetheless, Cal had to ask himself whether he — and others — had failed to intervene sufficiently, before Aaron's antisocial behavior could turn more violent.

Cal also remembered that when he was growing up in Laramie in the 1960s, the McKinneys "had been a solid family in town." Aaron's relatives had run a popular restaurant called the Diamond Horseshoe, which was always packed with diners on Sundays after church — including the Reruchas.

But Russell's story and Aaron's were very different, Cal said, "though both young men came from broken homes."

Asked if he'd been surprised when he heard it was Aaron and Russell who were involved in the attack on Matthew, Cal replied, "I wasn't surprised with Mr. McKinney. I was *very surprised* with Russell Henderson" (emphasis in original).

Cal elaborated on what he saw as fundamental character differences:

> [It] seemed like [Russell] had turned around his life and then . . . [he] met the wrong people. And went the wrong direction . . . [I'd been] very aware of his situation and the progress that he was making . . .
>
> [His grandparents] did an excellent job in raising him. And giving him that start. It's a sad ending to what could have been a good story . . .
>
> [Aaron] was a different individual . . . From the time that he was in school . . . he was violent. Physically violent. Almost a person without a conscience . . . Everybody in law enforcement knew Mr. McKinney because of his involvement with [the police] from the time that he was in junior high school . . . He liked to brag about killing other people. He liked to intimidate individuals. He would fly into rages . . . And he wouldn't hesitate to use a weapon.
>
> . . . McKinney certainly was the leader [in the attack on Matthew]. He was a person that you'd fear, I think. Just because of the way he acted . . .
>
> I don't think there's any doubt that the blows most probably were struck — especially the fatal blows — by McKinney with that .357 Magnum . . . Certainly McKinney was the person that was the more violent of the two . . . [He] was more culpable [as far as] the brutality . . .
>
> With these individuals I believe Henderson more than I believe McKinney . . . Henderson [is] more credible . . .

During the same interview with Cal Rerucha — nearly six years after the murder — he also had more to say about the role of drugs:

> . . . A lot of people didn't realize the devastating effects of methamphetamine. The addictive qualities . . . What it does to you . . . Just takes hold of you and takes away your soul . . . And [McKinney] was deeply involved in it, buying it, selling it, using it . . . You're not thinking about how you can help the family, you're thinking about how you can score your next big adventure . . .
>
> When you're into meth, nothing else matters . . . Relationships ares econdary . . .
>
> Methamphetamine was a huge part of this case. And . . . in some ways, the media really hadn't paid enough attention to that.
>
> Methamphetamine is not a one-time thing, it's a way of life. And once you get involved in this, then everything changes . . . It was huge in the lives of all those people around [McKinney] . . . [He] was a violent person. Not just [to] Matthew Shepard or people he came into contact [with] in the drug world, but also to girlfriends and people that he associated with . . .
>
> When you cast a play in Hell — and methamphetamine is Hell —you're not going to get angels for actors . . .

THIRTY

ACDC

Not long after Kristen Price had poured out her heart and soul to Detective Ben Fritzen — confessing everything that Aaron and Russell had allegedly told her about the crime, and acknowledging her own efforts to help cover it up — she continued to pledge her love to Aaron.

"Babe, I love you so much and I still want to marry you no matter what," she wrote to Aaron in a letter smuggled to him at the Albany County Detention Center ("ACDC"), where they were both jailed. "We can't have contact visits when you get to prison if we're not married. Just promise me you won't say anything to my mom about our second baby. I need to tell her in my own way . . . "

Other letters that Kristen wrote him were flattering — and sometimes sexually explicit.

"I saw you on TV, babe, you looked really good," she said.

On a different occasion, she referred to the prospect of Aaron showing off his genitals at the jail.

"I can't believe you was [sic] going to show everybody your dick," she complained in a sassy tone.

In the meantime Aaron stoked his sudden criminal celebrity by signing jailhouse autographs "Killer." He also bragged in a letter to a fellow inmate's wife, "Being a verry [sic] drunk homofobick [sic] I flipped out and began to pistol whip the fag with my gun."

Comments like the latter — along with his use of the epithets *fag* and *queer* in his statement to police — only served to reinforce Aaron's image as an unqualified homophobe. But these were also calculated attempts on his part to deflect attention from a side of himself that he was determined to keep hidden. In reality, Aaron had long been enamored of the bad-boy attitudes celebrated in "gangsta" rap and had used similar epithets with his friends. Sporting a bandanna, oversized cargo pants, and a thick chain around his check with the nickname DOPEY engraved in solid gold, he'd call them *bitch, nigga, ho,* et cetera.

The nickname Dopey was a handle Aaron had been proud of and had advertised everywhere, including his vanity license plate. He also had the Disney character tattooed on his shoulder, with another custom touch: Dopey is pouring a giant can of beer on his mother's grave — an unambiguous reference to the sudden death of his mother when he was sixteen, and to lyrics sung by the murdered rapper 2Pac and other "niggaz" who vowed to *pour a forty ounce on my homie's grave.* 2Pac, who was shot in 1996 when Aaron was nineteen, gave voice to the gangsta alienation that Aaron and many of his peers identified as their own.

(Kristen never had a second baby by Aaron. Presumably, she aborted the pregnancy or had a miscarriage after her release from jail. But within weeks of declaring her love to Aaron, she got pregnant by someone else and eventually gave birth to a second son.)

Russell and Chasity also exchanged love letters while they were incarcerated at ACDC, using a jailhouse system of "kites" to smuggle their correspondence. Mixed with occasional angry comments about Kristen, whom he blamed for their current predicament, Russell repeatedly swore his love to Chasity. She, in turn, addressed him as "Green Eyes."

Russell's collection of letters — which became part of the permanent case record — displayed a youthful sentimentality; he always began with "Hey Baby" and signed them "Yours Always":

> I wish I could see you more than once a week. I miss you so much. I miss everything about you. I wish more than anything that everything could go back to normal. I'm hoping and praying that we will be together soon . . .
>
> I wish I had a time machine so I could make everything right . . . Remember that I love you more than anything in this world. You will always have my heart. Also remember

that you will always be my baby. There is no one else that can fill that spot. I Love You.

My last letter to you didn't make it. It got in the wrong hands. It basically said how much I missed you . . .

I saw you when you came downstairs . . . thru a little window on a door, reflecting off the glass . . .

I found out the last time I cheated [that] you were the only girl for me. When you did it, it broke my heart and I learned how much I wanted you . . .

It would be nice to hear from you to know if you still care or [you're] already looking for a new life . . . I will always care for you no matter what happens.

I know that whore friend of yours snitched everyone out in the beginning w/out any hesitation. I am the only one that stayed strong and didn't talk . . . The way it looks to me is your [sic] planning your life so when you get out everything will be set. Set for me not to be in it.

I don't know what to do or think anymore. The only thing I do know is I can trust no one. Not even the most important person in the world to me. It's just me against the world . . .

I know in 5 years you won't be there for me . . . I don't think my grandma will be alive in five years. That leaves no one . . .

The whole world is against me and I need all the friends I can get . . .

. . . Please ask your mom to send at least one picture of you so I can at least have something to always remember my girl by. *I LOVE YOU.*

Chasity tried in several letters to allay his fears of abandonment and betrayal:

I am *not* trying to send you to prison, I am tying to get you out. I am trying to make it so you are an accessory [sic] just like me cuz [sic] I know that you didn't touch [Matthew] — at least I think that. Why would I be trying to get you out of my life, I love you so much.

. . . I was threatened by the police. I told them what I knew which was all heresay [sic] anyway . . .

Kristen is so lucky that Aaron loves her so much. He thinks we don't deserve to be here and he is so sorry for what we are going through.

If you want me to tell my lawyer fuck off and tell everyone I committed murder *I will*, at least then you will quit blaming me . . .

I will always be here for you and support you but I'm beginning to think that you don't need me anymore . . . If you want me to say murder, just say so. I love you.

For his part Russell continued to pour out his feelings, though he seemed only dimly aware — or was in denial — about what kind of sentence he could expect to receive:

. . . I was so glad to go up there and be able to see you. I wish I could come and hold you even if it were just for a minute. That would at least ease some of the pain of seperation [sic] . . .

I look forward to sleep so I can dream about being with you, even though it is hard to sleep without you by my side . . .

Your Sensless [sic] CD is in Doc's limo. [Aaron] took it one time he went in there, the time he cheated. Don't worry I didn't go in the limo . . .

My heart just grows a greater love for you every day I'm seperated [sic]. It lusts for you. It needs you . . .

I have not got [sic] any visits from anybody except my grandma and my 2 aunts . . . I'm even getting a lot of letters from people at my grandma's church . . .

My old boss was going to sell my picture to the newspaper

but Taco Bell said they would sue because of my uniform . . . This is all over the world Chasity. I need all the support . . . especially from you . . .

I don't expect you to wait for me. [But] I do expect you to remember what me and you [sic] had . . . That love will *never* leave my heart . . .

I still remember the last night we were together. That night was and will be the *greatest* night of my life even though we didn't make love.

Whatever you do and whatever you decide please don't forget me.

You shouldn't believe everything you hear cause I'm not getting death. They might try but I've been told I won't get it. I will probably get a little time. I still have a chance to beat it . . .

Like Russell, Chasity was struggling to be realistic about their future; at the same time she tried to convince him that there were reasons to remain hopeful:

From what I have heard you are going to get life in prison. If that is the case I don't know how we can keep our relationship going. If you don't get life then everything will be allright [sic]. If you do get life I will be here for you and support you the whole way through. I will keep in touch with you and try to see you . . .

If you guys go to trial Aaron is saying that you didn't touch [Matthew], just watched. Kristen is saying the same and I'm telling them what you told me, that you didn't touch him. I pray that you and I will be together someday and that you will get a lesser charge.

It sucks cuz [sic] I'm going to miss Thanksgiving and Christmas. I'm dying in here, it's going to make me crazy. But I take it day by day. I lost everything, you, my education, my job, and my home . . .

I wish it would all go away but thats [sic] just wishful thinking . . .

I hope that you and I get to have that baby we planned, someday. Just keep your head up and if you get down think of me. I think of you all the time and it helps me get through my day . . . I love you with all my heart.

With the passage of time Russell seemed more resigned to the likelihood that their relationship wouldn't survive his imprisonment, yet he continued to voice his love for her — even as he isolated himself more:

I love you more than the world itself. Nothing can or will ever change that. Not even if you stop caring . . .

I will survive. I'm not getting life. I might do a *little* time. I know you will want to move on and I will deal with that when the time comes. I try not to think about that . . . I will love you forever no matter what happens or where you go . . .

I've pretty much blocked everyone out of my life. There is no one I can trust anymore except for myself . . .

I want you to do anything to get out. I'm sorry for everything . . .

When I told you I loved you they locked me down but it was more than worth it . . . They could lock me down for the rest of my time here if they would give me 15 min [sic] alone w/you.

In a letter to Chasity's brother, Russell repeated something that he'd written to her several times, though his tone was very different.

"If there is one thing I learned from this is [sic] I can trust no one . . ." he said. "As your older brother I'm going to tell you to keep your ass out of trouble cause if you don't you might end up in my shoes."

Beyond the drug underpinnings of Matthew's murder, perhaps the most paradoxical discovery I made during my investigation was coming to realize that Russell, whom I've now known for nearly a dozen years, shows no signs whatsoever of being homophobic or hating gay people. Nor do I believe this is a convenient case of "convict's remorse."

Russell was a participant in a robbery that turned abhorrently violent and that led to Matthew's death, for which he has accepted responsibility. But all of the alleged anti-gay sentiments attributed to him came from the hearsay statements of second and third parties with a strong personal interest in the outcome of the case — notably Aaron's girlfriend, Kristen. The media then reported those statements endlessly until they were accepted as fact.

In my early conversations with Russell, beginning in 2002, I was extremely skeptical of everything he told me, including on the subject of sexuality. But as I became better acquainted with him and gradually conducted interviews with many who knew him, including prison personnel, it became apparent that he'd been telling me the truth right along.

When I first sent Russell a copy of the anonymous letter I'd found at the courthouse in the fall of 2000, which claimed that he and Aaron "were quite familiar with gay guys," he flatly denied the letter's allegations concerning himself. He also said he'd never seen Aaron involved in homosexual activities but "I can't speak for him." Yet it was the rest of Russell's letter that gave me pause and made me feel compelled to investigate further:

> I have never had intimate relations with another man in any way, shape, or form. This in no way makes me homophobic. I am far from this. I have no hatred towards anyone.
>
> . . . I don't know why so many people would say things about me that aren't true . . . It makes it hard because now when the truth is told, some people don't want to believe it.
>
> . . . It took a lot of consideration for me to talk to you. I do not have much trust in the media and I know they have a way of twisting words for their own purpose . . . I do trust you, which is not easily earned considering everything else that has happened to me . . .

I have never engaged in sexual activities with men. If I did, this is something I would not be ashamed of. This isn't the [19]50s. You don't have to hide from it. I am not hiding and I am being 100% truthful with you.

PART THREE

Rogers Canyon

THIRTY-ONE

The Little Bastard

In the summer of 1977 Russell Arthur Thompson was not born yet. He was still being jostled around in the womb of his nineteen-year-old mother, Cindy, when she griped wishfully to her girlfriend Michelle, "Let's flush the little bastard."

Michelle knew her friend's remark did not spring from momentary panic or one of the fleeting mood swings that typically accompany pregnancy. Cindy's desperate yearning to purge her baby was a refrain Michelle and others would hear often in the aftermath of Russell's premature birth on September 24.

Extracted from Cindy's uterus with stainless-steel forceps and weighing just an ounce over four pounds — his blood tainted by fetal alcohol poisoning and other drugs his mother had ingested — the boy was kept alive on a hospital incubator for two weeks. When his weight slipped to three pounds, the still-hopeful obstetrician who delivered Russell spoke of transporting him from Laramie to a Texas hospital with more advanced post-natal equipment. But there was good reason to fear that the tiny infant, with his jaundiced skin and lustrous green eyes, would not survive the trip.

According to town gossip, Cindy drank profusely in her hospital bed before being wheeled to the delivery room. For days after giving birth she refused to see the baby, and she neglected to visit his crib in intensive care before checking out of the hospital.

Cindy's temperamental, equally hard-drinking spouse, Gerry Farris, who couldn't give a damn about having a newborn son — or worse, becoming a parent — shared her indifference.

Exactly one year later to the day, another son fathered by Gerry — David Farris — was born to a different woman named Melinda. David Farris would later become inseparable friends with Aaron McKinney. A brawny, tough-talking amateur boxer and a hard drinker who has been in and out of jail in recent years, David, now thirty-four, prides himself on having been part of Aaron's tight inner circle and takes credit for introducing Aaron to his half brother, Russell.

For a brief time following Russell's birth, Gerry Farris seemed to have a change of heart. He promised Cindy he would give father-hood his best shot; both of them, in fact, vowed to make big changes. Cindy had decided she wanted to raise Russell and swore off alcohol and drugs. The first big step after getting custody from her parents, Bill and Lucy Thompson, was changing Russell's last name. He was now Russell Arthur Farris.

Like other men in Cindy's life, Gerry soon departed in a hail of rage amid her renewed threats that she would *flush the little bastard*. Russell, who had yet to speak his first word, would be an adult before he learned who his father was.

The full measure of Gerry's alcoholic desolation would not mani-fest until years later when he committed suicide in Arizona. He and Cindy had gone their separate ways by then, after a tumultuous three-year marriage.

Over Cindy's bitter objections, her parents, Bill and Lucy, a couple well respected around town as devoted, hardworking members of the Church of Latter Day Saints, assumed legal responsibility for Russell's care once more. Bill had a job at the post office downtown and Lucy ran a popular daycare center from their ranch home on South 26th Street.

When Russell turned five, Cindy was still in the throes of upheaval but buoyed by hopes of another fresh start. She convinced Bill and Lucy she was ready to be a mother and that her new husband, Bob Henderson — a long-haul truck driver — would be the father and family man Gerry Farris never wanted to be. Within two years Russell had two new half sisters, Carla and Stacey, and another new name. He was now Russell Henderson.

To the surprise of few, Cindy had another relapse; she also wanted a divorce. This time the court awarded her custody of her two daugh-ters, while Russell was given to Bob, his now-adoptive father.

Later, when Cindy married a fourth man, she changed her name again. She became Cindy Dixon, taking the family name of her carpen-ter spouse, Charlie, whose repeated crimes of domestic violence would eventually land him in the state penitentiary. But Charlie wasn't the only man to act out his frustration on Cindy with his fists. Nor was she the only victim. One of her roughneck boyfriends hurled Russell head-first through a plate-glass window. Another time Russell showed up at school badly bruised and assured his second-grade teacher that he'd been playing with his sister's boyfriend — though no boyfriend existed.

Those who followed Cindy Dixon's long, nearly unbroken path of decline, including a few in law enforcement, had a more mundane and pitiless explanation: They described her in the plainest of terms as "a hopeless alcoholic."

Born in 1955 as a "breech baby" with birth defects that limited her use of both feet, Cindy had surgery ten times before the age of fourteen. By high school, despite being a good student who talked about becoming a teacher, she was already addicted to prescription painkillers and soon turned to alcohol to numb herself more. Family members and friends would later say there was no kinder person than Cindy when she was sober. But when she was on a drinking binge, "someone else took over."

Long before Cindy was killed in January 1999 at age forty, and her body discarded by the side of a road in the subzero chill of a lonely Wyoming canyon, her girlfriend Michelle would think about the emotional turmoil Cindy battled during her teens. A sometimes-complacent witness to her friend's slow unraveling — one of many — Michelle would later wonder whether her "sweet friend" had come under siege by the devil. Maybe Cindy, a motel maid, had been prey to some ravenous ghost that would not rest until her soul was sucked dry.

But beyond the curse of alcoholism, another "ghost" had taken hold of Cindy, as well as untold others in her hometown: metham-phetamine. Not only was Cindy a chronic meth user herself, but her confessed killer — much like Matthew's — was an addict and a dealer. In late 1998 and early 1999 when these killings occurred, however, meth was still a dirty secret in Wyoming and a taboo topic in other parts of the nation — including urban gay enclaves, where an epidemic of crystal meth addiction had already begun.

THIRTY-TWO

Shadow People

My schooling in the grim realities of methamphetamine began more than a decade ago when a trusted source in Wyoming encouraged me to contact Diane Galloway, the former director of a statewide substance abuse program. At the time of our first phone conversation in May 2003, I was still investigating Matthew's murder for *The New York Times Magazine*.

Galloway quickly explained that in 1998 when Matthew was killed, the state had not yet established a substance division.

"When that murder was committed, Wyoming was just becoming aware of the size of the meth problem," she said. "We were just getting that wake-up call."

Galloway's words echoed what Cal had been saying — and also what Dave O'Malley, the current Albany County sheriff, would tell *20/20* the following year.

"We're educating on . . . methamphetamine use ten years after we should have started doing that," according to O'Malley. ". . . I wish we'd have started reacting to it before it got here."

I could tell that Galloway was surprised and relieved that someone from the national media was interested in Wyoming's burgeoning meth crisis. Along with briefing me on some alarming statistics, notably that the state had the highest rate of meth abuse per capita in the nation, she suggested I contact a circuit court judge in the western part of the state, Judge Tom Mealey of Evanston, whom she praised as an expert on meth.

A smart, plainspoken man, Judge Mealey was passionate about continuing to sound the wake-up call, not just in Wyoming but also to the country at large. In a phone interview he spoke of the unexpected changes that had taken place in his own thinking as the number of meth cases piled up in his courtroom, causing him to shift from harsh punitive measures to more of a treatment-based approach — to the extent the law would allow.

With gentle prodding from Cal, Judge Mealey, Diane Galloway, and others whose understanding of the intractable relationship between meth and crime far exceeded my own, I began to take a closer look at meth-related violence. More than anything, my curiosity was driven by my hunger to understand Aaron McKinney. I kept wondering if his statements about paranoia, hallucinations, uncontrollable meth rage, and "shadow people" were remotely plausible.

Aaron had already admitted to me that he had, indeed, hit Russell across the face with his .357 Magnum, spattered with Matthew's blood. At first Aaron tried to minimize his assault on Russell at the fence, calling it "a mistake," but eventually he was more forthcoming about the unstoppable rage that drove him to attack the man he considered his best friend.

Asked to describe the specific sensations he experienced when he was coming down from a meth binge, Aaron replied, "You hallucinate a lot, you're tired, you feel sick, you can't sleep."

Though I was skeptical and thought Aaron had been using his drug habit as another pitiful excuse for his murderous behavior — much as he'd used gay panic — his responses fit with something his father had told me. According to Bill McKinney, he had spent time with Aaron on Saturday evening, October 3, and Sunday, October 4, 1998 — the weekend before Matthew was attacked. On Saturday they had driven with Aaron's four-month-old son to Guernsey, Wyoming — a little over a hundred miles from Laramie — and arrived back at home by midnight. Bill said Aaron had slept on his couch that night and explained, "Kristen was out with the girls." ("The girls" were celebrating Chasity's twentieth birthday, which was the following day, Sunday the fourth.)

But Bill added, "On Sunday and Monday, [Aaron] couldn't get out of bed in the morning."

His recollections seemed to back up the claims of Aaron, his co-worker Joe Lemus, and others that Aaron had to tweak meth on Monday morning before he could pull himself together for work.

In a recorded interview with Aaron in 2004, he talked openly
about the recurring sensations he associated with his meth addiction:

> You start getting paranoid. You start hearing things.
> Everywhere . . . like I'd walk out of my house and every-
> body was calling my name. You start to hallucinate after
> you've been up for a while. Pretty graphically, too . . . I've
> seen all kinds of things. Roofs blowing off the houses. All
> kinds of colors. Things melting.

Aaron's descriptions were somewhat reminiscent of his confession
to police six years before.

"I don't know what happened," he told Detectives DeBree and
Fritzen. "I blacked out. It was like I was possessed or something. It
was like I left my body. I was furious."

Aaron's words were also consistent with Kristen's statement to
police, a full day before he confessed:

> [Aaron] said that [Matthew] was talking stupid. And I said,
> "Well, what did he say to you? Was he flirting with you or
> what?" and he said, *"I don't know."* (Emphasis mine.)
>
> He said, "Something just took over me" and he said, "I
> wasn't myself." He just kept on telling me that it was like
> he was possessed or something 'cause he was not himself.
> He could not imagine himself doing that in his right
> mind. 'Cause I kept on asking him, "Why did you do
> that?" and he kept on telling me, "I don't know. I wasn't
> myself" . . .

Six years after the murder Aaron's description of his mental state
while he was assaulting Matthew at the fence, and shortly afterward,
had changed little:

> It was almost like an out-of-body experience . . . [I] felt
> more like I was watching the whole thing . . . Stuff is real

out of focus . . . You see things move that aren't there. You
see people that aren't there . . . shadow people.

But Aaron also said that in the days immediately prior to the attack,
he'd been overcome with fatigue:

> It's like your mind's awake, but you can feel your body is
> really tired, and that you want to sleep, but you can't. You
> want to stop doing [meth], [yet] you want more . . . That
> causes a lot of anger.

As I spoke with experts fighting on the front lines of the meth crisis
in the Rocky Mountain West, I kept hearing of Dr. Rick Rawson, a
research psychologist and professor in the department of psychiatry at
UCLA. An internationally recognized authority on substance abuse,
Dr. Rawson was said to have a commanding knowledge of the impact
of prolonged meth use on individuals as well as its social impact. He
and his staff had also been training other professionals throughout
the region in how to deal with the growing epidemic.

Minutes into my first phone interview with Dr. Rawson, I understood why he had gained a reputation as something of a guru in his
field. Apart from a keen scientific mind and an impressive ability
to communicate complex ideas simply, it was evident that he cared
deeply about the devastating impact of substance abuse on all sectors
of society, including the gay community. He said he'd be happy to
help educate me about meth, "[since] it's a very serious public health
and criminal justice problem that's getting an insufficient amount of
attention and resources nationally."

At intervals over the next year, I conducted several interviews with
Dr. Rawson by phone and in person at his Los Angeles office, and then
on camera for *20/20*. Although he had no personal knowledge of the
Shepard case and therefore wouldn't address its specifics, he agreed to
discuss in broad strokes Aaron's drug history and the possible influence
of chronic meth use on his extremely violent behavior. Dr. Rawson's

opinions are based on his clinical observations and extensive studies of meth addiction:

> When someone's been addicted to methamphetamine for three years, particularly if they've been a dealer . . . it completely takes over their life . . .
>
> One of the most important effects . . . is that [it] can make you psychotic . . . Over time, the drug changes the way the brain works. The psychosis becomes more severe; the paranoia becomes intensified.

Dr. Rawson also said that he has frequently encountered descriptions like those given by Aaron, but he was quick to point out that they cannot be easily defined.

> To try to analyze what was underlying [Aaron McKinney's] rage is impossible to do. You really don't know, because . . . the brain manufactures these hallucinations and delusions. They may have something to do with some kind of reality that was underlying it, or they may be completely manufactured . . . You'll see people, literally, strike out at other people, thinking that they're monsters . . .
>
> The violence . . . is . . . not a logically laid out plan of being angry with someone, it's a complete loss of control . . . where people just act out without . . . any awareness of the consequences . . .
>
> Going through a meth binge . . . the propensity to violence gets much higher, because . . . it's sort of a building situation. And if they're in a situation where something important is going to happen, a drug deal, a robbery, or something like that, they become extraordinarily emotionally volatile . . . Not only is [paranoia] not unusual . . . it's normally what we see, and the paranoia gets very severe.

If what Dr. Rawson stated is true, that trying "to analyze . . . [Aaron's] rage is impossible to do," I was at a loss about how to reconcile that insight with the popular belief that Aaron's rage was an unmistakable manifestation of anti-gay hate. As a journalist and gay man, I was also unable to reconcile that belief with the added complications of Aaron and Matthew's personal relationship.

In the years immediately following the murder, methamphetamine was still something of a taboo subject not only in Wyoming but also in the nation's gay community. Within Matthew's circle of friends, several had struggled with meth addiction themselves. Jason Marsden, the former journalist who now serves as executive director of the Matthew Shepard Foundation (and also a friend of Matthew), told me in a 2004 interview:

> The quick and easy description of Matt Shepard gay bashed . . . is about as far from the actual nuanced truth of what happened as it can get . . . It's offensive to see the truth boiled down so much . . . that it's no longer the truth . . .
>
> The horrible irony . . . was that his death had an enormous amount to offer us in lessons and that many of those were missed opportunities because of the shorthand of the media . . .
>
> You see the icon and how it differs from the real person, but there's been such tremendous value in that icon having been created . . . Even if all you know is the barest misrepresentation of what took place, if it's important for you to know that, I'm glad that you do.

Later in the same interview when I asked Marsden about the possible role of drugs in Matthew's killing, he replied,

> Methamphetamine was a very big problem [and] very seldom discussed in Wyoming at that time . . . I remember thinking . . . especially when it started to come out that McKinney was surrounded by people who were deep into the methamphetamine problem, that this was perhaps

the most spectacular methamphetamine related crime that
had ever happened in Wyoming . . .

It was very clear ten years ago . . . to those who were
watching this problem emerge, that it was going to become
a scourge in Middle America, in our rural communities . . .
It dominates life for a lot of people in our state . . . We've
got needles on the side of the road in Wyoming . . . drug
lab materials that are thrown out the window of someone's
car on the interstate . . .

I remember thinking at the time that the Matt Shepard
case would forever go down in history as, you know, one of
the saddest examples of gay bashing, but what it also was,
was one of the saddest examples of the desperate lengths
people on methamphetamine will go to.

What Marsden and others may not have realized at the time was that
Aaron was not the only figure in this tragedy "surrounded by people
who were deep into the methamphetamine problem." The ravages of
meth, which helped destroy Matthew's life — not to mention the lives
of Aaron and Russell, and the shattering impact on the families of all
three — were never adequately examined or brought to light, and in
some cases were deliberately covered up.

THIRTY-THREE

Soldier Girl

For a long time I'd been asking Joan, a friend of Matthew who belonged to the Denver circle, to tell me how she first became involved with methamphetamine. She was very reluctant at first, but eventually she agreed to fill in pieces of her personal story and how it related to her friendship with Matthew, whom she met in Denver in 1997. She also agreed to an on-camera interview, which I conducted with my producing partner Glenn Silber.

In 1989, at the hopeful age of nineteen, Joan had already known what she wanted to do with her life. She saw two choices for herself and either one would have suited her well: join the Denver Police Department and move up through the ranks to a starring role in the war on crime, or scrape together the money to get to New York and train for a career in the performing arts — acting, singing, dancing.

Eight years later when Joan met "Matty" Shepard and they got close enough to talk "about anything," they confessed to each other how much they loved performing and their frustration at not being on stage.

Leggy and attractive, with deep-set brown eyes, high cheekbones, and a mane of shiny black hair, Joan exuded optimism and self-confidence. She also thrived on competition with an intensity some may have considered "un-feminine." To most, she was a natural leader.

But Joan said her 1989 application to the police academy got stuck in limbo, where it remained. A qualified Latina candidate, she felt she was at an ironic disadvantage in a season when the department was apparently recruiting African Americans. With money tight in her large family, dreaming of Broadway seemed naive and utterly beyond her reach.

Determined to make her mark, Joan did what generations of the young have always done: She enlisted in the army. She said that after eight weeks of basic training at Fort Benning, Georgia, at which she excelled, she was given advanced infantry training for another nine weeks, specializing in the lethal skills of hand-to-hand combat and biological warfare.

Before Joan and many of her buddies with whom she enlisted, male and female alike, had any clear idea of where Kuwait was situated, they received overnight orders for deployment to the Persian Gulf. There was little time for fear, family good-byes, or futile second thoughts. *You're in the army now, soldier.*

Whatever machinations led up to Saddam Hussein's military buildup against Kuwait — and the subsequent Iraqi invasion that sparked the First Gulf War — daily life for Joan and many of her fellow warriors would become a surreal blur as they encamped for months on the desert floor inside Saudi Arabia, and for years after returning stateside.

"It was war and it was traumatizing for all of us," she summed it up curtly almost two decades later.

When she and Matthew met in Denver in 1997 and became friends, she said, he was one of a tiny handful of people she could talk to about her experiences in the Gulf, especially since he had lived in Saudi Arabia and his parents still had a home there. The two bonded like older sister and younger brother, calling each other by the names "Sis" and "Matty."

Joan also trusted Matthew enough to confide in him about her experiences with methamphetamine on the battlefield — a drug she had never known until she went to war: the toxic assortment of every-day ingredients that soldiers gathered to make it; the hazardous cooking process; and how many of them came to depend on meth to keep them awake and alert when Saddam began blowing up Kuwaiti oil wells not far from their camp.

Much like her unnerving memories of service overseas, Joan said she continues to be haunted by the murder of her "little brother" in Laramie.

With great apprehension she'd agreed to revisit their friendship "to set the record straight on who Matty really was and why he was targeted."

Excerpts from a videotaped interview with Joan:

> **Joan:** Matt had a [routine]. When I heard that Matt
> didn't go for the ride-along — Tuesday [October 6]
> at one in the morning, when obviously the crime was
> going on — [I suspected that] whoever wanted Matt
> beat up or robbed or whatever, obviously wanted
> him taken out of town. By the time that ride-along
> would have been done and reached its Laramie point,
> Matthew was nowhere to be found. [*Note:* Joan is
> referring to "one in the morning" on *Wednesday,
> October 7,* not Tuesday, October 6.]
>
> Meth being the competitive little world it is . . . I think
> they wanted [Matt's] end of it . . . or . . . they didn't
> like Matthew and the power that he had at that time.
> They didn't want Matt anywhere in the [Laramie]
> circle . . .
>
> I think that it was planned from Jump Street . . .
> [Matt] was a businessman and so he was threatening
> to somebody. He threatened somebody the wrong way
> . . . [But Matt] didn't walk around hurting people. He
> wouldn't burn people or rob people. He really tried
> being straight with everyone that he ever met. And
> of all things, just everybody thinking he got killed
> because he was gay. I can't let Matthew — he hasn't
> been able to rest in peace for any of us . . . The record
> needs to be set straight.

During the interview, Glenn Silber and I asked Joan numerous
questions.

> **Question:** So as far as this being labeled the most
> heinous anti-gay hate crime, where do you stand on
> [that]?

Joan: It was heinous absolutely . . . but it wasn't because
Matthew was gay. NO way [emphasis in original].
Matthew was not beaten because he was gay . . .
Everyone around him that dealt with him, that knew
him, that met him, everyone knew he was gay . . . He
was just good at what he did. And somebody wasn't
happy about that.

Question: After you got over the shock and revulsion of
what you heard, what did you think [the crime] was
about? If it wasn't about him being gay?

Joan: I knew it was over drugs or money . . . The fact
that Matt didn't tell me what exactly was going on, I
knew it was over drugs or money.

Question: When you heard that Aaron McKinney and
another of his friends were the perpetrators —

Joan: I thought jeez, somebody wanted Matt dead. And I
guess [Aaron] would be the perfect person to do it, you
know. Somebody that was strung out looking for dope
and money . . . Aaron McKinney knew Matt. So just
by knowing that, I thought for sure Aaron was sent
by somebody to do it. Maybe he owed somebody a lot
and you know — they felt that Aaron was the perfect
person to do this to Matt because they had the bad
run-in previously [at the Library bar].

Question: In your circle of friends — people that knew
Matt — did you ever hear anything from any of them,
any speculations about why this had happened to
Matt?

Joan: The people that Matt and I knew, they all believed
the same thing. That [a Laramie rival] wanted Matt
dead. And [that] Matt knew something he wasn't
supposed to . . . I think that Matt was protecting the
circle. And he would have told the circle what was
going on and somebody didn't want that . . . it had to
be something pretty important though . . . So maybe
that person [is] gonna be protected for the rest of their

life just because Matt's dead. But there are some of us
that are hip to a lot of things that were going on at that
time. Who Matt was dealing with . . . There's [sic]
five of us that won't rest until we know exactly what
happened to Matthew and why.

THIRTY-FOUR

The Angel of Death

In the Albany County Courthouse on Wednesday, March 24, 1999, prosecutor Cal Rerucha and county public defender Wyatt Skaggs began choosing jurors for Russell Henderson's trial. The selection process was scheduled to last no more than two weeks, with opening arguments slated for Tuesday, April 6.

During nearly six months of trial preparation since the murder, both Rerucha and Skaggs had deliberately downplayed Matthew's homosexuality as a factor in the crime. But as far as public opinion was concerned, it was still widely believed that the chief motive behind the murder was anti-gay hate.

Shortly before Russell's trial was set to begin, Judy Shepard, Matthew's mother, traveled to Washington, DC, to lobby for a federal hate crime bill that had been stalled for months in Congress. At a news conference on Capitol Hill, she appeared alongside a nephew of James Byrd Jr., a forty-nine-year-old African American man who had been chained to the back of a pickup truck and dragged to death in Jasper, Texas, on June 7 of the previous year — just four months before Matthew was fatally beaten.

Days after the Laramie attack *The Boston Globe* attempted to explain a critical difference between the two cases, underscoring why a federal hate crime law was important.

"Unlike the aftermath of the racially motivated [murder] of James Byrd, Jr. . . . when the FBI rushed in to lead the investigation," the newspaper reported, "federal authorities have no jurisdiction in the Shepard case because the hate-crime law does not cover gays or lesbians."

While it was true that federal authorities had no direct jurisdiction in the Shepard homicide, I later learned from Cal Rerucha that the federal government had played a considerably larger, behind-the-scenes role in the case than the media had reported or may have understood at the time. Federal agents did go to Laramie to investigate the crime and to follow up on the case, Rerucha said, but there was a consensus based on the evidence that Aaron and Russell should be prosecuted under state law for felony murder and related charges. In Rerucha's opinion the evidence to prove a bias crime "wasn't there." He continues to hold that view today and has resisted attempts by federal officials to use the Shepard case as a model example of civil rights violations.

At her dying son's bedside in October 1998, Judy Shepard had decided she would do everything she could to keep Matthew's legacy alive. In addition to co-founding the Matthew Shepard Foundation with her husband, Dennis, she became active in the Human Rights Campaign, the nation's preeminent gay rights organization and a leading advocate of federal hate crime legislation. Matthew's parents hoped to work through their foundation "to promote tolerance in hopes of sparing others their son's brutal fate," according to a December 1999 article in *People* magazine.

"There is no guarantee that these laws will stop hate crimes from happening, but they can reduce them," Judy stated tearfully at the news conference on Capitol Hill. "They can help change the climate in this country, where some people feel it's okay to target specific groups of people and get away with it."

When asked about Russell's upcoming trial, Judy said she and Dennis wanted to "allow justice to run its course."

Over the next decade, both parents would lobby devotedly for the hate crime bill, even as it languished in Congress. They called it "the one piece of unfinished business" stemming from their son's murder.

(On October 28, 2009, during his first year in office, President Barack Obama signed into law "the Matthew Shepard and James Byrd, Jr. Hate Crimes Prevention Act." Better known as the Matthew Shepard Act, the bill, which was attached as a rider to the National Defense Authorization Act for 2010, expands the 1969 federal hate crime law to include crimes motivated by a victim's actual or perceived gender, sexual orientation, gender identity, or disability.)

———

The principal charges Russell would be facing at his trial were first-degree premeditated murder, kidnapping, and robbery — the same capital charges that Aaron would face in court later that year.

In their questioning of potential jurors, Russell's lead defense attorney, Wyatt Skaggs, and county prosecutor Cal Rerucha both emphasized that the murder case was not about "lifestyles."

"It's not about politics," Skaggs said. "It's about judging a human being, possibly even the life and death of a human being . . . The lifestyle of any one individual in this case is irrelevant."

Skaggs and his co-counsel, Jane Eakin — who were also married at the time— were more concerned with communicating to the large pool of potential jurors that Russell had only *watched* as Aaron beat Matthew with the barrel of a .357 Magnum, and had not participated in the beating himself.

Cal Rerucha was eloquent, yet firm, as he told jurors it was their duty to judge Russell Henderson — and by inference Matthew Shepard — without prejudice.

"It's not whether we're black or white, rich or poor, Catholic or Protestant or even atheist," he stated. "Whether we have power or no power, whether we are straight or whether we are gay, we are equal because the Wyoming Constitution tells us we are equal. If any of you cannot follow that element of the constitution, you cannot sit on this jury."

As the start of Russell's trial drew closer, the town of Laramie braced itself for another invasion of outsiders. A security zone of several square blocks was established around the courthouse, making the area look like an armed camp. The building could only be entered through a single side door, where a police checkpoint with two metal detectors had been set up. Every courthouse employee had been trained in bomb detection.

According to Cal, most of the security measures had been put in place by the federal government in Washington, mainly the FBI and Attorney General Janet Reno's office. But "other unidentified federal agents" were also keeping track of events as they unfolded in Laramie, he said. Even he and Detective Rob DeBree were being monitored constantly, "with people looking over our shoulders a lot."

On several occasions Cal watched in disbelief from his office window as bomb specialists used mirrors to search under cars and TV trucks for explosive devices. Marksmen with high-powered rifles also stood guard on nearby rooftops.

The quiet college town Cal had grown up in and loved "began to feel more like Northern Ireland."

In the first week of April 1999, just as Russell's trial was about to begin, a surprise plea bargain was announced. On the advice and admonitions of Wyatt Skaggs, his chief defense attorney, Russell agreed to change his long-held plea of not guilty and forgo a trial to avoid the possibility of a death sentence. Instead he would plead guilty to felony murder and kidnapping, while sidestepping the charge of premeditated first-degree murder. In exchange, he would be given two life terms. Whether those sentences would be served concurrently or consecutively was left up to Judge Jeffrey Donnell.

But only with the passage of time is it possible to examine the complex factors behind the plea-bargaining process — and Russell's decision — with any measure of objectivity or fairness.

One revealing fragment concerns the defense team's unambiguous view of the case, which was summed up by attorney Skaggs shortly after Russell had been sentenced. Skaggs told journalist JoAnn Wypijewski that "drugs were not involved in this case" (*Harper's,* 1999). Yet ironically, Cal Rerucha, his adversary in the courtroom, would later state the complete opposite: "It was a horrible murder . . . driven by drugs."

It was evident from the court record that Skaggs had strenuously avoided any mention of methamphetamine — and I was puzzled even more when I was given access to his confidential defense files. While combing through his trial preparation notes, I came across explicit instructions that said, "Stay away from meth" and "Meth – don't go into it."

If "drugs were not involved" in the case, why these notes?

Had Skaggs been aware of Aaron McKinney and Matthew Shepard's prior drug relationship and/or personal involvement, but made a strategic decision to avoid this incendiary element? The only way that essential evidence and facts could be elicited — and Russell could adequately defend himself against charges that he had targeted, robbed, and beaten Matthew because he was gay — was through a trial, yet Skaggs strongly recommended that Russell accept a plea bargain. The alternative would be the death penalty, Skaggs repeatedly told Russell and his grandmother.

In the relatively small world of Wyoming defense attorneys, Wyatt Skaggs was respected among his colleagues; Cal Rerucha had also spoken admiringly of him on several occasions. And although I had heard charges from many others in Laramie, including a former mayor, that Russell had been "railroaded," it was too facile an explanation in a high-profile murder case in which crucial information and evidence had been sidestepped on all sides.

A former boss of Skaggs — renowned criminal defense attorney and state public defender Leonard Munker, who died in 2005 — offered the simplest but perhaps most logical rationale for Skaggs's seemingly fainthearted approach to Russell's defense. Munker told me in an interview at his home on the outskirts of Cheyenne that he was "absolutely certain" Skaggs would never have taken the case to trial, "out of fear." With such high stakes, he said, Skaggs wouldn't risk the possibility of Russell getting the death penalty — though Munker and other legal experts thought the chances of that ever happening were slim.

The sentencing hearing for Russell on April 5, 1999, was only the latest chapter in a family tragedy that was no longer the Shepards' alone. Three months earlier, on the morning of January 3, Russell's mother, Cindy Dixon, had been found raped and frozen to death on a desolate road in Rogers Canyon, eight miles from town. A twenty-eight-year-old Florida man, Dennis Menefee, whose nickname was "Dinger" — a convicted felon, an alleged counterfeiter, a known meth dealer, and also a friend of Aaron McKinney — would eventually be found guilty of manslaughter in Dixon's death. Initially Menefee was charged with murder, but he was later offered a plea bargain and the charges against him were reduced.

The media paid scant attention to Dixon's killing, which Matthew's mother described as "mysterious" in her 2009 memoir, *The Meaning of Matthew: My Son's Murder in Laramie, and a World Transformed.*

Menefee was given a four-to-nine-year prison sentence by Judge Jeffrey Donnell and was released after serving the minimum four years. But nearly a decade and a half after Dixon was abandoned by the side of a road in freezing temperatures and left to die, one of my trusted law enforcement sources in Wyoming, who has intimate knowledge of the Shepard murder as well as the meth underworld, continues to maintain that Matthew's killing and Cindy Dixon's are "connected." My source believes that Dixon was abducted for one of two reasons, or both: to convince Russell to remain silent, especially had his case made it to trial; and as a form of retaliation for Matthew's robbery and murder in an ongoing dispute between rival drug factions.

Once again — according to official accounts — Cindy Dixon and Dennis Menefee were "strangers" who had met for the first time when Dixon got into his car on a Laramie street.

Very unlikely, my law enforcement source and others have told me. They said that both victim and perpetrator had associated with some of the same people locally, which may explain why Dixon had voluntarily gotten into Menefee's car.

And once again the suspected link between them was methamphetamine.

At the April 5 hearing in Judge Donnell's courtroom, Russell's grandmother Lucy Thompson stood up to make a statement on his behalf. Many in the courtroom knew Lucy personally. For four decades she had run "Lucy's Daycare" and was revered for the love and individual attention she gave all "her kids," as some liked to call them.

Visibly heartbroken, Lucy walked slowly to the lectern in front of Donnell's bench. Throughout the courtroom, tears were stifled before she started to speak. She turned first to Matthew's parents and brother, Logan, who were seated in the front row of the gallery behind Cal.

"We would like to thank the Shepards for allowing us this opportunity," she began. "You have showed such mercy to Russell. We know that there is nothing that can be said or done to ease your sorrow for your son and your brother, Matthew. You will always be in our prayers, as we know that pain will never go away."

As Lucy reminisced about her grandson, her words appeared to identify him with Matthew, though her tone was deeply felt.

"Russell was born premature with very severe health problems," she said. "His mother was young and she was not ready to be a mother. He faced many trials, more than any child ever deserved to go through."

After expressing Russell's "great sorrow and grief" to everyone in the courtroom, Lucy turned to Judge Donnell and with earnest conviction said that her family did not condone in any way what her grandson had done.

"But for the Russell we love, we humbly plead with you to sentence him to two life terms *concurrently*," she continued. "Please do not take Russell completely out of our lives forever. We believe that he can still make some goodness come out of his life."

Were Russell to receive concurrent life sentences he could conceivably become eligible for parole at some future time, while consecutive terms virtually ensured he would never be released.

Before Lucy returned to her seat she addressed her grandson, assuring him of her love and vowing to support him "throughout the times that may come."

Russell spoke next. A profound silence fell over the courtroom as he stepped up to the lectern and looked dolefully at the Shepards.

Dennis and Judy returned his gaze, while Logan shifted uneasily.

"Mr. and Mrs. Shepard, there is not a moment that goes by that I don't see what happened that night," he told them. "I know what I did was very wrong, and I regret greatly what I did. You have my greatest sympathy for what happened. I hope that one day you will be able to find it in your hearts to forgive me."

Russell turned then to his grandmother; his half sisters, Carla and Stacey; and several aunts and uncles in the seats behind his defense attorneys.

"To my family, thank you so much for being there with me," he said. "And I hope you can also one day forgive me."

At that moment forgiveness was not foremost in Cal Rerucha's mind. He knew the only outcome that could remotely console the Shepard family was justice.

But surprisingly, a couple of Matthew's college friends seated in the back of the courtroom were moved by Russell's plea. When Matthew had confided in them about his 1995 rape in Morocco, he said he still worried that the perpetrators might have been punished too severely when they were caught. After living in Saudi Arabia, he was aware of how harsh and unforgiving Islamic law could be.

According to Doc O'Connor, who said he had once asked Matthew what he did to people who hurt him, "Matt's reply was, 'I forgive them and go on with my life.'"

Russell's downcast eyes were facing Judge Donnell now. "Your Honor, I know what I did was wrong," he stated softly. "I'm very sorry for what I did, and I'm ready to pay my debt for what I did. Thank you."

"Thank you, Mr. Henderson," Donnell responded.

A mild tremor in the judge's voice may have stemmed from knowing that the lost young man awaiting his judgment had once been a shy and lost boy in this same courtroom, trapped in his mother's downward spiral of alcoholism and abandonment. And like Cal Rerucha and Wyatt Skaggs, Donnell could not escape the dull ache of regret.

After Russell returned to his place at the defense table, Donnell asked Cal if the Shepards wished to make a statement.

"Yes, they would, Your Honor," Cal said. He nodded reassuringly to Judy, who was already making her way to the lectern.

Calmly, and with the immensity of her loss written in her sad face and posture, Judy spoke of what Matthew's life and death had meant for her family. She spoke of her love for her firstborn son, who had known many disappointments and many successes; and how his experiences opened his eyes and heart to the differences in people.

Listening to her brought tears to Cal's eyes. He privately agreed with Dennis Shepard: Bastards who commit such heinous acts deserve to rot in hell. But in more reflective moments, usually in the solitude of a dark confessional at St. Laurence Church or during a sleepless night, Cal had felt many of his certainties fall away. And as he later confided to me, not a week had passed since Matthew's murder when he hadn't been to confession at least once. It was how he had held himself together when chaos and fatigue had become his daily routine.

Judy's weary gaze fell on Russell now, just a few feet in front of her.

"I have been told I can address you directly," she said in a low but determined voice. "I have debated whether or not to do so, and at times, I don't think you're worthy of an acknowledgment of your existence. But we all know you do exist. You murdered my son. You have forever changed my family . . .

"My hopes for you are simple. I hope you never experience a day or night without feeling the terror, the humiliation, the helplessness, the hopelessness my son felt that night. And I want you to understand that the decisions you made and the actions you took have done this to you and to your family and to my family. None of us would be here today going through this agony if it weren't for you."

After Judy thanked Judge Donnell, Dennis got up. With an aching sadness he talked about the singular mix of qualities that made Matthew who he was, including his "desire to work in human rights . . . saving the world through political means." Dennis also alluded to his son's "chance meeting at the Fireside bar with two friendly strangers."

What happens now? Who is there in this room to replace him to try and save the world?

My son was born blind; not physically, but to people's differences. He didn't see big people and little people, black, brown or white skin, religious or ethnic backgrounds. All he saw were people that needed a friend. His best friends included Japanese, Palestinians and Saudi Arabs. His friends included Muslims, Christians and Buddhists. His friends included gays and so-called straights.

Who will be their friend now? Who will worry about them? . . . Everybody needs a friend. Who will come forward now to be that friend?

. . . The smile that I see when I close my eyes is gone now forever.

Think of what has happened. Think of what Mr. Henderson has done; the impact of that mindless brutality to my family, to his family, to friends and to complete strangers. I no longer have a son with hopes and dreams, with problems and solutions.

. . . Matt's mother and brother watched him grow, and they grew with him while I traveled. They also watched him die. How do they continue? What does his brother say when he's asked, "Do you have any brothers or sisters?" What does his mother do when his birthday comes? Or Christmas? Or Mother's Day?

Judy held Logan's hand as tears streamed down her face. Seconds later, Dennis fixed his eyes on Russell, just as his wife had done.

Mr. Henderson, what about your life and your family? What do your grandmother and aunt, your sisters, cousins, say now? What about you? What future is there?

It takes someone quite unique to sit and watch someone else be beaten to death and do nothing about it. It takes a brave man to help another brave man tie up a person who did not know how to make and clench a fist until he was thirteen years old . . .

Mr. Henderson . . . There is a hole in my life that I can never fill. When we eat dinner, there is a place set for Matt, and we know it will not ever be filled again with his laughter . . . and his stories.

Remember this for the rest of your life.

Russell lowered his head in shame. Later he would say he was still too numb to know true remorse as he listened to Matthew's parents that day.

Behind him he could hear his grandmother's controlled sobs — the same muffled sounds he had heard on Father's Day in 1993 when his grandfather had died, and again in January when she'd come to the jail to break the news that his mother's body had been found.

After Dennis took his seat next to Judy and Logan, Judge Donnell asked Wyatt Skaggs if there was anything he wished to say.

Skaggs kept his remarks brief. To do otherwise would not only be insulting to the Shepards, he felt, but also put him on the wrong side of the judge. Skaggs already believed that Russell's chances of receiving concurrent life sentences were slim. But with Jeff Donnell you never knew for certain which way he was leaning. The judge had a statewide reputation for being fair-minded and independent, and ordinarily he liked to mull things over till the very end.

"Your Honor, I do believe that Russell deserves some consideration for being able to stand before you, and before the Shepard family, and take responsibility for his actions," Skaggs stated simply. "I will leave it to you to consider his sentence, Your Honor. Thank you."

Donnell nodded civilly, then looked to the prosecution table. "Mr. Rerucha?"

Cal rose from the table slowly. He was all too aware of the magnitude of what was before him, yet still unsure of the words he would choose. He had decided to let his sentiments be guided by the proceedings as they unfolded that morning.

Lucy Thompson's plea for Russell had stirred his emotions with the same intensity as Judy's and Dennis's statements had, though the Shepards' suffering and loss had been weighing on him for months already; he'd also gone over their victim impact statements more times than he could remember. But in Lucy's eyes he sensed a bottomless grief that was only partly veiled by her stoically strong faith. Lucy had endured the slow destruction of her daughter's life and was now watching and waiting as her grandson was about to be sucked hopelessly into a void of his own.

At the lectern Cal thanked Donnell and gazed solemnly over the courtroom.

"Each of us has the power to do many things," he said to all assembled. "We have power to do good things in big ways and in little ways, and it is inherent in man that some people have the power to create hell on earth in big ways and little ways."

Cal paused, his eyes on Russell.

"Mr. Henderson, you have created hell on earth for a family, for a community, for a state," he continued. "This is not a time to look at mercy because mercy was done before we came into this courtroom. It is now time that we look at justice. This case has always been about the pain, suffering, and death of Matthew Shepard. For his family, that pain and suffering will continue. For this community, there is pain which we will be left with forever."

With one hand still gripping the lectern, Cal turned to Donnell.

"Your Honor, I would ask for consecutive sentences," he said. "It is appropriate. It is correct. It's the right thing to do."

A moment after Cal returned to his chair at the prosecution table, Donnell asked Russell if there was any reason the court should not enter its sentence.

"No, sir," Russell answered faintly. His voice was so subdued that many in the courtroom noticed only that he shook his head slightly.

Donnell had been extremely circumspect during the media-driven chaos of the past several months. Though discretion was his usual judicial demeanor, he had been extra cautious to avoid a mistrial or do anything that could come back to haunt him on appeal. *State of Wyoming vs. Russell Henderson* was without question the most challenging case of the judge's career; he was also not naive about the lasting impact the Shepard case would have long after he retired from the bench. Some of Donnell's colleagues in Wyoming legal circles said his only remaining ambition was a seat on the Wyoming Supreme Court, for which he was eminently qualified, and that he was unlikely to render any decision that might jeopardize his chances of being appointed.

Nonetheless, Russell Henderson's sentencing hearing on April 5, 1999, was the judge's first real opportunity to publicly vent some of his carefully guarded thoughts on all that he had seen and heard since the October 1998 murder.

"Many people have called this a hate crime," Donnell told the packed courtroom. "Quite frankly, the Court does not find this matter to be so simplistic, for it is quite clear that a number of motives and emotions were involved here. The end result, whatever the motivation, was the brutal murder of a young man who was beaten to death with a three-pound revolver, perhaps in part because of his lifestyle, and perhaps because of a $20 [sic] robbery."

Almost every time that I went back over a transcript of the April 5 hearing, I stopped at those words: *perhaps in part because of his lifestyle, and perhaps because of a $20 robbery.* I assumed the judge was referring in his use of the word *lifestyle* to allegations that Matthew had made unsolicited sexual advances at the Fireside bar. There had been no mention of drugs during the hearing, which was in keeping with Wyatt Skaggs's position that drugs played no part. There had also been no mention of the complicated personal history between Aaron and Matthew, of which Russell was apparently ignorant on the night of the attack.

But after the series of discoveries I'd made during my investigation, I was astonished that Judge Donnell — along with both the prosecutor and defense attorneys — seemed to have had little or no knowledge at the time of the murder's drug component. The notion that Matthew's killing had "perhaps [come about] because of a $20 robbery" suggested a very different set of facts and circumstances than a rivalry involving interstate meth trafficking. It was the latter that had been behind Aaron's ill-conceived plan to rob ten thousand dollars' worth of methamphetamine from a family of competitors — Matthew's Denver-based "family" to be exact.

I understood by then that some police officials had made the decision long before to "let sleeping dogs lie," but what about the sacred duty of the court, both legally and morally, to establish what was true and to administer justice equitably?

Were the complexities of the case so much of a "hornet's nest" — to use Aaron McKinney's words — that leading participants decided it would be more prudent and practical not to poke deeper into the truth?

As I contemplated these questions, I was reminded of one of the few admissions Aaron has made since October 1998 that suggests he isn't totally devoid of empathy or remorse. In one of our recorded interviews, he stated,

> It's really hard for me to . . . see [Russ] in this situation, knowing that I'm the one that put him here. I ruined that

guy's life. . . . He didn't do nothing [sic]. The only thing that man's guilty of is keeping his mouth shut.

Judge Donnell arched forward in his chair, his tone strict and uncompromising.

"Mr. Henderson, you drove the vehicle that took [Matthew Shepard] to his death," he said. "You bound him to that fence. You stood by while he was struck again and again, his blood on your coat, doing nothing to stop it. You left him there for sixteen hours. This was a most savage crime, Mr. Henderson, evidencing a total lack of respect for human life, all life, whether different from your own or not."

Russell's eyes never strayed from the judge, just as his attorneys had instructed him, but more of a vacancy had crept into his expression. Behind him, Lucy bowed her head despondently, resigned to what was coming.

"The Court also considers, as it must, your own background," Donnell went on. "The Court notes that you have no significant criminal history by way of prior felony convictions; and notes as well that you did not, for the most part, grow up with any sort of parental influence. This Court most certainly does not criticize your grandmother, but that's not the same as having your parents available. It isn't. It can't be. But you are not a victim here because of your unfortunate background. You are a perpetrator. The pain you caused, Mr. Henderson, will never go away. *Never.* There may be days from time to time when people won't think about this or remember this, but it will always be here. The Court finds it appropriate, therefore, that your sentences be served consecutively, as follows . . . "

A wave of sighs and subdued whispers swept through the courtroom. Before Donnell could finish the sentencing order, a bevy of reporters leapt from their seats in the gallery and scurried into the corridor.

Cal stood on the courthouse steps a short while later and addressed the media and a gathering crowd of spectators who had just heard the news.

"It is my hope that Mr. Henderson will die in the Wyoming State Penitentiary and that the only time he leaves . . . is when they bury him," he stated.

Even on TV the moment registered with a biblical finality — an image that's been impossible for me to shake from memory. It's also a memory that I suspect Cal himself will never erase. It was he, after all, who had once argued zealously for Russell's protection as a boy but had now demanded — and won — two consecutive life sentences, effectively guaranteeing that Russell, then twenty-one, would never walk free again.

But if Cal harbored a secret of his own around the Shepard case, which didn't emerge until three years later while he was campaigning unsuccessfully for a fifth consecutive term as county attorney, it was this: In 1999, Albany County, Wyoming — the state's poorest jurisdiction — had only had enough money in its coffers for one trial of such magnitude, and even that required stretching the county budget to its limit. Although the Clinton administration had initially pledged its assistance, once the media and political spin began to die down, "the help never really materialized," according to Cal.

Cal had also raised the issue with the board of county commissioners, arguing fervently for the funds he needed to prosecute two capital cases fully, but he found himself overruled.

"If there was only going to be one jury trial," he later acknowledged, "there was never any doubt the person to be tried was Aaron McKinney."

That left Cal with little choice but to use the threat of the death penalty to strongly convince, if not coerce, Russell to accept a plea bargain. Court documents show that for six months Russell had steadfastly maintained that he was "not guilty" of Matthew's murder and had insisted he be given a trial. But because of the strict gag order in place, Russell had also been prohibited from discussing specifics of the crime — and his defense — with his grandmother and other family members.

According to Lucy Thompson, threats of the death penalty were constant as Russell's trial grew closer. "Every time I talked to Wyatt Skaggs he hammered the same thing," she recalled, "'Russell's going to get the death penalty if he goes to trial, Lucy.' From the beginning Russell always said he wanted a trial, so he could tell his side, and he wouldn't change that.

"But after they told us time after time, 'He's absolutely going to get the death penalty, you're in denial' — just like they kept telling Russell — I pleaded with him to avoid that. At least with a life sentence we we'd still have him alive . . . But the last time I went over to see Russell, he still said, 'No, grandma, I have to tell my part. If they give me the death penalty, then so be it.'"

Lucy said she didn't learn of the plea bargain until a reporter called her for a comment. "I kept telling the person who called me, 'That isn't true. Russell didn't take a plea, I was just over to see him.'"

Each time that Lucy recounted Russell's decision, I could sense her own impossible burden.

"How do you think I feel as his grandma?" she asked reflectively but without self-pity. "It was *me* who convinced Russell to accept that plea. If he was [sic] left on his own, that would never have been his choice. I just couldn't bear the thought of losing my grandson that way."

A week after Russell was sentenced, police handcuffed him at the Albany County Detention Center, escorted him outside, and loaded him into a vehicle for the hundred-mile drive to the state penitentiary in Rawlins.

As the car headed south on 3rd Street, he stared numbly out the window, watching his hometown and the only life he'd ever known slip away like fragments in a dream — but an irrevocable dream from which he feared he'd never awaken, not until he was dead.

Once the vehicle got out past the edge of town, Russell gazed at miles of empty, windswept prairie, losing himself there. A ranch fence with pine-log poles ran parallel to the interstate for many miles, stretching as far as he could see.

In the end Cal's strategy had succeeded: Russell agreed to change his plea in lieu of a trial that could potentially yield the death penalty. Yet Cal remained hopeful that Russell would testify against Aaron in his upcoming trial.

More than fourteen years later, however, the question remains: Did the enormous political, media, and financial pressures that overtook the Shepard case usurp Russell's right to a fair trial? Apparently that was another irrelevant detail in the media's relentless but often-superficial coverage of the story.

Several legal experts who commented at the time agreed almost unanimously that Russell's chances of receiving the death penalty for his role as an accomplice were slim to none. His case might also have had a different outcome, a manslaughter conviction perhaps, had the actual relationship between Aaron and Matthew been known publicly — a relationship of which Russell said he was unaware.

(In both the Daphne Sulk and Cindy Dixon killings the same court handed down manslaughter sentences that were considerably less severe than Russell's double life terms: In the former case Kevin Robinson was sentenced to a total of thirty-three years for a homicide in which he allegedly stabbed a pregnant teenager, then disposed of her body in the wilderness. As a result of "good time served," Robinson, who is said to have an excellent prison record, is currently eligible for parole. Dennis Menefee, the perpetrator in the Dixon case, served only four years of a four-to-nine-year sentence.)

JoAnn Wypijewski, who reported on the Shepard murder for *Harper's Magazine* and wrote an op-ed piece on the case for the *Los Angeles Times* six years after Matthew was killed, was the only journalist who seemed to notice the glaring disparities.

"Somehow that fact that Russell lost a mother — and Mrs. Thompson, a daughter — through another murder, a sex crime, never counted for much in all the stories about Laramie," she noted.

But during my research trips to Laramie over the years, I've heard the same opinion expressed numerous times, usually by women. Elaine Baker, who'd partied in Doc's limousine with Aaron and Matthew, and had also known Russell since he was a boy, stated pointedly:

> Where's the justice in this? [Menefee] is a grown man that took a woman out, raped her, threw her out in freezing . . . weather naked, and allowed her to stay out there and die a

slow, tortuous [sic] death. That must have been awful, to freeze to death.

And then you have these young kids [Aaron and Russell] that are barely old enough to be in a bar, on drugs . . . drugs controlling their whole lives . . . and [they] end up killing [Matthew] . . . And they're in prison forever, can never get out . . .

But this guy that deliberately took [Cindy Dixon] up there [to Rogers Canyon] and raped her and killed her spent four years in prison. What's wrong with this picture?

In the voluntary statement Russell had given to Detectives Rob DeBree and Jeff Bury after he was sentenced, he described how he felt when Aaron assaulted him at the fence. "Actually I was pretty scared," he said. "Scared of the same thing [sic] would happen to me, that was happening to Matthew."

The first time I'd read those words, I dismissed them as self-serving. But after I gained access to Russell's previously sealed defense files and family court records, I no longer doubted the intensity of the fear he said he felt after he got into the truck and drove to the fence with Aaron and Matthew.

As I studied the case files of public defender Wyatt Skaggs, I found confidential documents that seemed to shed light on Russell's silence — and why he might've been afraid to act more forcefully to stop Aaron from beating Matthew. A forensic psychiatrist who examined Russell while he was in jail awaiting trial reported to Skaggs that Russell was secretly terrified of Aaron: "He became more scared as [the crime] progressed . . . was too scared to even run away because McKinney knew where he lived . . . and won't admit he is scared of Aaron even now." The psychiatrist concluded that Russell "is not violent and . . . was scared to death."

I was reminded again that one of Matthew's friends, who had witnessed his extreme fear a couple of days before the attack, had overheard Matthew using those same words with Doc.

"[Matt told Doc] he was scared to death," according to the friend.

I also remembered what one of Russell's elementary school teachers had said: "The one thing Russell would never do is snitch — even when he came to school with bruises."

But Lucy, his grandmother, had her own thoughts on his passivity. She shared a story that she'd also related to reporter JoAnn Wypijewski.

Once, as a boy of twelve, Russell confided in his grandparents that he'd watched his mother, Cindy, suffer "a terrible beating" at the hands of a boyfriend. "The first thing we asked Russell is why he hadn't called us for help," Lucy recalled. "He told his grandfather and me that he just freezes on the spot, because if he does something he's sure to get a beating, too."

But Russell's regrettable history aside, he had done little to help his own cause following the attack on Matthew: He'd kept silent while Matthew was tied to the fence for eighteen hours, and he'd helped destroy evidence. At the time of his arrest, he'd also lied to police initially and then refused to tell them his version of events. And though he asked for a lawyer, even with his own attorneys he'd hesitated to speak out against Aaron.

Russell's unwillingness to incriminate Aaron helped seal his own fate. On the other hand, Russell must've surely realized that his chances of surviving in prison weren't good had he decided to talk.

I understood why both men had kept silent about certain subjects for their personal safety — each for his own reasons. Yet I was still baffled at how thoroughly the drug underpinnings of Matthew's murder had been concealed on all sides of the case.

It was not until Russell had served four years of his double life sentence that I became convinced he was telling the truth. His acceptance of responsibility for his actions, coupled with simple remorse, began to preoccupy me:

> It took me a long time to quit blaming [Aaron] . . . After a lot of thinking . . . about how I got here, I realized and understood that it was me. Whether influenced or not I

made my own choices and I chose to go along with what I thought was going to be a robbery. I involved myself by driving, tying [Matthew's] hands, and worst of all by not stopping it. I did that not [Aaron] . . . Although I made those decisions I did not murder Matthew, nor did I chose [sic] or want that to happen. But, not only am I paying for my choices, which I accept and deserve, but I am also paying for [Aaron's].

It was not only Russell's words that caused me to empathize with him more. I'd also spoken by then with a social worker who led an intensive group-style program that Russell had enrolled in at Nevada's High Desert State Prison — fittingly called "Victim Empathy." Due to her pledge of confidentiality, the social worker could only talk to me with Russell's consent. During a phone conversation, she quietly informed me that she'd been "impressed" by his participation in the group and that, in her professional opinion, he'd taken responsibility for his actions and seemed "truly remorseful." Part of the group process, she said, was Russell coming to terms with the pain suffered by Matthew and his family as a consequence of his actions.

I also stayed in regular contact with Russell himself, attended his high school graduation at the prison when he received his GED and honor-roll recognition, and periodically checked up on his other inmate activities as well. Surely I never imagined that I'd be Russell's lone guest at his graduation, but his grandmother and other family members hadn't been able to make the drive to Nevada. The somewhat unusual ceremony, with a couple of dozen prisoners clad in caps and gowns, was presided over by the warden, who picked up an electric guitar afterward and jammed on a few songs with the all-inmate rock band that provided entertainment for the event.

I had to remind myself that *prison is still prison* and *a life sentence is beyond my comprehension,* but it was reassuring nonetheless to see that Russell could avail himself of opportuntities to keep his humanity intact, and to mature as a man rather than degenerate.

Knowing how much the nation at large and the gay community in particular reviled Aaron and Russell as an indivisible pair — both said to be driven by the worst kind of hate — I hesitated to think where the rest of my journey might lead.

Had my growing concern for Russell compromised my ability to continue investigating the story as a journalist?

Though I kept those doubts to myself, I was not the only one to become sensitized to his plight. In late June 2004, after filming separate interviews with Aaron and Russell at the Nevada prison, I drove back to Las Vegas with *20/20* co-anchor Elizabeth Vargas. The first thing she said as I steered our rented Lincoln Navigator out of the parking lot was that interviewing Russell had been "heartbreaking." By contrast, after her ninety-minute interview with Aaron, she complained of feeling a stifling sense of confinement. As soon as it was over she was anxious to step outdoors for some sunlight and fresh air.

Earlier that day the prison's associate warden, "Mac" McBurney, had pulled me aside after he watched the filming of Russell's interview.

"What the hell kind of lawyer did that kid have?" he asked sourly.

"A court-appointed one," I replied.

I explained that since Russell and his grandmother had no financial resources he'd been represented by the county public defender — a lawyer whose alleged nickname among some of his Wyoming defense colleagues was "the Angel of Death."

Hard-bitten by decades of prison duty, with "few illusions about convicts or the justice system," Mac shook his head in disbelief that Russell, then twenty-six, was set to spend the rest of his life incarcerated.

"A shame," he added glumly. "He doesn't belong here."

PART FOUR

The Circle Unbroken

THIRTY-FIVE

Closet Case

In my early communications with Ted Henson, I could see that his grief over losing Matthew was still an open wound. Sometimes he became irritable and impatient with me for no apparent reason, but beneath his anger I sensed a tender melancholy.

"I know Matt was not perfect but none of us are," he wrote me in an email. "All I want is for the true meaning of Matt to come out, not something that is made up. Matt was far from [an] innocent person but he was a person that I loved and still do. No one in this world is innocent. Everyone has there [sic] little secrets."

For more than five years after Matthew's death, Ted kept many secrets of his own, safeguarding them along with Matthew's prized collection of old bottles and his high school class ring, and a necklace filled with Matthew's ashes given to him by the Shepard family. Ted said he had shied away from the media to protect his privacy, but also because several individuals had strongly advised him to conceal what he knew. Although he was reluctant to name those individuals at first, he eventually opened up.

Ted's candor made me realize that he was just as determined, in his own way, to learn the hidden truths behind Matthew's murder as I was — even when he found his efforts thwarted. He confided:

> i was doing some digging in laramie . . . and I was told to back off of [sic] it and leave things alone. and that person that told me that was doc [O'Connor]. doc told me that I should not come back to laramie and [should] move on with my life. well, I told doc that one day I am coming back. and that his idle threats mean nothing to me . . .

I decided to ask Ted about a comment that had been made to me by Elaine, the Laramie woman who recalled partying one evening in

Doc's limo and later at his home in Bosler with a small group that
included Matthew and Aaron. According to her description of the
threesome, Matthew was like "the little frail mouse, just no protection, and Aaron the cat, but yet Aaron has Doc the pit bull over him."
(I was careful not to identify Elaine by name to Ted.)

With little hesitation he responded:

> i think they said that because doc could corner matt and
> get matt to do anything doc wanted. doc . . . only admits to
> having sex with aaron, doesn't he? he sure didn't say anything
> about forcing matt one night into sex with him, did he?

Ted also claimed, "Doc ran the limos, yes, but he also ran guys . . .
When other guys wanted a male for the evening, well, Doc fixed that
up for them . . . [Doc] is dancing around with you."

Ted's revelations reminded me of my search for clues four years
earlier in the Denver demimonde, including the hustler bar formerly
known as Mr. Bill's. I asked Ted on several occasions how he knew
these things; I also explained that I couldn't write about them unless
he was more forthcoming.

In an email to me on February 18, 2006, he filled in another part
of the story:

> doc's relationship with aaron was basically a sex and drug
> issue . . .
>
> one night . . . we was [sic] in the limo, matt, me, aaron,
> and another older guy. I don't remember his name. all i
> knew about that guy was he was a president at some bank
> in Denver, that is all any of us knew about him. doc came
> straight out and told him in the limo that if he wants to
> play it is going to cost him. the guy then asked about me
> and matt, i told him no. but doc had us in the middle of
> nowhere. [He] stopped the limo [and] told me he wanted
> to talk to matt and me.
>
> doc said either we do this or we get left out where we
> was [sic]. and that he wasn't going no [sic] further until

after it was over. so we did it. in the back of a limo on the side of the highway.

when it was over and we went home i got out of the car, so did matt. doc told matt that matt owed [him] some money and that was payment. that pissed me off even more. i would not talk to matt for a couple of days after that.

Ted also had more to say about Aaron — and the incident when all four of them were at a Denver gay bar together. The bar was most likely Mr. Bill's, though Ted said he couldn't remember the name of the place, as some eight years had passed.

one guy when he came back [inside] I was drinking at the bar and he told me that he gave [Doc and Aaron] 40.00 so he could fuck aaron. i told him [Aaron] was nasty.

. . . aaron screwed matt at least 5 times that I know of. matt made me feel sorry for him a lot and I would do anything for matt. so when matt would go get high, his payment to aaron was ass, and aaron would only do it if aaron, matt and I would have a 3 way together.

as for me in the escort thing, i did it only 10 times with matt. and out of those, 6 times the limo was used. and aaron was there on almost all those times, but he was in the front with doc.

. . . it is not something that I am happy about either. in fact i feel trashy about it. if you want to . . . let [Aaron] know that I am telling you everything then do so . . . i wasn't scared of aaron then and i am still not. back then aaron was a loud mouth that could not back anything without help from someone.

. . . if you talk to russell tell him I said hello and i am going to do what I can [to help him]. and not to give up . . .

Ted mentioned something as well about Aaron's cousin "Bear" (Adrian McKinney), whose well-documented involvement with methamphetamine continued long after the Shepard case was over:

bear came to the bar in denver, and sold stuff there with
aaron from time to time. everyone knew that.

But Ted's statement about Bear also appeared to shed light on
another unresolved question. When I'd first interviewed Duane and
Rob, the bartenders at Mr. Bill's, they seemed convinced that *both* of
Matthew's assailants had hustled there, after seeing their photos on
TV. Actually, what Duane and Rob were most certain of is that the
men had come to the bar as a pair. Since I'd found no other information indicating that Russell had hustled or sold drugs — and Ted
acknowledged that he'd seen Bear at the bar but never Russell — I
concluded that the person Duane and Rob had probably seen at Mr.
Bill's, accompanying Aaron, was Bear.

If Aaron denied these truths again, Ted told me confidently, "Ask
[him] if he remembers a '90 Pontiac." Ted was sure Aaron, who loved
cars as much as he did, would remember his light blue Bonneville.

But Aaron had stopped talking to me by then. During our last
interview at a Nevada prison, he had let me know how infuriated he
was about the *20/20* report and what we'd revealed about his sexuality. Since I'd learned beforehand that he was very upset with me, I
asked one of the head correctional officers to search Aaron thoroughly
before leaving the two of us alone in an unguarded conference room
near the warden's office. Aaron had boasted more than once that,
with two life sentences, he had "nothing to lose," so I wasn't taking
any chances in the event he was concealing a razor blade or other
homemade weapon.

Ted's statement that Aaron "could not back anything without help
from someone" called to mind something Cal had mentioned years
before: "Aaron was dangerous if he had help."

I also remembered that Aaron, after pistol-whipping Matthew
repeatedly, had threatened to give Matthew's ID's to "certain people"
— an act of bullying in extremis.

"Hell, Aaron has no feelings," Ted wrote in another email more
than a year later, referring again to his joint encounter with Matthew
and Aaron. "I was there one night on a 3 way with Matt and Aaron,
and Aaron has no feelings, trust me. I [saw] that."

During an earlier interview with Doc O'Connor in one of his hangar-sized warehouses in Bosler — a few yards from the shiny stretch limo that both Aaron and Matthew liked to ride in — he was asked, "Did you think that Aaron was bisexual?"

"No, I know he's bisexual," he said. "There ain't no doubt in my mind. He *is* bisexual. Obviously."

Doc, who claims he doesn't know Ted and denies that he arranged for the sexual services of other males, was willing to talk about his decision to "out" Aaron, however.

"Did [Aaron] want you to keep his bisexuality a secret?" he was asked.

"Actually he did," Doc replied. "He said, 'Give me your word that this will never come out.'"

"Why was he so concerned about that?"

"Well, because he didn't want it to come out. And I told him, 'That's fine. No biggy.' The reason it's coming out [now] is because I've dwelt on this for . . . months and years; because he needs to face his reality in life, of what was going on at the time . . . Aaron was kind of like, in the closet . . . or [a] closet case, and he just never wanted to come out."

"Do you think [Kristen] knew he was bisexual?"

"I'd bet dollars that she knew."

"Why are you sure she knew . . . ?"

"She said that her [sic] and him and somebody else was in the same bed before. I can't remember the other guy's name. So, it wouldn't be a big deal. Everybody in the world wants to make bisexuality a big deal, or gay a big deal. And it's not really a big deal in Wyoming. It's just not really discussed."

We also asked Doc, "Why do you think . . . Aaron . . . was adamant about denying [to us] that he'd ever had sex with a man?"

He responded firmly, "I'll take a lie detector test any day you want about Aaron McKinney. Period . . . Aaron McKinney is not telling you guys the truth in that particular situation. It's not true. *Period*" (emphasis in original).

According to Stephanie Herrington, a Laramie woman who described herself as Doc's "part-time girlfriend" at the time of the murder, she,

too, had been with Doc, Aaron, and Matthew at an all-night party —
the same one Elaine recounted to me in telling detail.

My first conversation with Stephanie took place in a rickety, second-
floor apartment behind the Laramie post office, where she was living
at the time. She told me timidly that Doc had instructed her not to
speak with me unless he was present. But she said she wanted to talk
and didn't want Doc telling her what to say.

Later I interviewed Stephanie again at a sidewalk café in downtown Laramie — together with her ex-husband, Mark Herrington.
Both of them mentioned that Doc had tried to silence other people in
the past and that he sometimes made threats.

Eventually Glenn Silber and I filmed an interview with Stephanie
for *20/20*, but it wasn't included in the final program. We simply had
too many interviews to condense into a one-hour time slot.

Stephanie — like Elaine — said that Doc's party, which had started
in the limo and ended at his home in Bosler, took place "a couple of
weeks before [Matthew] was killed."

We told Stephanie that Aaron had informed us of his involvement
with methamphetamine and asked her, "Were you aware of that?"

"Yes," she answered.

"Is it your impression that Matt was into these things as well?"
Glenn probed.

"Yes, he actually tried to buy some from Doc . . . " she stated.
"Matthew Shepard actually bought some from Doc. He was giving
Doc money in the limousine at the time, so I know he was buying
drugs from Doc O'Connor."

When asked how she would describe Matthew, she said, "He was
an easygoing, loving guy, easy to get along with . . . But it wasn't a
hate crime."

"Is it your sense that when Matthew left [the Fireside Lounge] with
[Aaron and Russell] that he had drugs on him?"

"*Mm-hmm* [yes]," she nodded. "And they were trying to collect and
he wouldn't give it to them . . . They went out together because they
were interested in Matthew because he had drugs and . . . Matthew
didn't want to give them the drugs."

"How do you know this?" Glenn pressed.

"It's a fact."

"It's a fact?"

"*Mm-hmm.* I know he had drugs because he was trying to buy them from Doc . . . I was there when Matthew purchased the drugs from Doc."

"How long . . . before the attack?"

"That was the night when I was in the limo with them and I heard them talking about drugs and they were passing money in the back. I turned my head and looked at them."

Glenn pressed Stephanie again about her repeated references to "a drug deal gone bad."

"So is this just something that people [in Laramie were] talking about, that that's what they think happened?"

"I'm sure it happened," she said.

"You're sure it happened?"

"*Mm-hmm.*"

"Based on what?" Glenn continued. "Just talk to me. Based on what?"

"On what people said and . . . from what I know," she responded.

Later in the same interview, we asked Stephanie to revisit the night of Doc's party for us. She stated:

> Okay, we all met at the Buckhorn [Bar] . . . And then we just left the Buckhorn, gathered up in a limo and drove from there to [Doc's] house in Bosler. And then that's where they decided to play around . . . [Doc] asked me if I wanted to, with Aaron and Matthew, and I said "No," and that's when they paired off in . . . the small guest room that he had . . . Doc and Aaron McKinney and Matthew Shepard paired off . . . and did their thing . . . sexual activities.

But both Stephanie and Elaine agreed that the activities had started earlier in the limo, and that Doc had hired another chauffeur to drive that night.

"We were on the highway heading to Bosler and they were actually playing around in the back," Stephanie recalled. " . . . I was in the front seat and then [Doc] had the window rolled down . . . That's how I saw. I just turned my head and, 'Oops.'"

According to Elaine:

> I believe it started out with Doc telling Aaron and Matthew to do some stuff, and then Doc ended up getting involved in it later before we got to Bosler . . . It was mostly oral . . .
>
> I was trying not to look back at them too much because I just wasn't really interested in what was going on back there. But . . . the money exchange and stuff went on . . . before they started doing the oral . . . thing.
>
> I didn't really know exactly for sure what was going on at that point. Until Doc started talking . . . to mostly Aaron about . . . "You need to get my money from that son of a bitch" or something.

Earlier, I'd asked Elaine, "So what did you think was going to go on once you got up to Doc's place, given what you [saw] in the limo?"

"I have no idea," she responded, "I was pretty nervous about it. I didn't want to go up there. [Pause.] To be perfectly honest with you, I thought that there would be some drug exchange or . . . they were going to get some drugs or something. I thought that that's what would happen."

But Elaine said that while they were riding in the limo:

> I got the impression that Aaron already owed Doc some money for drugs or for — having sex with another man. And that Doc was unhappy about Aaron needing more [money] when they still owed him, and so they were kind of having a conversation about that . . .
>
> I can't really remember word for word . . . It was mostly Doc that did most of the talking. Aaron was just answering to Doc.
>
> . . . I just — I remember the feeling, the tense feeling in there. I remember the anger that Doc was expressing to

Aaron . . . something to the effect of, "I can't believe you let this son of a bitch get away with that . . . he owes me money."

. . . Doc would talk about [Aaron] being with somebody and, "Where's the money?" . . . Doc didn't try to hide it at all. He didn't try to hide the fact that Aaron was working for him. And Doc would come right out and tell people. He would offer Aaron to people, right, flat out. Flat out. He would just offer him . . .

I had [also] heard Doc and Aaron talking about pimping Matthew out . . . so I knew [the attack] wasn't because [Matthew] was gay and it made me angry. It made me really angry that it just blew over as a hate crime, that, you know, because Matthew Shepard was gay. It had nothing to do with Matthew Shepard being gay, nothing. It was about drugs and money.

. . . They were all friends . . . [but] Russell wasn't even really involved in that little clique . . . The main thing was — with Matthew and Aaron and Doc — was sex. And drugs.

During our interview with Stephanie, Glenn returned to the subject of drugs and asked Stephanie to tell us again what she remembered about the exchange of money.

". . . [As] I was riding [in] the limo and going to a party, [Doc] was exchanging money with Matthew Shepard," she said. "Aaron I'm not sure about at the time."

A few moments later Glenn inquired, "Has Doc ever told you, asked you, threatened you to . . . never talk about this stuff?"

"He said if I would confront a reporter by the name of Steve, not to mention anything to him because he's worried about this . . . "

"But was he saying that because he didn't want to really help Steve or because he wanted to protect himself?"

"I think to protect himself."

"Why are you telling us all this tonight, Stephanie?"

"Because I want to, I'm tired of hearing the false rumors that are going around about the gay hate crime and I just want to go on with my life and just . . . try to straighten it out."

"Are you worried about Doc at all trying to . . . come after you . . . or you think he'll just deny it? What do you think he'll do?"

"I'm — I'm worried. That Doc or somebody else might try to come after me."

"But you've just decided to sort of tell it like it is?"

"Yes. I want to tell it like it is and get the truth out there."

"Did you ever tell this to anybody else at the time, what happened?"

"No, I haven't."

"Not even your husband?

"My husband, he knew what was going on but he kept to himself about it."

Stephanie went on to say, "[Doc] wasn't being honest with me, I know that . . . Every time I've seen [him], he's told me not to say anything period . . . because he was worried about his safety."

But according to Stephanie and Elaine, Aaron and Matthew were definitely among the small batch of guests who stayed overnight at Doc's.

"The next morning, Doc decided to give them all a ride [back to Laramie], Matthew Shepard, Aaron McKinney, and the other people that were with them . . . " Stephanie said. "And then I stayed behind, which was really in the afternoon, and then he took me home as well."

THIRTY-SIX

An Easy Mark

Shortly after Russell arrived at the state penitentiary in Rawlins in April 1999 to begin his orientation as a "lifer," prison officials moved him into protective custody because he was apparently being preyed upon sexually. Word also came back to the jail in Laramie that Aaron could expect the same treatment when he got sent up.

From spring to early fall of that year, Aaron's court-appointed defense team — attorneys Dion Custis, Jason Tangeman, and Barbara Parnell — kept Cal Rerucha busy by filing scores of motions, most of them aimed at forestalling the possibility of a death sentence. On the public relations front, two Catholic chaplains from the University of Wyoming's Newman Center supported the attorneys' legal efforts by attacking Cal in the local press, mainly with the argument that capital punishment was a violation of Catholic doctrine. One of the priests, Father Roger Schmidt, was also Aaron's personal confessor.

As Aaron's trial drew closer, the animosity between Cal and the Newman priests intensified. Some Catholics in town, including a few parishioners at St. Laurence O'Toole — the church Cal had attended all his life — proposed that he be excommunicated.

A devoted Catholic, Cal said he was enraged by the priests' political maneuverings and their "complete disrespect for the separation of church and state." Not only did he fight back hard against their efforts, but by the time of Aaron's trial in the fall Dennis Shepard would join Cal in expressing his disdain. On the day Aaron was sentenced, Matthew's father stated in court:

> I find it intolerable that the priests of the Catholic Church
> and the Newman Center would attempt to influence the
> jury, the prosecution, and the outcome of this trial by their

castigation and persecution of Mr. Rerucha and his family by [their] newspaper advertisements and by their presence in the courtroom. I find it difficult to believe that they speak for all Catholics. If the leaders of churches want to speak as private citizens, that is one thing; if they say they represent the beliefs of their church, that is another. This country was founded on separation of church and state. The Catholic Church has stepped over the line and has become a political group with its own agenda.

But Dennis Shepard would also make a few statements in court that day that raised different concerns among some observers, including gay attorneys and activists who attended the trial. Some questioned whether the essential, time-honored boundary between an impartial prosecution by the state and the rights of crime victims had been breached in the Shepard case. Moments before he criticized the Newman priests, Dennis Shepard had acknowledged:

Mr. Rerucha took the oath of office to protect the rights of the citizens of Albany County . . . regardless of his personal feelings and beliefs.

At no time did Mr. Rerucha make any decision on the outcome of this case without the permission of Judy and me. It was our decision to take the case to trial just as it was our decision to accept . . . the earlier plea bargain of Mr. Henderson. A trial was necessary [for Aaron McKinney] to show that this was a hate crime and not just a robbery gone bad. If we had sought a plea bargain earlier, the facts of this case would not have been known, and the question would always be present that we had something to hide.

A New York–based gay activist, Bill Dobbs of Queer Watch, who was among the most vocal opponents of the death penalty while the Shepard case was in progress, later commented that he'd found "the very active role" played by Matthew's parents in the prosecution of

Aaron and Russell "troubling from a legal standpoint . . . insofar as justice was concerned."

After Russell's sentencing in April, Dobbs — who is also an attorney — had been quoted by the Associated Press.

"For us who are opposed to the taking of life, if we helped to stop an execution, that's a good thing," he said. "It's bittersweet. Matthew Shepard is not going to be brought back by this plea or this sentencing but it is a victory over violence because a possible execution, another death, has been averted."

But another gay activist, who asked not to be identified, said that it wasn't only the Catholic priests who had an agenda or a strong personal stake in the outcome of the case. According to the activist, the persuasive courtroom statements read by Matthew's parents at Russell's sentencing hearing and later at Aaron's trial had been carefully crafted with the help of gay organizations in Washington and Los Angeles.

With Aaron's trial scheduled to begin on the one-year anniversary of Matthew's murder in October, the eyes of the world would be on Laramie again. Meanwhile, in the intervening months, gay rights activists had continued to lobby for federal hate crime legislation, using the murder to rally support.

But the media frenzy around Aaron's trial would prove to be more intense than anything that had preceded it. More protesters came to town, requiring more security for blocks around the courthouse. In addition to the now-familiar band of hellfire fundamentalists led by the notorious preacher Fred Phelps, there were activists against the death penalty (ACLU, Amnesty International, Quakers); locals dressed as white-robed angels; numerous national and regional gay organizations, including Act Up, the Human Rights Campaign, Lambda, GLAAD, and Dykes on Bikes; and even a fringe group that staged a mock execution in front of the courthouse, showing Aaron being beaten to death just as Matthew had been beaten.

During a tedious jury selection process, Cal and the defense attorneys had screened hundreds of potential jurors.

Russell, who had been transported back to the county jail for the trial, was still expected to testify for the prosecution — which left many wondering if there would be any surprise revelations from the witness stand. But after the trial began, Russell changed his mind and refused to testify. His decision angered Cal, but with two consecutive life sentences Russell had little to gain and a great deal to lose: If fellow inmates got word that he had testified against Aaron, it would brand him forever as a snitch. (Russell later credited one of his attorneys, Jane Eakin, with helping him make that decision. Eakin, who today serves as a circuit court judge in the town of Rawlins where Russell is serving out his life terms, apparently understood the personal harm that could come to him if he took the stand.)

In his opening statement to the jury on October 25, 1999, Cal began: "Ladies and gentlemen . . . the evidence in this case will show that Matthew Shepard was 21 years of age. He was a student at the University of Wyoming, and he was openly gay. This case will not be about the life of Matthew Shepard. It will simply be about the pain, suffering, and death of Matthew Shepard at the hands of the defendant . . . Mr. McKinney." Cal promised to present evidence of kidnapping, robbery, aggravated robbery, and premeditated first-degree murder with malice.

By the end of the trial ten days later, he would sum up his case: "The only piece of the puzzle that is missing is Matthew Shepard. Even though he cannot testify, he fills every corner of the room . . . and I ask you to do justice." In actual fact, the trial itself offered few surprises yet it left many pieces of the puzzle missing — notably the story of how Matthew had become trapped in an underworld where Aaron was first his friend and occasional sex partner, then his competitor and adversary, and finally his killer.

Much as the media had done, Cal painted a picture of stark contrasts between Matthew's world and the world inhabited by Aaron and Russell. "Mr. Shepard paid in bills [at the Fireside bar]," he said, "he was immaculately dressed, he was polite, his shoes were shined, he had the air of someone who was educated and someone who was wealthy." Aaron and Russell, on the other hand, "spilled dimes and quarters to pay for a pitcher of beer, and they asked for the cheapest. Their manner is rough. They're not polite . . . and they look across the bar at Matthew Shepard. They could see he is . . . an easy mark."

Slowly and carefully, Cal outlined key facts and evidence in the case — most of them indisputable — and gave the jury a preview of the testimony they could expect to hear from his principal witnesses.

"At the conclusion . . . the evidence will be overwhelming for kidnapping, for robbery and aggravated robbery, and for premeditated first-degree murder with malice," he told the jury at the end of his statement. " . . . We will ask for your guilty verdicts on all three counts." (Robbery and aggravated robbery were merged as a single count.)

Laramie attorney Jason Tangeman, with whom Cal had faced off the previous year when he tried Kevin Robinson for the murder of Daphne Sulk, delivered the opening statement for the defense. (Cal and DeBree had earlier dubbed Tangeman "the Boy Wonder.") The thrust of Tangeman's message to the jury was that Aaron had admitted his involvement in Matthew's death, but it had not been premeditated:

> [Aaron McKinney] did not intend to cause the death of Matthew Shepard. Matthew Shepard did not die during the unbroken chain of events of a robbery. The defense . . . will argue that Matthew Shepard died during five minutes of emotional rage and chaos. The defense will argue that Matthew . . . died as a result of heat of passion. Matthew Shepard died because Aaron McKinney lost control of his emotions, and he became, in his words, furious.
>
> . . . You will hear his words in his confession. "I didn't mean to kill him."
>
> . . . The physical evidence will support and corroborate "I didn't mean to kill him" . . .
>
> The question that is going to be before you, the jury, is why it occurred. You . . . are going to have to answer that question for Aaron McKinney. Why was he furious?

Why did he blackout? Why did he feel possessed? Why did
Aaron McKinney do what he did?

During the weeklong trial that unfolded, Aaron's attorneys never
alluded to his personal relationship with Matthew, or what it involved.
On the contrary, Tangeman had declared erroneously in his opening
statement, "In fact, Aaron and Russell, when they leave for the bar
[on the night of October 6, 1998] have never even heard the name
Matthew Shepard."

The defense team also presented a very narrow view of Aaron's
sex-and-drug activities and what their impact may have been on his
explosive violence. Instead, both the defense and the prosecution
assumed — probably for the sake of their arguments — that Aaron
was straight, thereby reinforcing the impression that Matthew's
homosexuality was the trigger that set Aaron off.

Although Aaron's attorneys raised the issue of his chronic methamphetamine use and called an expert witness to testify regarding
the hyperactive behavior and paranoia that meth causes, they didn't
fully address the relationship between meth addiction, meth-induced
psychosis, and extreme violence. In addition, the attorneys steered
clear of Aaron's extensive dealing activities, including at least one trip
to a California meth lab.

I learned in the course of my investigation, however, that one of
Aaron's main drug suppliers — whose name never surfaced during the
case — was awaiting federal sentencing on interstate drug trafficking
charges on the night of Matthew's fatal beating in October 1998. The
supplier, who was arrested on a Nevada highway in 1997 with a Mexican
accomplice — while driving a vehicle loaded with meth and other drugs
— had been on his way back to Laramie with the shipment when he
was apprehended. According to several sources, Aaron and a few of his
friends had worked for the supplier, distributing product for him.

Knowing that the supplier had accepted a plea agreement and was
soon to be sentenced in federal court, Aaron lied to local police about
drugs to protect the supplier and keep his name out of the Shepard
case. Knowledgable sources have also alleged that a couple of high-
level police officers in Laramie were aware of Aaron's deception, yet

they had their own motives for allowing the story of an anti-gay hate crime to go unquestioned.

In retrospect, I recalled that a friend of Matthew from the Denver circle had said Aaron and Matthew reported to different "co-captains," and that both young men were at risk because of what they knew about the meth trade in Wyoming — and beyond. But my own investigation suggests there were more than two co-captains operating in Laramie at the time Matthew was killed, and that these rival operators weren't always competitors and adversaries; they cooperated when it was in their interest to do so. According to former dealing cohorts of Aaron, his Laramie-based suppliers and the "top dogs" in Matthew's Denver circle were well acquainted and, in some instances, were friends.

Just as global cartels engage in ruthless wars over territory, which are often followed by peacekeeping deals and the brokering of new business alliances, small-scale drug markets across the United States are characterized by similar turf battles and continually shifting power dynamics. In the late 1990s and early 2000s, Laramie — with its strategic location off I-80 — was no exception. During that same period, the buying, selling, and using of methamphetamine had also begun to ravage a staggering number of other communities across the country, including close-knit Native American reservations.

Cal Rerucha, who has spent most of the last decade on the front lines of the meth crisis as both a state and federal prosecutor, called it "the worst drug this country has ever seen." He also acknowledged, "Meth probably played a far larger role in the Shepard case than anyone understood at the time, including me."

Within a few years of Matthew's murder, authorities in Wyoming were attributing up to 70 percent of crimes to meth. Then-governor Dave Freudenthal, who had played a significant behind-the-scenes role in the Shepard case as US attorney, stated frankly, "It doesn't matter where we go in the state, meth is there. The whole issue is eating us alive." Wyoming's leading newspaper, *The Casper Star-Tribune*, agreed: "Wyoming faces no greater scourge than methamphetamine."

Statements like those would have been equally true in October 1998 when Matthew was killed, but the attention of the media, politicians, and special interests lay elsewhere.

By 2010, however, Barry McCaffrey, a retired four-star general who had served as Bill Clinton's drug czar from 1996 to 2001 — a period when meth abuse was spreading rapidly in the United States — spoke unflinchingly about the magnitude of the crisis.

"[Meth] is destructive of the human spirit like nothing we have ever seen," he said, ". . . it is rapidly addictive . . . [like] a blowtorch that melts your mental, spiritual and physical person."

To many observers of the Laramie tragedy (including me initially), Aaron's excessive rage could only mean one thing: pure hate.

In an article marking the murder's tenth anniversary in October 2008 ("Why the Shepard Murder was Different"), Cathy Renna, the former national news media director for the gay interest organization GLAAD — which played a decisive role shaping media coverage of the crime — emphasized again "the level of overkill, the brutality, and the graphic nature of the murder."

If, in truth, the attack on Matthew arose from an ongoing conflict over drugs and money and was further complicated by a covert sexual relationship between Aaron and Matthew, public understanding of what constitutes a hate crime deserves further debate. Ordinarily, hate crime is defined as a criminal offense motivated by bias — race, religion, gender, or sexual orientation — and usually involves violence, intimidation, or vandalism. But it is not the manner or degree of brutality or "overkill" that defines an act as a hate crime.

In thousands of execution-style killings that have occurred in Mexico as a consequence of ongoing drug wars, unprecedented acts of savagery have been committed, including decapitations, torture, and mutilation. Yet hate is seldom cited as the driving force behind these drug crimes.

It's also worth mentioning that at the time Matthew was killed and in subsequent years, up to 80 percent of the methamphetamine sold and used in Wyoming was produced not in homespun local labs but in Mexico or by Mexican cartels operating in the United States. Moreover, in the decade following the murder, there was a wave of other meth-related homicides across Wyoming, crimes notable not only for their grisly violence but their suspected links to drug rivalries.

According to the assessments of former drug czar McCaffrey in 2010, "[Firstly] meth is a cartel problem . . . [The cartels] are, hands down, the dominant criminal enterprise in America right now. They are the dominant criminal enterprise at the wholesale level in two hundred or more US cities."

These stark facts notwithstanding, the national outlook with regard to meth abuse has been improving over the past several years. Ambitious treatment programs and hard-hitting education programs warning of meth's corrosive impact are underway in Wyoming and many other states. Simultaneously, gay communities across the country have rallied to confront the crystal meth epidemic.

Nonetheless, I can't help but wonder why the wake-up call wasn't sounded earlier — and why the human injuries associated with meth addiction had to become catastrophic before we paid more serious attention. Such questions stand at the heart of nearly all tragedy, however, both personal and collective.

With the passage of fifteen years since Matthew's murder, it's now possible to see which truths were illuminated by Aaron's trial — and which remained hidden. It's also not inconceivable that Russell's case, and perhaps Aaron's, might have had a different outcome had their juries learned, as I did, that Matthew was part of an interstate meth-trafficking circle, and that the buying and selling of crystal meth was only one of the activities he and Aaron shared.

A few years ago, I finally gained access to court documents related to the case of former meth dealer Mark K, despite attempts by some officials in Laramie to prevent me from seeing them. According to several sources, Mark K established a friendship with Matthew in Denver in 1997 and eventually made him part of his dealing network in Laramie when Matthew moved there to attend the University of Wyoming. Mark K's name — like others — never came up during the Shepard case, but two and a half years *after* Matthew was killed, Mark K was arrested on a variety of interstate meth charges going back to 1997. By that year, he, Matthew, and several others in the Denver circle were already enmeshed in significant dealing activities together. According to those court documents, some Wyoming and Colorado cops were also implicated in those activities.

Although Mark K is said to be a born-again Christian now leading a very different life in a sparkling western suburb, law enforcement officers who arrested him in 2001 were astonished by the number of knives they found handily placed in the doorframes at his Laramie residence — along with an imposing sword over his bedroom door and several guns. TV cameras and in-house monitors also kept watch on the front of his house.

In 2002, when Matthew's one-time friend and associate stood before Judge Jeffrey Donnell — who three years earlier had presided over Russell's case — he claimed that knives were his "hobby." "I'm a part-time knife smith," Mark K said. "I refurbish knives, make knives."

But Donnell wasn't buying it. He pointed to Mark K's "admitted years . . . of delivery of this poison [to Laramie]" and described his home "set up like a fort, with surveillance cameras and weapons and all kinds of stuff."

Regarding Mark K's handling of monthly drug runs to the town since 1997, the judge added:

> By my mathematics . . . that adds up to around some-where between four and five pounds. That is a lot of meth. That is more than enough to ruin the lives of many, many people. And you're the guy that spread it around. That creates a consequence that you just can't walk away from . . . You're obviously a bright young man. And it is a real shame that you got yourself engaged in this kind of lifestyle; and even worse yet, that you chose to involve others in it with you . . .

Matthew was apparently one of the "others" whom Mark K helped initiate into the ruinous world of meth trafficking, but Matthew did not share his friend's luck of being "born again." Still, it isn't difficult to imagine that Matthew, had he lived, might have faced a similar harsh verdict from Judge Donnell.

Cal's best hopes for witness testimony in Aaron's trial rested with his former girlfriend, the mother of his son, Kristen Price. It was her convincing testimony that would help him win the day in court, yet she told only half-truths and left out key facts.

After my own initial interviews with Kristen, I began to examine what she'd withheld in her original accounts as well as her motives for helping to fabricate the alibi about Matthew making a sexual pass at Aaron and Russell. She gradually acknowledged to me that she'd lied to police and the media in the crime's aftermath ("I would have said or done anything . . . at that point to get [Aaron] out.")

But Kristen also revealed more about the ups and downs of her life with Aaron in Florida and Wyoming, including his anxiety over his sexuality; how she'd helped him deal meth; and why she'd lied about the extent of their drug involvement. Most surprising, however, was Kristen's personal suspicion — a suspicion shared by other key sources (including some in law enforcement) — about which individuals may have threatened Matthew on the weekend before the attack. Needless to say, the suspected individuals bear a strong resemblance to those alleged co-captains of the Laramie drug trade.

From the opening day of the trial, Aaron's attorneys tried to argue that he was really guilty of manslaughter, not first-degree murder. But the basis of their defense was split between four different factors. As Tangeman told the jury:

> Certainly you have the sexual advance itself [by Matthew Shepard] . . . starting to cause the anger. You have the drugs, and you have the alcohol fueling this. But there is a fourth piece of the puzzle that is important in this particular case. These are personal experiences that Aaron McKinney carried in his life. Personal experiences that he felt when this sexual advance was made on him.
>
> Aaron McKinney has [sic] some sexually traumatic and confusing events in his life . . .

Tangeman proceeded to describe episodes of homosexual abuse that Aaron had experienced as a boy of seven and then mentioned a later incident involving his cousin, though he didn't elaborate on the latter or explain its significance. It was also apparent again that: either Aaron's attorneys were ignorant about when he'd actually met Matthew the first time (in 1997), or that Aaron had withheld the truth from them.

> The question will be, did Aaron carry this with him 15 years later . . . At 15 [sic] Aaron's confusing, sexually traumatic past was still with him. He engaged in homosexual sex one time with his cousin.
>
> By age 20, just a year before he met Matthew Shepard, he is in Florida with his fiancée . . . Kristen. They go into a church . . . a gay and lesbian church. Aaron doesn't know it's a gay and lesbian church. He . . . sits with Kristen and he sees men holding hands and kissing, and he turned to Kristen and says, "We got to get out of here. I have got to go." And they go outside the church, and Kristen finds him sobbing outside, and she asks, what is wrong with you? Is there something in your past you need to tell me about? And he will say no. But she won't believe him.
>
> On October 6th, 1998, Aaron McKinney was certainly fueled by drugs and alcohol, but he was also haunted by a past. Haunted by a past that put him into a rage and triggered five minutes of emotional rage and chaos . . .
>
> The evidence is going to show that it is the . . . homosexual advance of Mr. Shepard that was significant to Aaron McKinney, that humiliated him in front of his friend, Russell Henderson. His past bubbled up in him. He was fueled by drugs. He was fueled by alcohol, and in his own words, he left his body.
>
> Did Matthew Shepard deserve to die? No, that is ridiculous. He didn't deserve to die. No manslaughter victim deserves to die . . . But that is what Aaron McKinney is guilty of, manslaughter. Five minutes of emotional rage

and chaos and Aaron McKinney committed manslaughter. Thank you.

While it's true that Aaron enlisted Kristen, Russell, and Chasity
in his improvised gay panic alibi, there are no statements by Russell
anywhere in the case record indicating that he saw Matthew make a
sexual advance on Aaron that "humiliated" him.

During this closely watched murder trial that offered little in the way
of surprise — the public, after all, had already been convinced of
Aaron's guilt a year earlier — the main question was whether he'd
receive the death penalty. But while the trial was in progress, the
moment that eclipsed all others was the defense team's attempt to
introduce a so-called gay panic defense. That defense was not only
rejected by the presiding judge, Barton Voigt, who today sits on the
Wyoming Supreme Court, but its rejection also came to define the
Shepard case itself — especially for gay Americans.

In an attempt to argue the point, Dion Custis, one of Aaron's attorneys, told Voigt, "We have never stated that this is a gay panic defense.
The only place that has ever come from are [sic] from these people out
here in the press. We are not putting on a gay, quote, panic defense."

But then Custis immediately reiterated what his co-counsel Jason
Tangeman had emphasized to the jury in his opening statement.

"The fact that Matthew Shepard made a sexual advance has relevance in this case, and it's a fact in this case," Custis said. "It's something that Aaron McKinney responded to."

By the time closing arguments were made in the case, little had
changed in the accepted narrative of the crime and its underyling
motives and circumstances. Cal Rerucha took the jury once more
through the alleged sequence of events when Matthew left the Fireside
Lounge with Aaron and Russell.

"Everything apperared to be normal," he explained. "There was
no disruption whatsoever. Why? Because McKiney and Henderson
were calm, cool, collected. They were pretending to be homosexuals.
Matthew Shepard left with them eagerly . . .

"What happened in this case? What happened to this . . . We have the deception where Henderson and McKinney pretended to be gay to lure Matthew Shepard out of the bar . . .

"In the area of the Walmart . . . that is when Mr. McKinney announced, 'Guess what. I'm not gay and you're getting jacked.'"

But those words, too, were part of the alibi Aaron had invented — and Kristen repeated.

During a lengthy interview that Russell gave voluntarily to police *after* he was sentenced to two life terms, Detective Rob DeBree asked him, "When it gets to the point where you are out by Walmart and Aaron demands the wallet, was there something that . . . it's gay week, or whatever, and you are getting jacked, can you remember . . . what that statement was . . . up there?

"I remember [Aaron] saying something like that, but I don't remember exactly what he said," Russell replied. *"I know he said, give me your wallet, you are getting jacked. I remember that"* (italics mine).

Attorney Dion Custis admitted that his client had murdered Matthew and he acknowledged once more that Aaron had used methamphetamine on a daily basis. But then Custis went on to underscore again Matthew's sexual interest in Aaron and Russell as a determining factor in the violence that followed:

> [Aaron and Russell] didn't deceive him. They didn't trick him. They didn't have to force him. They left. He had his own vehicle there. He could have gone anywhere he wanted to, but . . . he wanted to go with them. He was interested in them.
>
> . . . Aaron McKinney told you in his statement. That when they were driving from the Fireside Bar up to that fence, that Matthew Shepard was telling him that he could turn them on to drugs for sex. We know that Matthew Shepard was interested in this. We also know that it's consistent with his drug use. That he would say something to that effect. How else would Aaron McKinney know to say that? How could he make that up?

In his final remarks to the jury, Cal Rerucha was adamant that meth-amphetamine had nothing to do with the crime — a position he no longer holds today.

"The people at the [Fireside] bar . . . saw there was no apparent intoxication and no apparent situation, in fact, involving metham-phetamine," he said, "[and] you are left with a situation where that is what the [defense] lawyer wants you to believe, but that is not supported by the evidence in this case."

Nonetheless, Cal's parting words were eloquent and deeply felt — and they continue to reverberate today:

> Read Mr. McKinney's statement. It talks about fags and queers. Matthew Shepard was not an animal to be hung on a fence. Matthew Shepard was a human being. Matthew Shepard was somebody that loved and cried. Matthew Shepard is a person that deserves your dignity and your protection and your ability to follow the law in this case. You will do that and not be persuaded by half-empty jars. You will come back with a conviction for premeditated first-degree murder, robbery, and kidnapping because that is what the evidence shows.

While the jury was deliberating, Cal took a walk with his father, Elmer Rerucha, a retired cement factory worker, at the edge of a game preserve on Laramie's south side. A herd of antelope was grazing on the prairie.

"I was looking out my office window this morning, thinking that at one time they had hangings right in front of the courthouse," Cal told his father. "Everything seems to have changed, Dad, but maybe nothing has."

"You didn't go after the death penalty lightly, Cal," Elmer responded, as if he were reading his son's thoughts.

"You're never the same person after you make that decision, though. I've been sneaking off to church every other day, praying I know the difference between duty and revenge."

Elmer pondered the thought for a moment.

"When I got wounded in the Second World War, I was nineteen," he said. "Out there in the battlefield I used to pray for the same thing."

Cal pointed to the hills stretching out before them. "Whenever I come out here with the boys on our bikes, I think about that time when I was hunting with you. Remember the opossum? I couldn't have been more than ten."

Elmer raised one eyebrow as if he didn't remember — or at least he was pretending not to. "Which time was that?"

"You know which time. The opossum jumped up on my rifle and he's walking down the barrel, right there in my face, and I'm yelling at you to shoot him. And you wouldn't do it."

"Well, you lived to talk about it, right? He didn't bite you."

"Scared the hell out of me, though."

Cal's father glanced at him knowingly. "Something's gotta put the fear of God in us, Cal."

The jury of seven men and five women found Aaron guilty of kidnapping, aggravated robbery and second-degree murder, but not guilty of premeditated first-degree murder. His conviction could still bring him the death penalty, however.

The most unexpected turn in the case came when Matthew's parents agreed not to seek the death penalty in exchange for Aaron waiving all future appeals and refraining from talking to the media. It appeared to be a gesture of supreme mercy, but, in actual fact, multiple factors went into the decision to forgo the death penalty. Had the case proceeded to the penalty phase as required by Wyoming law, previously concealed information about Matthew, Aaron, and Russell — which had been inadmissible during the trial — could have been presented to the jury.

With the national media waiting in the halls of the courthouse and lining Grand Avenue outside, Cal had shown Judy and Dennis Shepard into the law library down the hall from his office. It was the only place where they could find some quiet refuge. The possibility that Aaron McKinney could be sentenced to die by lethal injection had infused an already-tense atmosphere with a new sense of urgency.

As soon as they sat down, Dennis spoke first. "Thank God we're almost done with it, Cal," he said. "I couldn't take another week of it."

Cal leaned his tired frame against the chair and looked at Dennis. After talking with Rob DeBree, Cal sensed what was coming.

Judy began slowly. "I need to ask you something, Cal."

"Of course, Judy," he replied. "Anything at all."

She hesitated at first, choosing her words delicately. "Would you mind if — after everything you've put into this — if we set aside the death penalty?"

Cal was more dazed than surprised. His eyes just held Judy's. Then he turned to Dennis, who quickly jumped in.

"You know how I feel about McKinney's lawyers, Cal — like we all do," he said. "They offered us life without parole, no appeals, no contact with the media. I just want this bastard to be forgotten."

Judy gazed strongly at Cal again. "What do you think about that?" she asked.

"*I don't want to hear it* is what I think," he answered reflexively.

"I know you're pissed at me about this, Cal," she went on.

"I'm not pissed at you, Judy. I just don't know how you can do this."

"Do you think less of me for asking you to do this?"

"No — *God, no*," Cal said. "I think more of you."

Cal paused and looked at Dennis, and then at both of them. "But this son of a bitch deserves to die. He'll do worse if he can get away with it, we all know that."

Judy nodded wearily and leaned in closer to the table.

"I lost my son, Cal, I'm not getting him back," she explained. "All I've been thinking is, what would Matt want? Can more be accomplished? Everyone's expecting us to be vengeful now. What if we step back from the violence, despite what they did to Matt? How will people look at this years from now?"

"We want them to remember Matt," Dennis added, "what he stood for."

Cal was silent for a moment as he took in their words.

"Whatever you both want, I'm with you on it," he told them. "This can't be about my personal emotions. It's a lot bigger than me."

Judy's moist eyes met his again. "It's bigger than all of us, Cal," she said.

THIRTY-SEVEN

Big Stone Gap

My investigative journey held many surprises, but none was as unlikely or unthinkable as the friendship I've witnessed between Ted Henson, Matthew's longtime friend and lover, and Russell Henderson, who is now in the fifteenth year of his double life sentence.

Ted had been telling me for a couple of years that he wanted to meet Russell in person. While the idea sounded noble in principle — it signified the hopeful possibility of atonement and perhaps forgiveness between one of the many victims of Matthew's murder and a perpetrator of the crime — I also felt wary about being the person to facilitate it. But Ted kept pressing me, insisting that we go together to the Virginia prison where Russell was then incarcerated.

Four years had already passed since Ted and I began communicating. He mentioned several times that he'd grown to trust me and was confident I'd give him the support he needed to face Russell. I was gratified by his trust but nervous just the same.

In a string of emails to me, Ted had written:

> The only problem I am having with Russell is, how come he didn't call someone when he got back in town [after they left Matt at the fence] . . .
>
> The only thing I want from Russell is for him to be honest [with] me and open. That is it. I have an open mind on hearing from him and what went on . . . I think he is just trying to find the right words to say to me . . .
>
> Matt was a very forgiving person and I know that everything I am doing Matt would have done the same if he was [sic] alive today . . .
>
> I would like to meet [Russell] in person and hopefully you would be there with me on that.

By then Ted had been having regular phone conversations with Russell's grandmother Lucy Thompson and had even sent her flowers. He said their talks about Matthew were "comforting" to him and that he could unburden himself easily about other issues in his life. As a single, gay parent who had adopted his son at birth, Ted felt Lucy "knows a thing or two about caring for kids."

"I think Lucy and I have gotten a very good friendship going," he stated in the same email. "I sent those flowers . . . because I was thinking about her."

But the following week, on Valentine's Day, I sensed again the rawness of Ted's emotions. He wrote about "how much love matt and i [had] for each other," yet went on to say:

> Matt was a person who could not hold his liquor too well at all. He always got emotional when he was drunk . . . [Matt] would be passed out and [he] would wake up like nothing happened . . .
>
> I guess I should have kept him under lock and key sometimes. Then none of this mess would have happened to him.

I wondered if Ted had confided in Lucy about this, as her daughter Cindy had suffered from alcohol and drug abuse, but I didn't ask.

I'd also been curious for months about Ted's motives for communicating with Lucy, and now Russell. I couldn't tell if it was a gesture of compassion, however unusual, or if there was an element of conscience or guilt that had prompted him to break his silence about Matthew.

Ted's reference to Matthew being passed out from alcohol reminded me of other incidents he'd recounted — times when he said Matthew became nauseated and physically ill from excessive drug use, especially crystal meth. According to Ted, these were problems Matthew had coped with while living in Denver in 1997–98 — before he moved to Laramie — and even prior to 1997.

> Matt's drug habit got worse and I could not take seeing someone that I love so much doing it, so I left him one day

while he was gone to a friend's house. Then Matt would call me telling me that he would not do drugs anymore, and if I did not come back he would kill [himself]. I knew that Matt did what he said he would do.

I waited a long time before I got up the courage to ask Ted if he knew any of Matthew's friends from the Denver circle. Though he'd grown to trust me, I was afraid of losing him as a source again. But someone from inside the circle had already admitted knowing Ted and confirmed his close association with Matthew in 1997–98.

When I finally broached the subject, Ted responded:

yes, i know of them. i had a feeling that carl [head of the Denver group] and matt messed around some, and i asked matt about it and all matt said was "no." but I didn't believe that at all. i can honestly tell you i have not talked to any of them in a long time . . . everyone thought of me as an ass, because i didn't do a lot of the things that they did and I tried to keep matt [away] from all of them.

On a crisp November afternoon in 2008 — a decade after Matthew's murder — Ted and I met at the airport in Knoxville, Tennessee. As I came through security, I could see him waiting next to a sun-splashed fountain in the middle of the terminal. Water cascaded over a long bed of rocks, simulating a mountain stream in the Ozarks. Three days later when I returned to the airport, patches of artificial snow would decorate the rocks, signifying another change of seasons.

Ted and I greeted each other warmly. I was relieved to find him smiling, with his round, boyish cheeks exuding a healthy glow. A few days earlier, as we were firming up plans to travel to Wallens Ridge State Prison in southwestern Virginia, he'd been suffering from migraines, chest pains, and other ailments. The last time I'd seen Ted face-to-face he was in a Memphis hospital recovering from surgery for congestive heart failure.

But he was determined to make the trip to meet Russell. He told me several times that he wasn't going to let his heart condition get in the way of that. We just had to make sure in advance that prison authorities would allow him to bring along his nitroglycerin prescription, in case he needed an emergency dose while we were inside. Once they agreed, Ted was good to go.

A short while after we left the airport, coasting in a rented white Pontiac across the Tennessee border into Virginia, we quickly lost ourselves in conversation — and without realizing it lost our sense of direction as well. Our two-hour road trip to the town of Big Stone Gap, home of the prison in the heart of Appalachia, turned into a four-hour, winding journey through the darkened hills of Jefferson National Forest.

Despite a lot of joking back and forth about who was to blame for getting us lost, I could feel Ted's trepidation about meeting Russell the next morning. He admitted as much but tried to reassure both of us.

"Look, I bet you anything Russell's feeling the same thing right now," he said. "Don't you think he's got a million things running through his mind, too?"

The following morning, after a country breakfast of eggs, bacon, ham, and grits, topped off with biscuits and gravy ("the Hungry Man Special") — Ted had picked at his food while I anxiously stuffed myself — we got in the car and climbed another steep road to the flattened hilltop where the prison sits.

Ted later recalled how he felt during the trip and afterward:

> On the plane ride there all I thought about was what to say and how to react towards [Russell].
>
> The morning of going to visit [him], I was very nervous and confused. I was wondering if what I was doing was right or was it wrong.
>
> But I knew I had to see Russell; he was one of the last people . . . to have touched Matt when Matt was alive.
>
> When we got [into] the prison there was a very long walkway to the visiting room . . . That seemed like the

longest walk. [I had] knots in my stomach but felt alright since Steve was there with me.

Once I met Russell, I just sat there and listened to [him] speak for a while. He said, "I'm sorry," I cannot remember how many times . . .

And Russell told me exactly what happened that night. I knew — I could see it in his eyes and face that he was not lying to me.

Russell and I spoke of a lot of things and the visit became more relaxed and more comfortable.

The reason I had to see Russell is because I felt the need and also [because] Matt was a very forgiving person. I felt that if Matt would have lived he would have done the same thing that I did and [gone] to see Russell.

Since my visit, and before my visit, we've written back and forth many times and are continuing to [write]. I feel that Russell is all I [have] left of Matt . . . I do believe in Russell and I am going to continue my friendship with [him] for the rest of my life. Or until Russell no longer wishes to stay in touch with me.

The hours of our prison visit hurried by. Three or four times I got up and went to the vending machines on the opposite side of the room, returning with cans of soda, chips, candy bars, and other junk food. But really I just wanted to leave the two men alone for a while and allow them some semblance of a private conversation without me noting every word they uttered. For this same reason, I won't attempt to reproduce here the many things that were spoken about that day, with the exception of one brief exchange that has stayed with me over the past five years.

Early in the visit, Ted looked at Russell sternly. Ted's face was drained of color and his lips were trembling slightly, as he confronted Russell with the question that had been troubling him more than any other.

"Why didn't you let someone know Matt was out there — just call someone?" Ted asked in a muted voice.

Russell nodded gently for several seconds, yet the two men never broke eye contact.

"It's the biggest regret of my life," he said. "It's something I think about every day and wish I could change."

Ted continued to stare at Russell. Gradually his face began to soften and the blush returned to his cheeks.

I was at a loss about how to interpret this moment — and even how to "report" it.

But later that afternoon when the presiding officer announced over the loudspeaker that visiting hours were over, I said my good-byes to Russell and then watched as Ted leaned over the low barricade that ran down the middle of the table, separating visitors from inmates. As the two men shook hands, Ted extended his other arm around Russell and hugged him warmly. I saw Russell reciprocate but then I looked away, aware again that this shared gesture belonged to them alone.

THIRTY-EIGHT

Missing Pieces

During the years that I've been preoccupied with Matthew's murder, I've come to believe that the complex truths of his tragedy — and the parallel tragedies of Aaron and Russell — have a universal meaning that defies and transcends the politically correct mythology that's been created as a substitute. There's no doubt that the violence inflicted on Matthew triggered a national awakening about the harsh realities of anti-gay hate, just as there is no doubt that other positive developments followed on the heels of his murder, including a long-overdue expansion of civil rights — a mission that remains incomplete as of this writing. But the more I learned about Matthew's life and his suffering, the more convinced I became that clinging to a partly false mythology could never yield the subtler, more powerful meanings of his sacrifice. It would also be a disservice to Matthew's memory to freeze him in time as a symbol, having stripped away his complexities and frailties as a human being.

An obvious paradox is that I didn't know Matthew personally. Nonetheless, I grew suspicious of the truncated portraits of him that I found in media accounts and official records. It seemed as if everyone who knew Matthew (and many who did not, me included) had their own take on his vulnerabilities and misadventures and how they all came to be. Over time, a handful of Matthew's friends — together with the insightful public testimonies of his parents — persuaded me of the value that could be gained from peering into those corners of his life that have been invisible or mostly cast in shadow, and attempting to understand the part they may have played in the tragedy of October 6, 1998.

Early on, I'd read a variety of remembrances by people who had known Matthew intimately, which only amplified my interest in him. Though these statements sometimes obscured as much as they revealed, they invited further exploration of Matthew as a human being.

One particular quote that I'd come across in a 1999 *Vanity Fair* article stayed with me over the years — made by Romaine Patterson, a lesbian friend of Matthew.

"Matt had emotional scars — he had faced this kind of attack throughout his life," she said. "He was a perpetual victim. That's how he became the person that he was."

Not only was I curious about her mention of "emotional scars . . . throughout his life," but I also noticed that it differed somewhat from an observation Matthew's father had made. "Violence was not part of [Matt's] life until his senior year in high school," Dennis Shepard stated. He spoke explicitly of "the mental anguish that Matt dealt with on a daily basis after his rape in Morocco."

Yet Matthew's mother had commented at various times that "he never had a best friend"; "he had a real restless, searching quality"; and "I think he always felt out of place." Five years after the murder, though, Judy noted that her son had lived his life true to himself. "[Matt] didn't live a lie," she told a reporter for the *Casper Star-Tribune*. "He was happy in his skin. I don't know how many people can say that."

Still, I continued to reflect on Romaine's belief that Matthew "became the person that he was" because he'd been "a perpetual victim." Like Tina Labrie, Ted Henson, Lewis Macenze, and other confidants of Matthew, Romaine seemed to be suggesting that her friend's emotional scars had older roots than Morocco.

My reason for probing into this sensitive territory is that I hoped to understand what may have been behind Matthew's addiction to drugs and alcohol; what drew him into the Denver circle; and, ultimately, why he may have befriended Aaron.

Lodged in the back of my mind was the timeworn metaphor Cal had used in court during the Daphne Sulk case. "Some people have said that Daphne was not afraid of [her killer]," he'd told the jury. "Well, a fly is never afraid of the spider's web until it's too late."

According to informed sources who requested anonymity on the subject of Matthew's childhood and adolescence — presumably because some records remain sealed and others have been expunged

— Matthew was a victim of sexual abuse and molestation as a boy and as a teenager. Just days before he was killed, while in the throes of fear and depression, he identified three of the perpetrators. According to my sources, all were adult males: an alleged member of his Casper church, an older friend whom he'd turned to for guidance, and a relative (not a member of his immediate family).

These same sources believe it was these earlier traumatic experiences — and not Morocco — that precipitated Matthew's history of psychiatric ailments and self-medicating with alcohol and drugs. Apparently, his wounds from being sexually victimized also manifested in another common, but tragic pattern: The victim becomes a perpetrator himself.

At age fifteen Matthew was arrested for molesting two eight-year-old boys in his Casper neighborhood. According to a relative of one of the boys, Matthew received counseling to help him deal with the incident; he'd also attempted suicide and been hospitalized, she said. But a former Casper police officer who was assigned to the case expressed discomfort at how the later attack in Laramie had been mishandled by the media, as well as the fact that Matthew's juvenile arrest record had been quietly concealed. (Court files show that on February 25, 1999, Cal filed a motion requesting that "the defense be barred from reference to or testimony regarding any information . . . which may be contained in police reports regarding Matthew Shepard, obtained from the Casper Police Department as well as juvenile records of Matthew Shepard obtained from any Natrona County [Wyoming] court records.")

As a result of these and other discoveries, my view of Matthew as a perpetual victim took on new meaning, but not for the reasons suggested by the popular mythology. I also came to see some of the personal insights of his family and friends in a new light.

"Whenever [Matt] learned of someone suffering, it affected him personally," his friend Tina had said. As a witness to his deepening crisis in his final days, she also recalled that he'd been "in a lot of emotional pain . . . wishing he had more security . . . feeling very alone, lonely, isolated."

It was no longer such a mystery to me why Matthew had fallen in with an improvised "family" of dealers — or why he'd become a dealer himself. Since his teen years, Matthew had used a variety of drugs to cope with his isolation, not to mention the pain of being victimized sexually. But as a part of the Denver circle he gained a sense of belonging and even empowerment, however illusory or short-lived. His dealer friends whom I interviewed talked about how much they respected and looked up to him; and I imagine he, in turn, mistakenly looked to them to provide the security he longed for.

With this new understanding, I reconsidered some of the insights offered by Matthew's father — and others.

"[Matt] was naive to the extent that, regardless of the wrongs people did to him, he still had faith they would change and become 'nice,'" Dennis Shepard had said. "They would hurt him and he would give them another chance." He also spoke of his son as "the perfect nego-tiator" who "would walk into a fight and try to break it up. He could get two people talking to each other again as no one else could."

Tragically, these same attributes could be dangerous if you were negotiating in a criminal underworld — or with Aaron McKinney while he was strung out on meth.

EPILOGUE

In April 2013 I returned to Wyoming for my last visit in connection with the writing of this book. Over the years the trip had become a welcome — and by then necessary — ritual: pick up a rental car at the Denver airport, drive north on I-25 to Fort Collins, and then head northwest on Highway 287 to Laramie.

No trip to Laramie would be complete if I didn't check in with Cal Rerucha and his family, and with Russell's grandmother Lucy Thompson. I'd made several good friends and met many acquaintances there, but it was the Rerucha family and Lucy who invariably made me feel welcome in their homes and their lives. Despite the sensitive nature of my research and reporting — and my continual delving into their lives — I was never made to feel like an outsider once they grew to trust me. On the contrary, their steady friendship encouraged me to pursue the truth wherever it might lead, at whatever cost.

Whenever time allowed, I'd also spend a day visiting Russell — initially at the prison in Torrington, Wyoming; and more recently at the state penitentiary in Rawlins, where he's expected to remain for the foreseeable future, if not the rest of his life. Aaron broke contact with me in 2005 for reporting on "that sex stuff" and for mentioning on TV that he has a son.

As I drove through Fort Collins that afternoon, I could see the skies beginning to change dramatically. Earlier in the day Denver had appeared to be in the throes of spring, but in parts of northern Colorado and Wyoming a late-winter snowstorm had already hit. It was the third week in April, which meant little if you were trying to predict what kind of weather you'd encounter in the Rockies.

Perhaps I'd made a mistake not renting a four-wheel-drive SUV. If I got stuck on the sixty-five-mile stretch of highway between Fort

Collins and Laramie — an expanse of rugged, hilly plains — it would be awhile before help came. I also wondered if the Wyoming interstate would be open the following day, so I could make the drive to visit Russell at the penitentiary. The car radio was saying that portions of I-80 had been closed due to heavy winds and snowfall.

I'd spent time in Wyoming during every season and had learned from the locals to pay close attention to the weather — especially the fierce winds.

Oddly, though, as I left Fort Collins and drove north on 287, I had only a dim sense that a thirteen-year journey would soon end. I was finishing a story, *yes*, but the story and its characters had become etched into my life, as had Wyoming and its "hometown."

I'd watched from a distance as Cal's two sons had grown up: from enthusiastic teenagers to hardworking college students, and, now, mature young men with careers. I'd sat in Lucy's living room when it was overflowing with kids and she was still running her beloved daycare program, but also in more recent days when her leg has been crippled by disease and a pensive quiet hangs over her home. And I remembered Russell as a young "lifer" in his early twenties when we'd first begun to talk, and reminded myself he was now approaching the age of thirty-six.

They were no longer characters in a story. They'd become friends whose lives had enriched me. It was true that the story I'd written would end shortly, but on that cloudy afternoon with the plains blanketed in snow in every direction, I knew with certainty that I'd return to Wyoming — not only to see friends and feed my nostalgia, but also to visit Russell. As a gay man with no sons or daughters of my own — and an intimate understanding of the tragedy that took Matthew's life and sent Russell away for the remainder of his — the least I can do is offer my friendship and do some small part to see that he, like Matthew, is not forgotten.

In that stark but bracing landscape — and again the following day as I drove to the prison in Rawlins — I conjured up some familiar ghosts. I thought of Matthew and his love of Nelson Mandela, and the dream that he'd one day work in human rights. I missed this young man whom I'd never known, whose father once called him Dandelion Head and the Bad Karma Kid.

I remembered just a few of the lost and the fallen, and the dead whose voices still speak.

The pregnant girl, Daphne Sulk.

Steve Heyman, the professor whose murderer has never been found.

Denise McKinney, a mother who departed too young.

Cindy Dixon, frozen in the falling snow.

High on a ridge I saw a long row of tall, white windmills, spinning slowly.

I knew this highway, I'd driven it many times before. Soon I'd be sitting with Russell in a windowless, fluorescent-lit room with vending machines, trying to put some of the ghosts behind us.

And then I'd be back on the road again, traveling home.

LIST OF SOURCES

Subjects interviewed for *The Book of Matt* and the ABC News *20/20* story produced by author Stephen Jimenez:

Cal Rerucha — Former County Attorney, Albany County, Wyoming. Currently the Carbon County Attorney.

Aaron McKinney

Bill McKinney — Father of Aaron McKinney.

Adrian "Bear" McKinney — Cousin of Aaron McKinney

Kristen Price — Former girlfriend of Aaron McKinney.

Kim Bierema — Mother of Kristen Price.

Russell Henderson

Lucy Thompson — Grandmother of Russell Henderson.

Linda Flynn — Aunt of Russell Henderson

Pat Flynn — Uncle of Russell Henderson.

Lisa Johnson — Aunt of Russell Henderson.

Carla Henderson — Half Sister of Russell Henderson.

Stacey Teel — Half Sister of Russell Henderson.

Wyatt Skaggs — Former Albany County Public Defender and Lead Counsel for Russell Henderson.

Paul Sonenberg — Legal Assistant, Henderson Defense Team.

Priscilla Moree — Investigator, Henderson Defense Team.

Tim Newcomb — Appellate Counsel for Russell Henderson.

Chasity Pasley — Former girfriend of Russell Henderson.

Linda Larson — Mother of Chasity Pasley.

Rod Pasley — Father of Chasity Pasley.

Doug Larson — Uncle of Chasity Pasley.

Lois Pasley — Grandmother of Chasity Pasley.

Ben Fritzen — Former Detective, Laramie Police Department. Currently Lieutenant and Head. Administrator, Albany County Detention Center.

Dave O'Malley — Former Laramie Police Commander. Currently the Albany County Sheriff.

Rob DeBree — Former Sergeant Detective, Albany County Sheriff's Office. Currently the Albany County Undersheriff.

Flint Waters — Former Agent, Wyoming Division of Criminal Investigation and Former Deputy, Albany County Sheriff's Office.

Lynne Callaghan — Former Agent, Wyoming Division of Criminal Investigation.

Jason Tangeman — Attorney for Aaron McKinney.

Dion Custis — Attorney for Aaron McKinney.

Maribeth Galvan — Attorney for Chasity Pasley and Kevin Robinson.

Kevin Robinson — Convicted of manslaughter in the 1997 murder of Daphne Sulk.

Jean Shaw — Mother of Kevin Robinson.

Stacy Simpson — Sister of Kevin Robinson.

Buddy Carroll — Attorney for Kevin Robinson

Judge Jeffrey Donnell — Presiding district court judge in the cases of Russell Henderson, Kevin Robinson, Dennis Menefee, Mark K. Rohrbacher, etcetera. Richard Bohling — Current Albany County Attorney.

Ken Brown — Former Deputy County Attorney, Albany County, Wyoming. Current Deputy County Attorney, Goshen County.

Ken Haselhuhn — Former roofing co-worker of Aaron McKinney and Russell Henderson.

Judy Shepard — Mother of Matthew Shepard.

Sean Maloney — Former Attorney for the Matthew Shepard Foundation and Current Member of the US House of Representatives, representing District 18 of New York State.

Ted Henson — Friend and Lover of Matthew Shepard.

Tyler Kern — Friend of Matthew Shepard.

Alex Trout — Friend of Matthew Shepard.

Walt Boulden — Friend of Matthew Shepard.

Ronnie Gustafson — Friend of Matthew Shepard.

Tina Labrie — Friend of Matthew Shepard.

Phil Labrie — Friend of Matthew Shepard.

Chris Cesko — Friend of Matthew Shepard.

Ryan Bopp — Friend of Aaron McKinney and Kristen Price.

Katie Bopp — Friend of Aaron McKinney and Kristen Price.

Cory Warpness — Friend of Aaron McKinney.

David Farris — Friend of Aaron McKinney.

Melinda Farris — Mother of David Farris and friend of Aaron McKinney. Now deceased.

Dale Harper — Drug dealer who was convicted of a 1996 drug-related murder in Albany County, Wyoming. Former cellmate of Aaron McKinney. Now deceased.

Freya Harper — Widow of Dale Harper.

Daisy Harper — Daughter of Dale Harper.

Faye Harper — Daughter of Dale Harper.

Trudy McCraken — Former Mayor of Laramie.

Deana Johnson — Friend of Lucy Thompson and Russell Henderson.

Gene Pratt — President of Latter Day Saints congregation in Laramie and friend of Lucy Thompson and Russell Henderson.

Shaundra Arucby — Former girlfriend of Russell Henderson.

Matt Mickelson — Former owner, the Fireside Lounge.

Doug Ferguson—Former bouncer, the Fireside Lounge.

JoAnn Wypijewski — Journalist.

Bill Dobbs — New York-based gay rights activist who opposed the death penalty for Aaron McKinney and Russell Henderson.

Andrew Sullivan — Journalist and Gay Advocate.

Jason Marsden — Former journalist and currently the executive director of the Matthew Shepard Foundation,

Charles Levendowski — Journalist for the Casper Star-Tribune, Casper, Wyoming. Now deceased.

Mary Vrooman — Owner of the former Overland Restaurant, Laramie, Wyoming.

Jason Palumbo — Former bar owner, Laramie, Wyoming.

Stephanie Herrington — Former girl-friend of Doc O'Connor.

Mark Herrington — Ex-husband of Stephanie Herrington.

Elaine Baker — Friend of Stephanie Herrington.

Christopher Baker — Son of Elaine Baker and friend of Aaron McKinney.

Lynell Rayos — Daughter of Elaine Baker.

Jay Pinney — Friend of Aaron McKinney. Committed a murder at the age of twelve in his hometown of Riverton, Wyoming.

Norman K. Mabbitt ("Little Norm") — Former driver for Doc's Class Act Limousine Sevice.

Marge Bridges — Former driver for Doc's Class Act Limousine Service.

Tom Pagel — Former police chief, Casper, Wyoming, and former director of the Wyoming Division of Criminal Investigation.

Travis Brin — Friend of Aaron McKinney.

Justin Pinter — Former bartender, the Library Bar.

Brad Kaufman — Former bartender, the Library Bar.

Scott A. Barker — Former Laramie resident who was a victim of attempted murder.

Jason Spencer – Former bartender at the Buckhorn Bar and confessed methamphetamine dealer who served time in federal prison.

Deb Thomsen — Editor, The Boomerang.

Tillma Giesse — Ex-wife of former police officer Bob Giesse of the Albany County Sheriff's Office.

John Earl Baker, Jr. — Auto mechanic and repeat methamphetamine offender.

Robert Bromley — Currently serving long prison term for multiple drug offenses. Communicated with Mr. Bromley through his mother, Norma Bromley, and his appellate attorney, Clifford Barnard.

Teri Kindler — Proprietor of Laramie tattoo shop.

Karol Griffin — Author and former Laramie resident.

Len Munker — Criminal defense attorney and former chief public defender, state of Wyoming. Now deceased.

Robert Vogele – Laramie teacher and father of the late Dale Vogele, a tattoo artist who designed Aaron McKinney's "Dopey" tattoo and died in 1999 of a drug overdose.

Debra Hinkel — Owner, the Ranger Motel and Bar.

Jerry Coca, Jr. – Auto mechanic and coach at the Laramie's Cathedral School. Now deceased.

Brian Gooden — Friend of Matthew Shepard.

Lewis Macenze — Friend and lover of Matthew Shepard.

Michele Rodriguez — Friend of Cindy Dixon (Russell Henderson's mother).

Shannon Shingleton — Friend of Aaron McKinney and Matthew Shepard.

Jenny Malmskog — Friend of Aaron McKinney.

John Mills — Friend of Aaron McKinney.

Rick Rawson, Ph.D. — Psychologist and substance abuse expert, UCLA Medical Center, Los Angeles, California.

Duane Powers — Former manager and bartender, Mr. Bill's, Denver, Colorado.

Rob Surratt — Former bartender, Mr. Bill's, Denver, Colorado.

Orelius Berkel ("Shadow") — former DJ, the Fireside Lounge.

Nicole Cappellen — Friend of Russell Henderson and patron at the Fireside Lounge.

Mike St. Clair — Patron at the Fireside Lounge.

Mark Beck — Former detective, Albany County Sheriff's Office.

Father Roger Schmidt—Former chaplain, the Newman Center at the University of Wyoming.

Judge Thomas Mealey – Former circuit court judge, Evanston, Wyoming.

Diane Galloway – Former director, Wyoming substance abuse program.

Glenn Duncan — Friend of Aaron McKinney.

Chris Hoogerhyde — Former bartender, the Silver Dollar Bar, Cody, Wyoming.

In addition, the author interviewed more than twenty other sources who requested anonymity. Some of them appear in this book under pseudonyms.

ACKNOWLEDGMENTS

This book had a long gestation and required the help, expertise, patience, and generosity of many individuals, to whom I am immensely grateful.

Without the honesty and personal integrity of one man — prosecutor Cal Rerucha — *The Book of Matt* would not have been written. It was he who cautioned me about jumping on "the media bandwagon" and encouraged me to search out the difficult truths of the Shepard murder case before authorizing myself to write about it. I extend my deepest gratitude to Cal, his wife Jan, and their sons, Luke and Max, for more than a decade of friendship and hospitality.

This book has also come to fruition because of the vision and tenacity of my publisher Chip Fleischer and his dedicated staff at Steerforth Press: Helga Schmidt, Devin Wilkie, and Rebecca Hecht. I'd also like to thank the entire Random House sales force for their invaluable pre-publication feedback, and for spreading the word about *The Book of Matt* to booksellers everywhere.

Michael Denneny, my editor, guided me through many phases (and pitfalls) of writing this book with his salty wisdom and wit — and the fierce poise of a Buddhist master. Time and again he whacked me with his little baton to be sure I was awake and paying attention. Many thanks, Michael.

Very special thanks to my attorneys Richard Hofstetter and Mark Merriman, and legal assistant Lise Horton at Frankfurt Kurnit Klein and Selz; and to my extraordinary agent Kim Witherspoon and her colleagues at Inkwell Management. Thank you, Kim and Richard, for your counsel and friendship.

My fond appreciation as well to my publicist Scott Manning, cover designer John Gall, copy editor Laura Jorstad, compositor Peter Holm, social media consultant Karen Louie Joyce; and to William Callahan and Carla Jimenez.

I have numerous people to thank in Wyoming — for favors large and small — but especially for their generous cooperation over the years (in alphabetical order): Elaine Baker, Orelius "Shadow" Berkel,

Ken Brown, Lynne Callaghan, Jerry Coca, Jr. (deceased), Kevin Cox, Dion Custis, Judge Jeffrey Donnell, Glenn Duncan, Melinda Farris (deceased), Doug Ferguson, Linda and Pat Flynn, Ben Fritzen, Mary Elizabeth Galvan, Tillma Giesse, Tim Gosar, Karol Griffin, Ronnie Gustafson, Alyson Hagy, Stephanie Herrington, Debra Hinkel, Lindsay Hoyt, Deanna Johnson, Lisa Johnson, Jim Kearns and the University of Wyoming News Service, Tyler Kern, Tom Mealey, Trudy McCraken, Bob McKee, Bill McKinney, Matt Mickelson, Priscilla Moree, Len Munker (deceased), Tim Newcomb, Thomas "Doc" O'Connor, Dave and Jennifer O'Malley, Jason Palumbo, Gene Pratt, Ruth Proctor (deceased), Janice Sexton, Jean Shaw, Susan Simpson, Wyatt Skaggs, Paul Sonenberg, Mike St. Clair, Deirdre Stoelzle, Jason Tangeman, Deb Thomsen, Michele Trabing, Robert Vogele, Charlene Wallen, Flint Waters, and Julie Yates. (There are quite a few others whose names I'd like to include here, but they have asked me to omit them for their protection and/or privacy.)

Three men whose stories are told in *The Book of Matt* — Russell Henderson, Ted Henson, and Lewis Macenze — have left an unexpectedly strong imprint on my life. I thank them for their astounding candor and the gift of their friendship. In the same spirit, I'd like to express my appreciation to Tina Labrie, Kristen Price, Chasity Pasley — and especially Joan, a confidante of Matthew Shepard who agreed to be interviewed at great personal risk.

A substantial portion of the research and investigation documented in this book was made possible by ABC News *20/20* and the show's Executive Producer, David Sloan. I also extend my sincere thanks to Elizabeth Vargas, Carla Delandri, Richard Gerdau, Sara Holmberg — and especially to my reporting and producing partner Glenn Silber. (*The Book of Matt* would not have been possible without you, Glenn.)

My heartfelt gratitude to Sharon Dynak, Raymond Plank, Ruthie Salvatore, and the staff of the Ucross Foundation — and to Michelle Sullivan and Elizabeth Guheen — for simultaneously nourishing my love of writing and the breathtaking beauty of Wyoming. I'm profoundly grateful as well to Larry Schiller, Greg Curtis, the staff of the Norman Mailer Center, and my fellow writers in the 2012 nonfiction fellowship program. In your company last summer, this book finally took flight.

I was equally blessed by the behind-the-scenes support of several individuals at critical junctures in the writing of this book: attorney Robert H. Montgomery, Jr. and Georgetown University professor Thomas M. King, S.J. (both deceased); Dick Nodell and Karin Aarons, who have been my longtime teachers and never fail to light my way; Pamela Talese, Andrew Boylan, and Ann Donaldson, who provided research and investigative assistance and have been impeccable fellow travelers; JoAnn Wypijewski, the first journalist to map the terrain of this story; activist and attorney Bill Dobbs; Nan and Gay Talese, whose vote of confidence carried me further than they know; my goddaughter Sarah Nodell, keeper of the dreams; and my band of friends who provided logistical assistance and helped me keep the faith — Kelly Johnson, Alexandra Eldridge, Karen Mauch, Diane Zilka, Kevin Baker, Lory Pollina, Darcy Nicholson, Troy Fernandez, James Bristol, Julia Cameron, Gayla Bechtol, Sterling Zinsmeyer, Louis Bixenman, Hampton and Anne Sides, Jean Gardner, Paul Ryan, Katie Leishman, Pamela Tudor, Doug Wiggin, Barbara Sullivan, and Dave Minear.

I owe a special debt of gratitude to David and Catherine Skinner for supporting this book during a critical stage in its development; and also to Michael Gill.

Finally, I want to express my love and thanks to my father, Daniel Jimenez, for his generous support of *The Book of Matt*; to Lucy Thompson, whose faith and friendship have sustained me; and to my partner, Miles Fairris, for joining me in the Big Adventure.